MEDELLÍN

ANDREW DIER

Contents

Discover Medellín 4
Planning Your Trip 6
The Best of Medellín and Coffee Country 8
Medellín Walking Tour 10
Medellín and the Coffee Region 13
Background 111
Essentials 147
Resources 162
Index 180
List of Maps 184

Clockwise from top left: a friendly devil in Salamina; Jardín Botánico del Quindío; colorful doors in Salento; the Plaza Botero in downtown Medellín.

DISCOVER
Medellín

Dynamic Medellín offers all the culture, restaurants, and nightlife any cosmopolitan visitor might desire. But what makes it unique is its location amid Colombia's countless coffee plantations and colorful pueblos.

In a landscape dotted with towering wax palms and brightly colored birds, Paisa pueblos abound. Jardín, Jericó, Salamina, and Salento are the most photogenic.

Lush mountain landscapes, perfect weather, and gorgeous haciendas should be enough to put this region on your list. But the can-do spirit and contagious *alegría* of its people will make your visit unforgettable.

Clockwise from top left: coffee beans; the Parque de las Luces in Plaza Cisneros; saffron-crowned tanager; Jardin; wax palms in Valle de Cocora.

Planning Your Trip

When to Go

Because Colombia straddles the equator, the temperatures and length of days are nearly constant year-round. There are, however, distinct dry and rainy seasons. Throughout most of the country, the months of **December through February** and **July through August** are considered *verano* **(dry season).** *Invierno* **(rainy season)** is usually between **April and May** and again between **September and November.**

High tourist seasons run from **mid-December through mid-January,** during **Easter week (Semana Santa),** and, to a lesser extent, school vacations from **June to August.** Medellín empties out during the end-of-the-year holidays from December 15 to January 15, and also during Semana Santa (Holy Week). This is peak time for regional pueblos and coffee region haciendas. During school vacations (June-July), natural parks and reserves and coffee haciendas get busy again.

Passports and Visas

Travelers to Colombia who intend to visit as tourists for a period of under 90 days will need only to present a **valid passport** upon entry in the country. You may be asked to show **proof of a return ticket.** Tell the immigration officer if you intend to stay up to 90 days, otherwise they will probably give you a stamp permitting a stay of 60 days. Language schools and universities will be able to assist those who may require a yearlong **student visa.**

Vaccinations

There are **no obligatory vaccination requirements** for visiting Colombia. However, if you are traveling onward to countries such as Brazil, Ecuador,

the Parque Principal in Jardín

a Satena airplane

or Peru, you may have to provide proof of the vaccine upon entry to those countries.

The Centers for Disease Control and Prevention (CDC) recommends that travelers have **hepatitis A** and **typhoid** vaccinations. **Hepatitis B, rabies,** and **yellow fever** vaccinations are recommended for some travelers. If you plan to visit the Amazon region, **antimalarial drugs** may be recommended.

Transportation

Most travelers arrive by plane to Colombia, with the vast majority arriving at the modern **Aeropuerto Internacional El Dorado** in Bogotá. There are numerous **daily nonstop flights** into Bogotá from the eastern seaboard of the United States, as well as from Houston, Dallas, Los Angeles, and Toronto. However, **Medellín** is also served by nonstop flights from the East Coast of the United States.

Intra-country flights are easy, safe, increasingly more economical, frequent, and, above all, quick. Taking the **bus** to just about anywhere in the country is an inexpensive and popular but slower option. **Medellín** has a clean and efficient **Metro. Private buses** and **taxis** are ubiquitous in cities, although cabs should be ordered in advance. The best way to see the city's sights is usually **on foot. Renting a car** is a viable option for exploring the **coffee region,** where roads are good.

The Best of Medellín and Coffee Country

DAY 1

Arrive in the evening at the Aeropuerto Internacional José María Córdova in Rionegro, outside of Medellín. Make the one-hour trip via cab or bus into town. Get settled at **Charlee Lifestyle Hotel,** then linger over perfectly paired Argentinian wine and food at one of the city's most renowned restaurants, **Carmen.**

DAY 2

Discover downtown Medellín by taking a ride on the Metro. Here you can check out the finest art museum in the region, the **Museo de Antioquia,** and have your picture taken in front of your favorite rotund **Fernando Botero** sculpture in the adjacent plaza. Visit the moving **Museo Casa de la Memoria**, the country's first museum dedicated to the memory of victims of Colombia's decades-long armed conflict.

Then check out symbols of the new Medellín: the **Metrocable gondola** network and the **Biblioteca España,** a boldly designed public library built on the side of a mountain. From there, transfer once more to another Metrocable line to the **Parque Arví,** a huge recreational area.

Head back to your hotel and freshen up before checking out a tango show at **Salón Málaga.**

DAY 3

Take the three-hour bus ride through the southern Antioquia countryside to the picture-perfect Paisa town of **Jardín.** Hang out with the locals in the

one of Medellín's Metrocable gondolas

Hacienda Guayabal

Valle de Cocora

sublime **Parque Principal,** a park bursting with flowers, where you can enjoy a beer or sip a locally produced coffee.

Relax at the low-key hostel **Casa Selva y Café,** a pleasant walk away from the town center. Birding and nature enthusiasts will want to stay at **Hacienda La Esperanza.**

DAY 4
Set off for the coffee region by heading to **Manizales** in the morning on a five-hour bus ride. Once in town, have a coffee under the shadow of the remarkable **El Cable** tower, the gondola system that once transported coffee over the mountains to the Río Magdalena.

Check in to a **coffee farm** in the verdant valleys near Chinchiná such as **Hacienda Venecia** or **Hacienda Guayabal,** only about a half hour away.

DAY 5
Take a tour of a coffee farm today, and admire the orderly rows of deep green coffee plants adorned with bright red beans. In the afternoon, take a bus to one of the region's cutest pueblos, **Salento,** a five-hour trip.

Stay at the bright orange **Tralala** hostel and have dinner at wonderful **La Eliana,** followed by dessert and coffee at **Café Jesús Martín.**

DAYS 6-7
Hitch a ride on a Jeep Willy through pastureland and tropical forest to the **Reserva Acaime,** where you can watch hummingbirds flit about while you warm up with a hot drink. Then head back down through a wonderland of 60-meter-high (200-foot-high) wax palms, Colombia's national tree, in the **Valle de Cocora.**

Spend the night again in Salento. Before retiring for the night, stroll the atmospheric **Calle Real.** The next morning, drive back to Medellin to bid the city farewell.

Medellín Walking Tour

Plaza Botero to the Plaza de los Pies Descalzos

Medellín's brash downtown makes for a compact history tour comprising stoic remnants from the colonial era, brick-and-mortar evidence of Medellín's reign as Colombia's most important industrial center in the early 20th century, and the vibrant public spaces, modern transportation systems, and futuristic architecture showing this proud city's 21st-century optimism.

Begin the tour at the Parque Berrío Metro station and walk five minutes north to the Plaza Botero.

Plaza Botero

Most visits downtown begin under the shadow of the **Palacio de la Cultura Rafael Uribe Uribe** (Cra. 51 No. 52-03, 8am-5pm Mon.-Fri., 8am-2pm Sat., free), which occasionally hosts of art exhibits. The **Plaza Botero** (in front of the Museo de Antioquia, Cra. 52 No. 52-43) gets its name from its 23 corpulent bronze sculptures by Fernando Botero. Passersby often pose for snapshots in front of the sculptures, such as *La Mano (The Hand)* and *Eva (Eve)*. One of the most prolific, and by far the best known, of contemporary Colombian artists, Botero donated these works to his hometown of Medellín. His paintings and sculptures of rotund people often portray campesino (rural) life, but many of them are also commentaries on the violence in Colombia.

Peatonal Carabobo

To the south, the **Peatonal Carabobo** is a pedestrian walkway that extends for eight blocks. Lined with shoe shops, five-and-dime stores, and snack bars, it's busy, loud, and colorful. (Although there is usually a police presence, be sure to watch your stuff.)

On the right-hand side is Medellín's oldest church, the brilliantly white **Iglesia de la Vera Cruz** (Cl. 51 No. 52-38, tel. 4/512-5095), which dates to 1682. It is often filled with working-class faithful, sitting or standing in meditation and prayer. It's a refuge of quiet in this busy commercial area.

The Belgian architect who designed the grandiose **Palacio Nacional** (Cra. 52 No. 48-45, tel. 4/513-4422) in the 1920s probably never expected that it would become the domain of around 400 vendors of discount tennis shoes and jeans. Built to house governmental offices, today the corridors of this historic building are filled with the chorus of *"a la orden"* ("at your service") from hopeful shop attendants. Toward the end of Peatonal Carabobo is **Donde Ramón,** a small kiosk in the middle of the walkway that is jam-packed with antique objects like brass horse stirrups or old *carrieles* (leather handbags) from Jericó.

Parque de las Luces

After years of abandonment and urban decay, in 2005 the artificial forest of the **Parque de las Luces** or **Plaza Cisneros** (Cl. 44 at Cra. 52) was opened in an effort to rejuvenate the area. The park, consisting of 300 illuminated posts, looks somewhat odd during the day but is spectacular at night when it shines. Check it out by car at night; it is not safe to roam about after dark. On the east side of the plaza are two historic early-20th-century brick buildings: the **Edificio Carré** and **Edificio Vásquez** (Cl. 44B No. 52-17, tel. 4/514-8200). When they were built they were the tallest buildings in Medellín. These buildings were important warehouse facilities during the industrial boom of the early 20th century. The plaza used to be the home of the main marketplace. On the western side of the plaza is the **Biblioteca EPM** (Cra. 54 No. 44-48, tel. 4/380-7516, 8:30am-5:30pm Mon.-Sat.), a stunning public library sponsored by the electric company EPM (Empresas Públicas de Medellín), built in 2005. In addition to reading rooms, there are occasional exhibitions and cultural events held at the library.

Across from the Parque de las Luces on the southern side of Calle 44 is the **Estación Ferrocarril** (Cra. 52 No. 43-31, tel. 4/381-0733), the old main train station. There's not much to see here, except for a train engine and forgotten old tracks.

Plaza Mayor

To the west of the Estación Ferrocarril is the **Centro Administrativo La Alpujarra** (Cl. 44 No. 52-165), which houses the Departamento de Antioquia government offices. The sculpture *Homenaje a la Raza,* by Rodrigo Arenas Betancur, stands in the middle of the large intermediary plaza. Just beyond is the **Plaza de la Libertad** (Cra. 55 between Clls. 42-44), a complex of modern office space and interesting public space complete with urban gardens.

Cross the pedestrian bridge over the lanes of the Metroplús bus station.

Parque de las Luces

Plaza de los Pies Descalzos

(Opened in 2013, Metroplús is the latest addition to Medellín's transportation network.) Here is the **Plaza Mayor** (Cl. 41 No. 55-80, www.plaza-mayor.com.co), the city's preeminent convention and event venue; it has a fair share of nice restaurants. The **Teatro Metropolitano** (Cl. 41 No. 57-30, tel. 4/232-2858, www.teatrometropolitano.com), a 20th-century brick building, hosts concerts.

Finally, the **Plaza de los Pies Descalzos** (Cra. 58 No. 42-125) is a plaza filled with a *guadua* (Colombian bamboo) forest and fountains, where you can take off your shoes and play. It's flanked by eateries on one side and the massive **Museo del Agua** (Cra. 57 No. 42-139, tel. 4/380-6954, 8am-6pm Tues.-Fri., 10am-7pm Sat.-Sun., COP$4,000) on the other. In the distance is a long-standing Medellín architectural icon: the **Edificio Inteligente** (Cra. 58 No. 42-125). Built in the late 1950s, it has served as the headquarters of EPM, the utility company.

Medellín and the Coffee Region

Medellín........................ 18	Southern Antioquia............. 52
Northern and Eastern Antioquia.. 44	The Coffee Region.............. 60

Look for ★ to find recommended sights, activities, dining, and lodging.

Highlights

★ **Museo de Antioquia:** The galleries of this art museum are filled with works from the best Colombian artists spanning nearly four centuries. And the terrace café has the best people-watching in the Centro (page 20).

★ **Museo Casa de la Memoria:** Go to this museum to hear the heartwrenching stories from victims—and survivors—of the country's decades-long armed conflict (page 22).

★ **Parque Arví:** Chill out in the cool climes of this park and enjoy a ride on the Metrocable, an innovative public transportation system using gondolas (page 23).

★ **Reserva Natural Río Claro:** This jungle paradise is set along a canyon that was discovered only recently. This private natural reserve offers caving, river rafting, and a surplus of peace (page 46).

★ **Jardín:** Just a few hours south of busy Medellín, life slows to a crawl in this picture-perfect town, which is surrounded by lush green mountains full of recreational opportunities (page 52).

★ **Salamina:** Life goes on much as it always has in this remote Paisa town known for its superb architecture and warm hospitality (page 71).

★ **Parque Nacional Natural Los Nevados:** Dozens of hikes leading through tropical jungles afford fantastic views of snowcapped volcanoes and mountain lakes in this easily accessed national park (page 74).

★ **Jardín Botánico del Quindío:** In the best botanical garden in the region, you can take a guided tour through a tropical forest (page 84).

★ **Valle de Cocora:** One of the most dramatic and photographed scenes in Colombia is this valley filled with towering wax palms, the national tree (page 93).

This region has it all: lush countryside, beautiful mountain landscapes, welcoming locals, a plethora of recreational activities, vibrant cities, and gorgeous haciendas.

Medellín, the surrounding department of Antioquia, and the coffee region departments of Caldas, Risaralda, and Quindío comprise the central, mountainous section of Colombia, covering the Cordillera Central (Central Range) and Cordillera Occidental (Western Range). The mountains then flatten out into the coastal lowlands.

Despite its inaccessible terrain, Antioquia was an important province of colonial Nueva Granada thanks to its abundant gold deposits. It attracted settlers who panned the rivers or cultivated food for the mining camps. Santa Fe de Antioquia, founded in 1541, was the main colonial settlement.

After independence, the province continued to prosper, even attracting foreign investment in gold mining. Demographic pressure triggered a southward migration known as the *colonización antioqueña*. Waves of settlement brought Paisa families to unoccupied lands in the south of Antioquia, the coffee region, and the northern part of the Valle del Cauca.

During the early part of the 20th century, coffee was a major source of prosperity in Antioquia. Medellín grew rapidly and became the industrial powerhouse of Colombia. The last decades of the 20th century were difficult times for Antioquia, which suffered from the triple scourge of drug trafficking, paramilitary armies, and guerrillas. In the past decade, the government has made huge strides in bringing back the rule of law, and today Antioquia is one of the safest and most prosperous regions in Colombia.

Previous: Medellín at night; coffee plantations near Manizales.

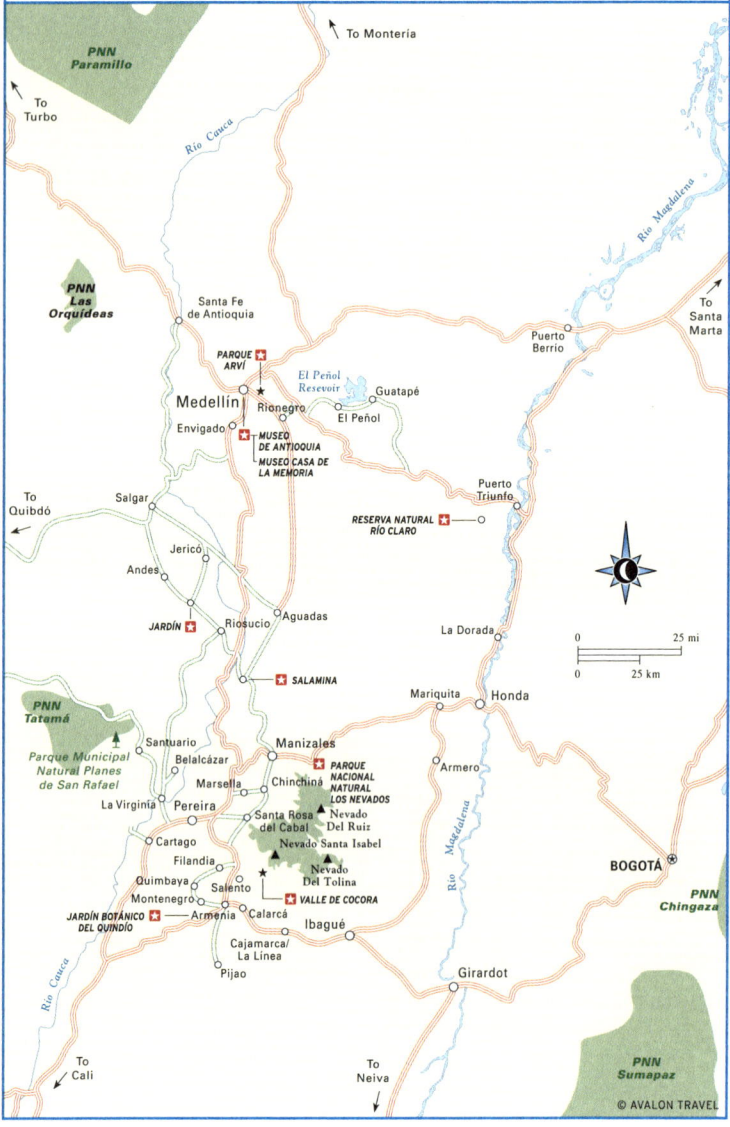

PLANNING YOUR TIME

Weather-wise, any time of the year is a good time to visit Medellín and the coffee region. The entire region has a temperate climate, which is why they call Medellín the "City of Eternal Spring."

Give Medellín three days. In that amount of time, you can experience "old Medellín" sights in the Centro, such as the Museo de Antioquia, as well as the modern Medellín icons that are the subject of great pride: the Metrocable, Biblioteca España, the café culture of cool El Poblado, and the Parque Explora. Consider spending a weekend in Medellín, when hotel rates drop, and especially if you're interested in checking out the city's nightlife scene. Those staying a week can add one or two other destinations in Antioquia, such as the Reserva Natural Río Claro or one of the picture-perfect Paisa pueblos, such as Jardín or Jericó. These are within about a three-hour bus ride from Medellín.

Many visitors experience the gorgeous colonial town of Santa Fe de Antioquia to the north of Medellín as a day trip, but it's better to spend one night there in order to enjoy its quaint streets after the sun has gone down; on the banks of the mighty Río Cauca, Santa Fe is one of the hottest towns in the region. Guatapé, with its famous rock, El Peñol, makes for a nice overnight on the way to or from the Río Claro reserve, where two nights are necessary. These three destinations are popular on weekends and holidays. The stunning natural beauty of Río Claro is best enjoyed during the week.

To the south of Medellín are two picture-perfect Paisa pueblos, Jardín and Jericó. A couple of days in one of those should be enough. You can continue from there southward into the coffee region on winding country roads.

The cities of Armenia, Manizales, and Pereira, and the town of Salento, make ideal bases for visiting the coffee region. Pereira and Armenia have good air connections, while the Manizales airport is often shrouded in fog.

One of the joys of this region is spending a few days at a coffee hacienda. Many tour operators will pack your days with day-trip activities, but resist this urge. Because it gets dark at 6pm every day, it would be a shame to miss spending some daylight hours strolling the grounds of the *finca* (farm), lazing in a hammock or rocking chair, or doing nothing at all.

A week or more is needed to decompress on a coffee farm and see the region's top sights: the Valle de Cocora, Salento, the Jardín Botánico del Quindío, and one or two of the national and regional parks. There are very good transportation links between the three major cities and Salento. Roads are generally excellent. While renting a car in Colombia is not often the best option, here it makes sense.

Medellín

While Medellín is the country's second city in terms of population and importance, perpetually behind Bogotá, this metropolis of around 2.7 million is truly on the move and an example of Colombia's ongoing transformation. It's the country's only city with an urban train system. It's also the first city with a gondola and modern trolley transportation network.

The first settlement in the region, near the present-day Poblado sector, was established in 1616. Medellín proper was founded in 1675, and was designated the capital of Antioquia in 1826.

In the 1980s, Pablo Escobar, born in nearby Rionegro, established a cocaine-trafficking empire based Medellín. In its heyday, the Medellín Cartel controlled 80 percent of the world's cocaine trade. When President Virgilio Barco cracked down on the cartel in the late 1980s, Escobar declared war on the government. He assassinated judges and political leaders, set off car bombs to intimidate public opinion, and paid a bounty for every policeman that was murdered in Medellín—a total of 657. In 1991, Medellín had a homicide rate of 380 per 100,000 inhabitants, the highest such rate on record anywhere in the world. In 1993, Escobar was killed while on the run from the law.

During the 1990s, leftist guerrillas gained strength in the poor *comunas,* or sectors, of Medellín, waging a vicious turf war against paramilitaries. At the turn of the century, the homicide rate was 160 per 100,000 inhabitants, making Medellín one of the most dangerous places on Earth.

Shortly after assuming power in 2002, President Álvaro Uribe launched Operación Orion to wrest the poor *comunas* of Medellín from the leftist guerrillas, and violence decreased notably. By 2005, homicides were still high by international standards but a fraction of what they had been a decade before. Under the leadership of Mayor Sergio Fajardo, elected in 2004, and his successors Alonso Salazar and Aníbal Gaviria, Medellín has undergone an extraordinary transformation. In partnership with the private sector, the city has invested heavily in public works, including a new cable car transportation system, museums, and libraries. In recent years, the city has become a major tourist destination and has attracted significant foreign investment.

Orientation

Medellín is in the Valle de Aburrá, with the trickling and polluted Río Medellín dividing the city into east and west. Both the Metro (Line A) and Avenida Regional or Autopista Sur, a busy expressway, run parallel to the river.

The main neighborhoods are **El Poblado,** including the mini-hood of Provenza; the **Centro;** and the **Carabobo Norte** area (often referred to as **Universidades**).

If you arrive in Medellín from the Rionegro airport, you will descend the hill into the valley and land more or less in El Poblado. The neighborhood is packed with great restaurants, bars, hostels, hotels, and glitzy shopping malls. It is also full of tall brick high-rise apartment buildings, home to the well-to-do. Luxury hotels and malls line Avenida El Poblado. Parque Lleras is the center of the **Provenza** neighborhood, a small, leafy, and very hip part of El Poblado on the eastern side of Avenida El Poblado. To the west, down Calle 10, is Parque del Poblado, and a few blocks farther is the El Poblado Metro station.

The Centro is between El Poblado to the south and Carabobo Norte to the north. The heart of the Centro is the Plaza Botero and Parque Berrío Metro station area. Avenida El Poblado, also known as Carrera 43A, connects El Poblado with the Centro, as does the Metro.

Across the river from El Poblado is the Terminal del Sur bus station and the Aeropuerto Olaya Herrera. **Cerro Nutibara** (Nutibara Hill), home to the Pueblito Paisa, is north of the airport. Northwest of Cerro Nutibara is the quiet neighborhood of **Laureles,** and farther west is the **stadium area.** The B line of the Metro connects the Centro with the stadium area.

Between El Poblado and the Centro is an up-and-coming area with new hotels and high-rises being built in what is known as **Ciudad del Río,** where the Museo de Arte Moderno de Medellín is located. **Barrio Colombia** is also home to many nightspots.

In the far south of town are the municipalities of **Envigado** and **Itagüi.** Avenida El Poblado connects El Poblado with Envigado, which has some good restaurants, a busy main plaza, and the Parque El Salado. Itagüi is an industrial town with little of interest for the tourist except for bars and clubs, many of which are open until the wee hours.

Safety

The streets of the Centro should be avoided after dark, and valuables should be secured during the daytime. It is not a good idea to take a carefree stroll in the northern or western neighborhoods or, especially, in the *comunas* (city sectors) on the surrounding hills, but specific sights mentioned can be visited. The Metro, Metrocable, Metroplús, and Tranvía are not only clean and efficient, but are also safe.

It's best to avoid hailing taxis on the street, particularly at night. Instead, order a cab from a taxi app like Tappsi or EasyTaxi or a ride-sharing app like Uber. Be careful at clubs and bars, and don't accept drinks from strangers.

SIGHTS

To see Medellín in full motion, visit the Centro during the week. On Saturdays it's quieter, although the Peatonal Carabobo bustles with activity. Downtown is practically deserted on Sundays. Most visits to the Centro start from the Parque Berrío Metro station, and the main sights can easily be seen on foot in a few hours.

Centro

★ MUSEO DE ANTIOQUIA

The **Museo de Antioquia** (Cra. 52 No. 52-43, tel. 4/251-3636, www.museo-deantioquia.org.co, 10am-5pm Mon.-Sat., 10am-4:30pm Sun., COP$18,000 non-Colombians) is one of the top art museums in the country, with an extensive permanent collection of works from Colombian artists from the 19th century to modern times. The building itself is an architectural gem, an art deco-style structure from the 1930s that originally served as the Palacio Municipal. Inside, look for the iconic painting *Horizontes* (*Horizons*) by Francisco Antonio Cano, a romantic 1913 work portraying the *colonización antioqueña,* the period when families from Antioquia headed south to settle in what is now known as the coffee region. In the contemporary art rooms, you'll see *Horizontes* (1997) by Carlos Uribe. This painting presents the same bucolic scene, except in the background a plane sprays pesticides over the countryside to eradicate coca and marijuana crops. Native son Fernando Botero has donated several of his works, over 100 of them, to the museum. There is also a small room with a series of works, contemplations on mortality, by Luis Caballero. There is a free guided tour at 2pm every day.

Carabobo Norte

Over 37,000 students are enrolled at the **Universidad de Antioquia** (Cl. 67 No. 53-108, tel. 4/263-0011, www.udea.edu.co), one of the country's top universities. Its campus, full of plazas and public art, buzzes with vibrant student energy. In addition to a busy calendar of cultural events, the university has an excellent museum, **MUUA** (Cl. 67 No. 53-108, Bloque 15, tel. 4/219-5180, www.udea.edu.co, 8am-5:45pm Mon.-Thurs., 8am-3:45pm Fri., 9am-12:45pm Sat., free), featuring contemporary art exhibits and a permanent natural history exhibit. Visitors to the UA campus must show their passport at the Portería del Ferrocarril gate for entry.

the Museo de Antioquia

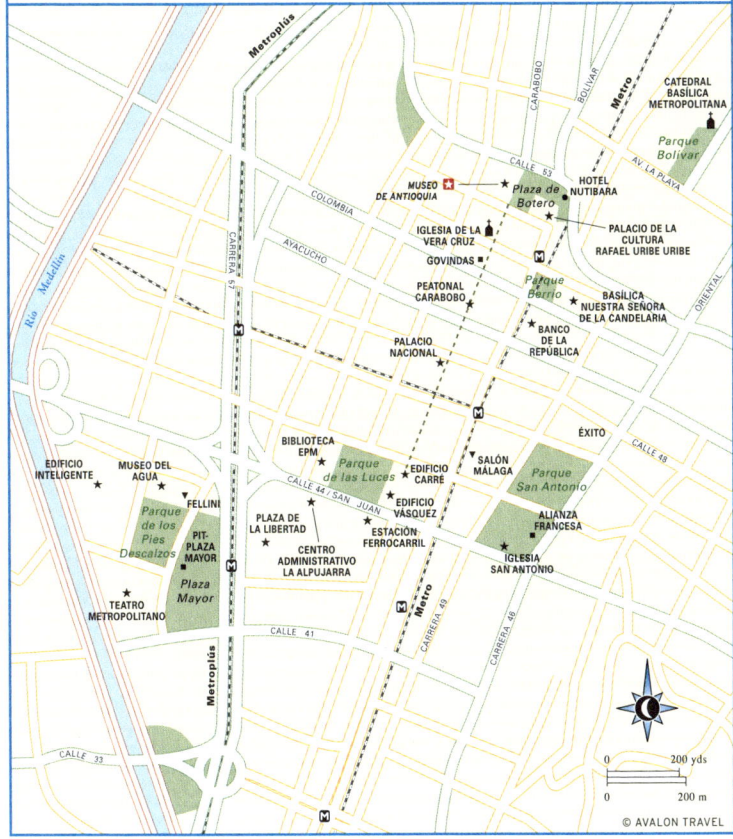

Adjacent to the university near the Metro station is the photogenic **Parque Explora** (Cra. 52 No. 73-75, tel. 4/516-8300, www.parqueexplora. org, 8:30am-5:30pm Tues.-Fri., 10am-6:30pm Sat.-Sun, COP$24,500), one of the most iconic architectural landmarks of modern Medellín. It is a complex of science and natural history museums, with a highly regarded **aquarium,** one of the largest in Latin America. The ticket office closes 90 minutes before closing time. The **Planetario Medellín** (Cra. 52 No. 71-117, tel. 4/516-8300, www.planetariomedellin.org, 8am-5pm Tues.-Wed., 8am-7pm Thurs.-Fri., 10am-6pm Sat.-Sun., COP$15,000) is across the street from the Parque Explora.

Up for a walk in the park? Across from Parque Explora is the **Jardín Botánico de Medellín** (Cra. 73 No. 51D-14, tel. 4/444-5500, www.botanicomedellin.org, 9am-4:30pm daily, free), a pleasant green space in the city. The highlight here is the Orquiderama, an open-air wood lattice-like structure where events—even thumping raves—are held. Inside the gardens, the **In Situ restaurant** (tel. 4/460-7007, www.botanicomedellin.org, noon-3pm Mon., noon-3pm and 7pm-10pm Tues.-Sat., noon-4pm Sun., COP$35,000) boasts gorgeous views and is a posh choice for lunch. Behind the park is an overlooked homage to notable women from the area: the **Esquina de las Mujeres** (Cra. 51 at Cl. 73), a small public space with busts of accomplished women from Medellín and Antioquia from the colonial era to the present day.

Presidents, artists, and writers rest in the **Museo Cementerio de San Pedro** (Cra. 51 No. 68-68, tel. 4/516-7650, www.cementeriosanpedro.org.co, 8am-5:30pm daily, free). Marble statues and elaborate tombs pay tribute to influential Antioqueños from the 19th century onward, but the reminders of the city's turbulent past may strike you as more interesting. One plot near the tomb of Fidel Cano, founder of the *El Espectador* newspaper, contains the tombs of several of drug kingpin Pablo Escobar's associates and guards. Some tombs have stickers identifying allegiance to one of Medellín's soccer clubs; others have touching handwritten notes from children left behind. There is usually a free tour on Sunday afternoons. Check the cemetery's up-to-date website for a schedule of activities, including evening tours.

Cerro Nutibara

To see an authentic Paisa pueblo, go to Jardín, Jericó, or Salamina. They're just a couple of hours away and are as real as you can get. Can't do that? Then go to the **Pueblito Paisa** (Cl. 30A No. 55-64, tel. 4/235-6476, 5am-midnight daily, free), a Disney-esque celebration of Paisa architecture and culture, set atop Cerro Nutibara. Plenty of food (including an overpriced restaurant) and handicrafts are on sale here. On a clear day the views of Colombia's second city aren't bad. The hill is also a popular place for an early-morning jog.

Northern Medellín

★ MUSEO CASA DE LA MEMORIA

Tourism campaigns promoting Colombia highlight the country's natural beauty, welcoming people, and cultural diversity, understandably not dwelling on its sad recent history of bloody armed conflict. Opening in 2016, the **Museo Casa de la Memoria** (Cl. 51 No. 36-66, tel. 4/383-4001, www.museocasadelamemoria.gov.co, 9am-6pm Tues.-Fri., 10am-4pm Sat.-Sun., free) nudges Colombians and international visitors alike to face those dark years head-on. Dedicated to the memory of victims of the world's longest-running war, the museum documents the disappeared, the displaced, and the fallen. Exhibits (most descriptions are in Spanish) put faces to the numbers of victims, and give them—the survivors and the deceased—a chance to recount to the world their stories. Outside is a wall of memory, with names of victims etched on bricks. To get to the museum, you can take the Metro to Parque Berrío station and walk up Calle 52 and Avenida La Playa, just beyond the Teatro Pablo Tobón.

CASA MUSEO PEDRO NEL GÓMEZ

In the barrio of Aranjuez is the **Casa Museo Pedro Nel Gómez** (Cra. 51B No. 85-24, Barrio Aranjuez, tel. 4/444-2633, ext. 102, free). This delightful, small museum houses an extensive collection of the painter's works, including several murals for which he is best known. Much of his work portrays the plight of campesinos (rural peasants), workers, and indigenous people. The house, now the museum, was designed by Gómez, its location was chosen by his Italian-born wife. The hills overlooking the city here reminded her of Florence, somehow. In the new wing of the museum there is a small public library. The courtyard holds a snack bar-café. The museum is not easy to get to via public transportation, so it may be best to cab it.

BIBLIOTECA ESPAÑA

When this public library was opened in the low-income neighborhood of Santo Domingo, King Juan Carlos came from Madrid for the ceremony; as the facility's name implies, Spain helped fund the project. It's one of many newly created *biblioteca parques* (public library parks) in Medellín. More than a place for books, these library parks have become community centers and sources of pride in neighborhoods that continue to struggle with poverty and violence. Of them, the **Biblioteca España** (Cra. 33B No.107A-100, tel. 4/528-9495, www.reddebibliotecas.org.co, 8am-7pm Mon.-Sat. and 11am-5pm Sun.) boasts one of the most daring designs: It resembles giant boulders clinging to the edge of the mountainside. It was designed by architect and Barranquilla native Giancarlo Mazzanti, who won a prize for this work at the VI Bienal Iberoamericana de Arquitectura y Urbanismo in Lisbon in 2008.

Getting to Santo Domingo is an attraction in itself. The neighborhood is connected to the metropolis by the Metrocable cable car system. Take the Metro toward Niquía station and transfer to the Metrocable at Acevedo. The Santo Domingo station is the third and final stop. Many visitors are content to view the library from the Metrocable gondola as they continue onward to the Parque Arví.

When the Metrocable K line was opened in 2004, it was the first of its kind: a gondola-like public transport system with a socioeconomic purpose, connected to a metro. The system has eliminated eternal climbs up and down the mountain for low-income residents.

★ PARQUE ARVÍ

For some fresh, crisp, country air, a visit to the **Parque Arví** (Santa Elena, tel. 4/444-2979, www.parquearvi.org, 9am-5pm Tues.-Sun., free), covering 16,000 hectares (40,000 acres) of nature, hits the spot after a few days of urban exploring.

Highlights in the sprawling park include some well-marked nature paths that meander through cloud forests thick with pine and eucalyptus trees, over brooks, along ancient indigenous paths, and to mountain lakes and lookout points with fine views of the Valle de Aburrá and Medellín below.

Most paths are less than three kilometers (two miles); they are not strenuous whatsoever and require no guide, although there are often free guided nature walks as well.

Other recreational activities on offer include horseback riding, zip-lining, and visiting a butterfly farm. The park's layout, based around different *nucleos* (nuclei), is somewhat confusing, but park staff can orient you.

Many visitors enjoy the trip to the park—on the Metrocable—as much as or more than the park itself. To get there from the city, take the Metro to the Acevedo station in the north of the city (Línea A toward Niquía). From there, transfer to the Metrocable (Línea K) to the Santo Domingo station. From there you must transfer to the Línea L, an additional COP$4,850 one-way.

The temperature can drop substantially and abruptly in the park. Pack a light sweater and a lightweight rainproof jacket. Various snack bars and restaurants are located throughout the grounds. Aim for an early start in order to enjoy the park at your leisure.

Southern Medellín

One of the city's most important cultural spaces is the **Museo de Arte Moderno de Medellín** (MAMM, Cra. 44 No. 19A-100, tel. 4/444-2622, www.elmamm.org, 9am-5:30pm Tues.-Fri., 10am-5:30pm Sat., 10am-5pm Sun., COP$10,000), set in a revamped steel mill, Talleres Robledo, that began operations in the 1930s. Exhibitions (usually two at a time) are hit or miss, but the facilities are gorgeous and there are often film screenings in the modern auditorium. The museum store, the *tienda,* is an excellent place to pick up a whimsical Medellín souvenir.

The **Parque El Salado** (Cra. 27A No. 41S-58, Envigado, tel. 4/270-3132, www.parqueelsalado.gov.co, 9am-5pm Tues.-Sun., COP$3,000), a well-organized municipal park covering 17 hectares (42 acres) in Envigado, has trails and activities, such as a zip line (COP$7,000) and a rock-climbing

The Parque Arví is an excellent break from the city.

wall (COP$3,000), and makes for a relaxing excursion. On weekends it gets packed with families on a *paseo de olla*. Literally a soup-pot excursion, *paseo de olla* usually means *sancocho,* a hearty beef stew. Essential gear for a day out at the park includes giant aluminum pots for slowly heating a *sancocho* over a campfire; it can get smoky on the weekends. Getting to the park is easy using public transportation. From the Envigado Metro station look for a green bus with a sign that says Parque El Salado (COP$2,000). It's about a 20-minute ride toward the mountains; you can also cab it (COP$10,000).

ENTERTAINMENT AND EVENTS
Nightlife

Except for the very traditional music venues and bars, Facebook pages are the best resource for what's up at the clubs.

Since 1969, **El Social Tienda Mixta** (Cra. 35 No. 8A-8, tel. 4/311-5567) has been selling the basics to neighborhood residents (soap, sugar, coffee); it's only a recent phenomenon that it's the hippest place to be seen at night, when it is converted into the most popular bar in Provenza. It's so popular on weekend evenings that you can forget about finding a vacant plastic chair.

On Thursday and Friday evenings, the Medellín microbrewery **3 Cordilleras** (Cl. 30 No. 44-176, tel. 4/444-2337, 5:30pm-9pm Thurs.-Fri., COP$21,000-26,000) offers tours of its brewery, tastings of five beers, and friendly socializing. There's live music on Fridays.

Calle 9+1 (Cra. 40 No. 10-25, cell tel. 313/753-8392, 6pm-2am Mon.-Sat., cover varies) is a hipster's paradise in El Poblado. Music varies wildly from salsa to house to folk. The dim lighting and well-worn couches provide the perfect chilled-out atmosphere.

Cuchitril Club / Sala Bombay (Cl. 10 with Guayabal, cell tel. 313/745-6349, 9pm-4am Fri.-Sat.) is a happening venue that packs in exuberant crowds for live music and DJs. **Salón Amador** (Cra. 36 No. 10-38, www.salonamador.com) often hosts international DJs.

Working-class locals, intelligentsia, and students converge on the Parque del Periodista downtown to meet friends over a few beers and listen to music. It may very well be the coolest corner of Medellín. **Bar El Guanábano** (Parque del Periodista, Girardot with Maracaibo, tel. 4/216-3742) is a faithful—and funky—friend at the center of it all. Rock (like Bowie) plays on the sound system in this dark and cozy hangout, the centerpiece of which is the sacrilegious (yet good-natured) depiction of the Divino Niño made from the bizarre-looking guanabana fruit.

Short on cash? Head to the beer stalls (there are dozens) at the **Parque San Antonio** (Cra. 46 with Cl. 45). Pull up your red plastic chair and mix it up with the locals over a Poker beer.

Getting Up the Hill

During the late 1990s to the 2000s, thousands of families from rural areas in Antioquia, Córdoba, and Chocó were forced to leave their homes due to violence. Moving to Medellín to start a new life, many arrived in the *comunas*, the low-income neighborhoods along the steep slopes of the mountains surrounding the city. But here, where many live in meager brick homes covered with corrugated zinc roofs secured only by large stones, horrific violence has followed them. First it was turf wars between guerrillas and paramilitaries in the early 2000s. Today the bloodshed is caused by drug-trafficking gangs with links to former paramilitaries. This wave of violence has given birth to a new phenomenon: intra-urban displacement, during which families have been displaced within the city due to urban violence. For many, this is the second displacement that their families have had to endure.

City leaders have sought to improve the quality of life in the *comunas* in a variety of innovative ways. Two lines of the Metrocable gondola system have made a huge difference in allowing residents to travel to work or school in the city without having to walk up and down the mountainside. Spectacular modern public libraries have been built in many low-income communities, providing a safe and pleasant space to study, read, and connect to the Internet. These have developed into important cultural centers, with an active schedule of films, children's activities, and other cultural activities. New homes have been built and donated to 200-300 displaced families, with funds from the national government under President Juan Manuel Santos.

In 2012, the city debuted its latest project, one aimed at improving life in the numerous neighborhoods making up Comuna 13, the most notorious of the city's *comunas*. The project involved the creation of open-air escalators in this neighborhood, and today a series of six dual, interconnected escala-

SALSA, TANGO, AND JAZZ

Salsa has its aficionados here. If the musical genres *son, la charanga, el guaguanco*, and *la timba* don't mean anything to you now, they might after a night at **Son Havana** (Cra. 73 No. 44-56, tel. 4/586-9082, www.sonhavana.com, 8pm-3am Wed.-Sat., cover Sat. COP$8,000), which often has live performances. Nearby is **El Tíbiri** (Cra. 70 No. 44B-01, cell tel. 310/849-5461, hours vary Wed.-Sat.), an underground salsa and Afro-Colombian music joint on Carrera 70 that is hugely popular on the weekends. They say the walls sweat here, as after 10pm it gets packed, especially on Friday nights. El Tíbiri also regularly offers an array of dance classes.

The downtown **Salón Málaga** (Cra. 51 No. 45-80, tel. 4/231-2658, www.salonmalaga.com, 9am-11pm daily, no cover) has plenty of character. It's filled with old jukeboxes and memorabilia, and has its clientele who come in for a *tinto* (coffee) or beer during the day. The Saturday tango show at 5:30pm and oldies event on Sunday afternoons are especially popular with locals and travelers alike, but a stop here is a fine idea anytime.

Near the Parque de la Periodista, a major weekend hangout for the grungy set, there are some small bars big on personality. Tuesday nights border on legendary at **Eslabón Prendido** (Cl. 53 No. 42-55, tel. 4/239-3400,

tors extend down the slopes for some 384 meters (1,260 feet). The system operates from early in the morning until about 10pm. They are monitored by city employees, and their use is free. It is the first time in the world escalators have been used to improve the lives of the less fortunate.

The escalators have made a difference in the lives of the 134,000 Comuna 13 residents, although there are some who believe that the money spent on the project (around US$6 million) could have been better used otherwise. There have been alarming reports as well that some gangs have been intimidating residents by charging them to use the escalators, under the threat of dire consequences.

Despite the high levels of violence affecting residents (never foreign tourists), the escalators have become a tourist attraction, and even appear in the city's tourism-promotion materials. Celebrities and dignitaries from President Juan Manuel Santos to French fashion designer François Girbaud have taken a ride on the escalators.

It is indeed a strange kind of tourism, with which some may feel uncomfortable. However, if you would like to see this escalator project, you certainly can. Go during the day, don't wander too far away, and avoid being in the neighborhood after dark. To get there, take the Metro Línea B to San Javier station. As you depart the station, in front are *colectivos* (small buses) that regularly transport passengers to Comuna 13. It's about a 15-minute trip and costs under COP$1,500. Ask anyone which bus to take, and let the bus driver know that you'd like to go to the *escaleras eléctricas*.

From San Javier, there is also a Metrocable line (Línea J) that has three stops and travels to the top at La Aurora.

To get a local's perspective on life in Comuna 13—and take pics of cool graffiti—contact the **Grafitour** (cell tel. 312/889-5564, tel. 4/252-0035).

3pm-11pm Tues.-Sat., cover varies), a hole-in-the-wall salsa place that really packs them in. **El Acontista** (Cl. 53 No. 43-81, tel. 4/512-3052, noon-10pm Mon.-Thurs., noon-midnight Fri.-Sat.) is an excellent jazz club downtown. It has a bookstore on the 2nd floor and live music on Monday and Saturday evenings. It has great food, too, making it an excellent stop for unwinding following an arduous day of tourism.

In Envigado, **La Venta de Dulcinea Café Cultural** (Cl. 35 Sur No. 43-36, tel. 4/276-0208, www.laventadedulcinea.jimdo.com, 2pm-11pm Mon.-Sat.) is a somewhat bohemian spot where live performances (salsa, *milonga*, bossa nova, and tango) are often held. Check the venue's website or Facebook page for the latest.

DANCE CLUBS

Jesús Dulce Mío—Mi Pueblo (Cra. 42 67A-151, tel. 4/444-6022, www.fondadulcejesusmio.com, 8pm-4am Thurs.-Sat., cover varies) is a long-running and colorful nightspot that plays mostly crossover music. It's on the Autopista Sur, and there are other locations around the city, too.

There's a big electronic music scene in Medellín, but it's not obvious what's going on and where. Your best bet is to check the international website www.residentadvisor.net or the Medellín Underground Facebook page.

GAY BARS AND CLUBS

The online guide **Guia Gay Colombia** (www.guiagaycolombia.com) has a complete listing of bars.

There is a lively and youthful gay nightlife scene in Medellín. **Donde Aquellos** (Cra. 38 No. 9A-26, tel. 4/312-2041, cell tel. 313/624-1485, 4:30pm-2am daily) is an easygoing kind of place near the Parque Lleras in El Poblado. This friendly bar is a good place for a terrace drink. **Purple** (Cl. 10A No. 36-29, COP$10,000) is where the boys (and some girls) go to dance to pop and electronica.

Theater and Cultural Centers

Intellectuals, wannabes, artists, students, and downtown purists congregate at **Ateneo** (Cl. 47 No. 42-38 Local 9901, Torres de Bomboná, tel. 4/216-0708, www.ateneomedellin.com), which has an ongoing cultural program of concerts, theater performances, and art exhibtions. At its café you can drink *micheladas* all night and listen to live music or conversation.

A cool theater with 1960s flair is the **Teatro Pablo Tobón** (Cra. 40 No. 51-24, tel. 4/239-7500, www.teatropablotobon.com). Almost every day there's something happening here—concerts, theater, yoga, lectures, parties, chess—and even when there isn't, you can just hang out in the lobby café.

Otraparte (Cra. 43A No. 27AS-11, Envigado, tel. 4/448-2404, www.otraparte.org, 8am-8pm Mon.-Fri., 9am-5pm Sat.-Sun.) is a cultural center that offers a dynamic program of free concerts, films, book launches, and even free yoga classes.

Festivals and Events

The **Festival Internacional de Tango** takes place each year during the last week of June, commemorating the anniversary of the death of Carlos Gardel. This festival, and in fact the perseverance of tango culture in Medellín, is largely due to one man's passion and efforts: Argentine Leonardo Nieto visited Medellín in the 1960s, primarily to get to know this city where tango icon Gardel died in an airplane crash. He fell in love with the city, stayed, and created the Festival Internacional de Tango. During this festival, tango concerts and events take place across the city, the culmination of which is the **World Tango Championship** (www.worldtango-championships.co), held at the **Teatro Pablo Tobón** (Cra. 40 No. 51-24).

Since 1991, Medellín has hosted an impressive **Festival Internacional de Poesía de Medellín** (www.festivaldepoesiademedellin.org), which routinely attracts poets from dozens of countries; they share their work in more than 100 venues across the city. It's held in either late June or early July each year.

As the leading textile manufacturing center in Colombia, Medellín is

International Day of Laziness

Paisas are known throughout Colombia to be some of the most hardworking and driven people in the country. The Medellín Metro, routine 7am business meetings, the orderly pueblos in the Antioquian countryside, and even former president Álvaro Uribe, a native Paisa, are examples of this industriousness. Uribe's famous words upon taking office in 2002 were *"trabajar, trabajar, trabajar"* ("work, work, work"). Laziness is quiet simply anathema to Paisas.

But you can't be productive *all* the time. The people of **Itagüi,** an industrial town bordering Medellín, have taken that to heart. In fact, on one day each year they not only take it easy, they embrace and celebrate the virtues of slothfulness during their **Día Internacional de la Pereza** (International Day of Laziness) celebrations. On that day in August, residents rise at the leisurely hour of 10am, put out their hammocks and beds in front of their houses, and laze the day away, sometimes still in their pajamas. The day's events include a bed (on wheels) race and general goofing off. Ironically, most of the action (or inaction) of that day takes place in the Itagüi Parque del Obrero (Worker's Park).

---

the obvious choice for the most important fashion event in the country: **Colombiamoda** (www.inexmoda.org.co). It attracts designers and fashionistas from across the globe, and during this week, the Plaza Mayor becomes a fabulous model-fest. Taking place in late July, Colombiamoda often coincides with the Feria de las Flores.

The **Feria de las Flores** (www.feriadelasfloresmedellin.gov.co) is the most important festival of the year in Medellín, and is when the city is at its most colorful. It's a weeklong celebration of Paisa culture, with horseback parades, concerts, and the highlight, the Desfile de los Silleteros. That is when flower farmers from Santa Elena show off incredibly elaborate flower arrangements in a parade through the city streets. The festival, which includes a staggering number of events, is mostly free of charge and takes over the city for around three weeks in late July-early August each year.

At Christmastime, Medellín sparkles with light, every night. It all begins at midnight on December 1, during the **Alborada.** That's when the sights and sounds of fireworks and firecrackers envelop the entire Valle de Aburrá. On December 7, the **Alumbrado Navideño,** the city's Christmas light display, begins. The Cerro Nutibara and the Río Medellín, along with other city sites, are illuminated with 14.5 million multicolored lights. Sponsored by the electric company, it's quite a sight to behold.

SPORTS AND RECREATION
Biking
On Sundays and on holidays, Medellín residents take to the streets on their bikes and blades, or in their running shoes, during the **Ciclovía** (8am-1pm Sun.). There are several routes, including along Avenida El Poblado and along the Río Medellín. On Tuesday and Thursday evenings there is

a **Ciclovía Nocturna** (8pm-10pm) on two routes: one along the river and another around the stadium.

Encicla (www.encicla.gov.co) is Medellín's free bike-share program. Visitors can check out a bike, though it will take a week for permission, which can be obtained online. Some nice bike paths are along Carreras 65 and 70 and around the universities, connecting the Estadio and Universidad Metro stations.

Bike Rent (Cra. 35 No. 7-14, cell tel. 310/448-3731, www.bikerent.com.co, 9am-7pm Mon., Wed., and Fri.-Sat., 9am-10pm Tues. and Thurs., 8am-1pm Sun., COP$25,000 half day, COP$35,000 full day) rents good bikes cheaply, and the prices decrease as the number of hours you rent them increases. It also has information on routes and suggestions at this convenient Provenza location. Bike shop **Giant** (Cra. 43A No. 10-38, tel. 4/444-3850, COP$40,000-60,000) has a few road and mountain bikes available for rent, as well as details on group rides and races in the region.

Barranquero Cicloturísmo (tel. 4/538-0699, cell tel. 314/806-5892, ciclobarranquero@gmail.com, www.barranquero.co, COP$70,000-90,000 pp) organizes interesting day-trip bike rides for all levels of cyclists in the city and beyond, such as in the nearby pueblo of Santa Elena and in Guatapé. Bikes and necessary equipment are included in the price, but transportation to the meeting point is not.

Paragliding

For incredible views of both the verdant Antioquian countryside and the metropolis in the distance, check out a paragliding adventure organized by the **Aeroclub San Felix** (Km. 6 Vía San Pedro de los Milagros, tel. 4/388-1077, www.parapenteencolombia.com, 20-min. flight COP$125,000, complete course COP$2,500,000). Bus transportation toward the town of San Felix is available from the Portal del Norte bus station, and buses can drop you off at the Estadero El Voladero. Numerous other outfits offer paragliding (*parapente* in Spanish), including **DragonFly** (Vía Sanpedro de los Milagros, cell tel. 300/333-0080, www.parapenteenmedellindragonfly.com).

Hiking

Ecoturismo Arewaro (Cra. 72A No. 30A-21, tel. 4/444-2573, cell tel. 300/652-4327, www.ecoturismoarewaro.com, COP$30,000) organizes day-trip walks and bike trips in parks and pueblos near Medellín. *Arewaro* means "gathering of friends" in the Wayúu language, and this is an interesting option for those looking to meet outdoorsy locals.

Soccer

Medellín has two professional teams, and Envigado has one. By far the most famous team, with rabid followers across the country, is **Atlético Nacional** (www.atlnacional.com.co). Nacional, wearing the green and white of the Antioquian flag, has been playing since 1947. It's one of the most successful teams in Colombia and has won the top division 11 times. Nacional is wildly popular with young men and boys in Medellín, Antioquia, and beyond. The cheap seats at Nacional games are always packed with kids from the barrios. It's an intense affair. The other team in town is **Deportivo Independiente Medellín** (www.dalerojo.net). This is the oldest club in Colombia and was originally called Medellín Foot Ball Club when it was established in 1913. Both teams play at the **Estadio Atanasio Girardot** (Cl. 48 No. 73-10, www.inder.gov.co). Meanwhile, the new kid on the block is **Envigado FC,** a club that curiously has quite a visible following of European and North American expats ("La Familia Naranja") living here. Tickets can be purchased at **Ticket Factory Express** (tel. 4/444-4446, www.ticketexpress.com.co).

Tours

Turibus (www.turibuscolombia.com, 9am-7:40pm daily, COP$35,000 24-hour pass) operates a hop-on, hop-off service that has seven stops in the city, including the Plaza Botero and the Cerro Nutibara/Pueblito Paisa. It also offers tours to other parts of the Antioquia department, such as to Jericó and Guatapé.

A popular walking tour catering mostly to backpackers is **Real City Tours** (www.realcitytours.com), which offers free tours twice a day Monday-Saturday, although a tip is expected. It also has an exotic fruit tour (COP$40,000) in the mornings. Book tours on the website. A five-hour bike tour (22 km) of the city is on offer from **BiciTour** (www.bicitour.co); a portion of the proceeds go to the children's nonprofit, Fundación Niños del Sol.

While some may find it unseemly to go on a tour of Pablo Escobar's Medellín, others find it fascinating. During the three-hour **Pablo Escobar Tour** (cell tel. 317/489-2629, www.paisaroad.com, 9:30am Mon.-Sat., COP$60,000) offered by Paisa Road, you'll see where the world's most notorious drug baron grew up, learn about the violent world of the cartels,

the Estadio Atanasio Girardot complex

and visit his tomb. The meeting point for the tours (offered in English) is at the Black Sheep and Casa Kiwi hostels in the Provenza area of El Poblado. If you'd like to visit Escobar's grave independently, you can take the Metro to the Sabaneta station. The **Parque Jardines Montesacro** (Cra. 42 No. 25-51, Autopista Sur Itagüi, tel. 4/374-1111, 9am-5pm daily, free) is within walking distance from there.

Colombian Bike Junkies (cell tel. 318/808-6769, www.colombianbiekjunkies.com) offers several exciting multiday trips in the area, including bike adventures with white-water rafting on the Río Buey (Class 3-4) and other thrills. **El Dorado Trips** (cell tel. 321/874-3440, www.eldoradotrips.com) offers more conventional day tours to coffee farms, Guatapé, and Río Claro.

SHOPPING

The Provenza neighborhood and the area around Parque Lleras are home to several boutique clothing and accessories shops. The **Milla de Oro** in El Poblado is the pride of modern Medellín: a strip of modern shopping malls, hotels, and office buildings. **Santa Fe** (Cl. 43 No. 7 Sur-107, www.centrocomercialsantafe.com) is one of the largest and flashiest of all.

FOOD

Twice a year, typically in April and in September, around 75 of the city's top restaurants participate in **Medellín Gourmet** (www.medellingourmet.com), during which they offer special prix fixe menus.

El Poblado
COLOMBIAN

Popular with a local crowd, ★ **3 Típicos** (Cl. 34 No. 7-05, www.3tipicos.com, tel. 4/322-3229, 11am-4pm Mon.-Tues., 11am-9pm Wed.-Thurs., 11am-10pm Fri.-Sat., 11am-6pm Sun., COP$23,000) is a pleasant open-air place where you order grilled meat and fish. For dessert, there's figs with *arequipe*. Vegetarians can have the beans and rice with avocado salad.

Along Avenida Las Palmas above El Poblado are several large and famous grilled meat and *comida típica* restaurants. They are especially popular on weekend afternoons. Open-air and under a giant thatched roof is **Hato Viejo** (Cl. 16 No. 28-60, Av. Las Plamas, tel. 4/268-5412 or 4/268-6811, www.hatoviejo.com, noon-11pm daily, COP$25,000), a popular place for a weekend lunch with the gang. On Friday nights they have live music. **San Carbón** (Cl. 14 No. 30-10, tel. 4/444-7602, www.sancarbon.com.co, noon-10pm weekdays, noon-2am on weekends, COP$29,000) often has live music Wednesday-Sunday. Specialties include barbecue pork ribs and pepper steak.

FUSION

★ **Carmen** (Cra. 36 No. 10A-27 tel. 4/311-9625, www.carmenrestaurante.com.co, noon-2:30pm Tues.-Fri., 7pm-10:30pm Mon.-Sat., COP$38,000)

El Poblado

is considered one of the top restaurants in the country, and this sophisticated dining spot has a fantastic location on the fringes of El Poblado. Reservations are required. The open kitchen allows you to observe the attention to detail from your table.

★ **La Provincia** (Cra. 42 No. 3Sur-81, tel. 4/322-0192, www.laprovinciarestaurante.com, noon-3pm and 7pm-midnight Mon.-Sat., COP$35,000) is a Medellín classic, always ranked at the top of the city's restaurant list. It is a fusion of Mediterranean cuisine (lots of seafood) and Colombian flair. Try for a table on the romantic patio out back. Try the exotic grilled fish fillet in a peanut sauce with green papaya strips. At La Provincia you're guaranteed a memorable evening out. Reservations are recommended.

El Herbario (Cra. 43D No. 10-30, tel. 4/311-2537, www.elherbario.com, noon-3pm and 7pm-11pm daily, COP$24,000) has an inventive menu with items such as lemongrass tuna, turmeric prawns, and artichoke risotto. Spacious and minimalistic, it can feel a little like eating in a warehouse, though. The attached store sells exotic jams and chutneys and the like.

Feeling guilty for consuming too much fried food, carbs, and alcohol? You'll start to feel better just by stepping into slow-food believer **Appetit** (Cl. 8A No. 35-40, tel. 4/268-9901), a clean and fresh corner restaurant in in Provenza. Under the watchful eye of its German owner, Appetit specializes in organic ingredients. Mains include grilled octopus with hummus (COP$23,500) and organic lentils with shrimp (COP$26,000).

Set in a modernist house with interior gardens is sophisticated **Barcal** (Cl. 7D No. 43A-70, tel. 4/268-8714, www.restaurantebarcal.com, Mon.-Sat. noon-3pm and 7pm-10pm, COP$34,000), which specializes in Mediterranean fusion dishes. Start your meal with the octopus popcorn.

Wagon wheel lamps and antiques add to the atmosphere at long-time favorite **La Tienda del Vino** (Cl. 9 No. 43B-93, tel. 4/311-5822, www.latiendadelvino.com.co, Mon.-Sat. noon-10pm, Sun. noon-5pm), where a menu of mostly grilled meats and pastas is served in an open-air environment.

FRENCH

Stylish French bistro **Ganso & Castor** (Cra. 36 No. 7-46, tel. 4/268-9572, 8am-7:30pm Mon.-Sat., 8am-1pm Sun., COP$16,000) serves breakfast anytime and dishes up menu items such as croque monsieur, quiches, steak tartare, and escargots. There are two tables outside. It has a second location at the Museo de Arte Moderno.

Entrecôte (steak) and *pommes frites* (fries) await diners at upscale **Le Loup** (Cra. 43C No. 9-50, tel. 4/311-8986, noon-7pm Tues.-Sat., COP$32,000), which is set on a street full of interesting antique shops.

MIDDLE EASTERN

Tabun (Cra. 33 No. 7-99, tel. 4/311-8209, www.eltabun.com, noon-10pm Mon.-Wed., noon-11pm Thurs.-Sat., noon-5:30pm Sun., COP$22,000) serves standard Middle Eastern fare in generous portions, and they also have a few Indian dishes. Belly dancers perform on weekends.

ITALIAN

Fantastic artisanal pizzas pair with Argentinian wine at **Da Filippo** (Cra. 40 No. 10A-30, tel. 4/266-3489, noon-3pm and 6pm-midnight Tues.-Sat., noon-5pm Sun., COP$26,000). It's run by the same people as neighboring Il Castello.

There's a nice atmosphere at the small Italian restaurant **Seveníssima** (Cra. 40 No. 10A-13, tel. 4/311-8593, noon-10:30pm Mon.-Sat., noon-3:30pm Sun.), which has a rustic old-world feeling about it.

Whereas most restaurants in El Poblado face rather busy and noisy streets, ★ **Toscano** (Cl. 8A No. 34-20, tel. 4/311-3094, cell tel. 314/739-6316, noon-2:30pm and 6:30pm-9:30pm Mon.-Thurs., noon-2:30pm and 6:30pm-11pm Fri.-Sat., noon-4pm Sun., COP$13,000 lunch set menu, COP$24,000) is on a quiet stretch. It's a delight to sit outside and have a pasta dish with a glass of wine.

VEGETARIAN

Most restaurants except the hard-core Colombian *parilla*-type places now offer at least one lonely vegetarian dish on their menus. In Provenza, there's no need to pity the herbivore any longer: Make a beeline for the cool atmosphere and fantastic vegetarian food at two-story ★ **Verdeo** (Cl. 12 No. 43D-77, tel. 4/444-0934, www.ricoverdeo.com, noon-10pm Mon.-Wed., noon-11pm Thurs.-Sat., noon-4pm Sun., COP$18,000). This vegetarian haven could be the best vegetarian restaurant in Colombia. Veggie burgers go down well with an artisanal beer, but there are also Asian- and Italian-inspired a la carte options. Lunch menus are inventive, and are a bargain.

Lenteja Express (Cra. 35 No. 8A-76, tel. 4/311-0186, cell tel. 310/879-9136, 11am-9pm Mon.-Sat.) specializes in veggie burgers: chickpea burgers, lentil burgers, and Mexican burgers. They have several locations in the city.

ASIAN

Authentic Asian restaurants are few and far between in Medellín. **Royal Thai** (Cra. 8A No. 37A-05, tel. 4/354-2843, www.royalthaicolombia.com, 6pm-10pm Mon.-Wed., noon-3pm and 6pm-11pm Thurs.-Fri., 1pm-4pm and 6pm-11pm Sat., 6:30pm-9:30pm Sun., COP$27,000) is a welcome change of pace serving authentic Thai cuisine.

Naan (Cra. 35 No. 7-75, tel. 4/312-6285, noon-3pm and 7pm-10pm Mon.-Wed., noon-3pm and 7pm-11pm Thurs.-Fri., noon-11pm Sat., noon-4pm Sun., COP$24,000) is a small and trendy Indian place in the Provenza area.

BURGERS AND SANDWICHES

The original ★ **Fellini** (Cra. 37 No. 10B-04, www.fellini.com.co, tel. 4/444-5064) has a gorgeous location amid gardens and trees, and it's home to a friendly cat. They serve lots of burgers here, and vegetarian dishes as well (falafel burger and portobello pesto). The owner moved to Medellín from the Netherlands years ago.

Hip, good, and popping up all over Medellín is chain **Chef Burger** (Cl. 11A No. 42-05, tel. 4/448-2378, noon-10:30pm Sun.-Wed., noon-11:30pm Thurs.-Sat.), where they stake the claim of serving the best burger in town. There are quite a few from which to choose.

Sandwiches don't have to be boring. At **Espresso Sanduchería** (Cra. 40 No. 10A-37, tel. 4/268-8300, cell tel. 318/343-6827, noon-10pm Mon.-Sat., COP$18,000) you can order a bahn mi or a blue cheese-and-beef sandwich. It's a smart little place on a pleasant side street.

CAFÉS AND QUICK BITES

The **Juan Valdez Café** (Cra. 37A No. 8A-74, 10am-9pm daily), atop the Parque Lleras, is a point of reference for the area and the place to meet up with someone for a cappuccino. It's popular with travelers and locals alike.

If you're feeling decadent, as in you'd like your latte in an actual coffee cup and served to you at a table, try **Pergamino Café** (Cra. 37 No. 8A-37, tel. 4/268-6444, 10am-9pm Mon.-Fri., 11am-9pm Sat.). It's on a relatively quiet street in the Provenza area. This could become your favorite coffee place. A few blocks from the hordes of cappuccino-seeking tourists is **Urbania Café** (Cl. 8 no. 43B-132, Mon.-Fri. 7am-8pm, Sat. noon-8pm, Sun. 10am-6pm), a cool place with organic chocolates, light pastries, and a little style.

La Maga (Cl. 10B No. 36-38, tel. 4/386-0673, 8am-7pm Mon.-Thurs., 8am-6pm Fri., 10am-5pm Sat.) may be on the nicest block in Medellín. It's tree-lined and quiet. In the front of the Perceptual interior design store is this tiny coffee and pastry stand, where you can sip coffee and savor a piece of cinnamon bread on the divine terrace.

They serve food at **El Codo de San Lorenzo** (Cra. 36 No. 10A-71, tel. 4/580-4022, noon-8pm Mon.-Tues., noon-9pm Wed., noon-11:30pm Thurs., noon-1:30am Fri.-Sat.), but the café's terrace may be nicer for a beer or two on a pleasant spring evening.

Centro
COLOMBIAN

A cheerful option downtown with a decent lunch menu is **El Tunel Café y Cocina** (Cra. 42 No. 54-62, tel. 4/239-6536, noon-10pm Mon.-Sat., COP$15,000).

FUSION

★ **In Situ** (Jardín Botánico, tel. 4/460-7007, www.botanicomedellin.org, noon-3pm Mon., noon-3pm and 7pm-10pm Tues.-Sat., noon-4pm Sun., COP$35,000) may have the nicest view of any eatery in Medellín. It's surrounded by a million shades of green on the grounds of the Jardín Botánico. It's an elegant place for a lunch, but if you've been sweating while visiting the city you may feel out of place among the sharply dressed business and society crowds. In Situ has an interesting menu with items such as apple sea bass (COP$30,000) and beef medallions in a coffee sauce with a plantain puree (COP$29,000).

Next to the Museo de Arte Moderno de Medellín is hip **Bonuar** (Cra. 44 No. 19A-100, tel. 4/235-3577, www.bonuar.com, 10am-7pm Tues.-Fri., 11am-6pm Sat., noon-4pm Sun., COP$22,000), where the burgers (including a portobello and lentil version) are famous and so is the brunch. It's a cool place with a nice outdoor seating area. During weekdays, it's better to go in the evening when the atmosphere is livelier. Try the fish in coconut creole sauce.

VEGETARIAN

Govinda's (Cl. 51 No. 52-17, tel. 4/293-2000, www.govindas.co, 11am-3pm Mon.-Sat., COP$14,000) is a Hare Krishna restaurant downtown serving delicious vegan lunches.

BURGERS

Fellini (Plaza Mayor, Cl. 41 No. 55-80, Local 105, tel. 4/444-5064, www.fellini.com.co, noon-8pm Mon.-Fri., noon-4pm Sat., COP$15,000) specializes in burgers, but it also serves sandwiches, salads, and pastas. Plan to eat here after your long day of sightseeing downtown.

Laureles and the Stadium Area
COLOMBIAN

★ **Mondongo's** (Cra. 70 No. C3-43, tel. 4/411-3434, www.mondongos.com.co, 11:30am-9:30pm daily, COP$20,000) is a well-known and popular place for typical Colombian food and for drinks with friends. *Mondongo* is a tripe stew, a Colombian comfort food. In addition to the Carrera 70 location, there is another Mondongo's on the busy Calle 10 in El Poblado (Cl. 10 No. 38-38, tel. 4/312-2346) that is a popular drinking hole as well. They even have a location in Miami.

Another popular place on the Carrera 70 strip is **La Tienda** (Cra. 70 Circular 3-28, tel. 4/260-6783, 10am-2am daily). It's a festive restaurant that morphs into a late-night drinking place as the Medellín evenings wear on. Their *bandeja paisa* is famous. It's a signature Antioquian dish that includes beans, rice, sausages, and pork rinds.

Maru Rico Guayabal (Cra. 51 Sur No. 6-8, tel. 4/354-5565, 11am-7pm Mon.-Sat., COP$14,000) is famous for its beans.

MIDDLE EASTERN

★ **Fenicia** (Cra. 73 No. C2-41, Av. Jardín, tel. 4/413-8566, www.fenicia-comidaarabe.com, noon-8pm Mon.-Thurs., noon-9pm Fri.-Sat., noon-4pm Sun., COP$22,000) is an authentic Lebanese restaurant run by a family who immigrated to Colombia years ago. *Pastel cartageneros* (rice tamale) are served only on weekends, while delicious desserts like date pastries and fig flan with coconut are always awaiting after a delicious meal.

ITALIAN

At **Crispino** (Circular 1A No. 74-04, Laureles, tel. 4/413-3266, noon-11pm Mon.-Thurs., noon-midnight Fri.-Sat., noon-5pm Sun., COP$20,000), owner Salvatore, direct from Naples, offers authentic Italian cuisine and freshly baked bread in an agreeable atmosphere.

Bandeja paisa is made of beans, rice, sausage, and pork rinds.

ASIAN

Korea House (Transversal 39B No. 77-56, tel. 4/412-1874, 11:30am-8pm Mon.-Sat.) has the bulgogi you've been craving, as well as zucchini pancakes.

CAFÉS AND QUICK BITES

Four in the morning and you've got the munchies? Join the legion of taxi drivers, college kids, and miscellaneous night owls at **Trigo Laurel** (Circula 1A No. 70-06, tel. 4/250-4943, 24 hours daily), where it never closes. They specialize in baked goods, but they also serve cheap lunches. It's on a quiet corner of Carrera 70.

Envigado
SPANISH

Cozy and chic Spanish restaurant **El Barral** (Cl. 30 Sur No. 43A-38, tel. 4/276-1212, noon-10pm Mon.-Sat., COP$30,000) specializes in paella, tapas, and sangria, and does them well in sophisticated surroundings.

STEAK

With Colombian newspapers plastered on the walls displaying headlines of yesteryear, the Argentinian steak house **Lucio Carbón y Vino** (Cra. 44A No. 30S-40, Envigado, tel. 4/334-4003, noon-midnight Mon.-Sat., COP$32,000) specializes in grilled steak, paired with a nice Malbec.

ACCOMMODATIONS

Accommodation options to fit every budget and taste are plentiful in Medellín. El Poblado has the most options, with luxury hotels along Avenida El Poblado and hostels and boutiques in the walkable Provenza area, close to a smorgasbord of restaurants and bars and close-ish to the El Poblado Metro station. Laureles is a quiet and green residential area with a growing number of fine options for those wanting an escape from the madding crowd. Some may choose to stay in the Centro, but note that it's an area of town that feels unsafe at night. As is the case in cities in the interior of the country, hotel prices fall on weekends, and vacancies increase.

El Poblado
UNDER COP$70,000

Medellin is a top destination on the international backpacker trail, and hostels geared toward that market have sprung up throughout the city. Hostels have distinct "vibes," from mild to wild, with the latter tending to be close to the action near Parque Lleras in Provenza.

Waypoint Hostel (Cra. 48B No. 10 Sur 08, cell tel. 300/671-9912, www.waypointhostel.com, COP$25,000 dorm, COP$80,000 d) is close to the EAFIT university and has friendly staff and clean facilities. A big selling point here is the pool. It's a bit of a hike to the Parque Lleras area, but the property is close to the Metro. The hostel has bikes for rent. Some dorm rooms have a lot of beds in them.

COP$70,000-200,000

Acqua Hotel Express (Cra. 35 No. 7-47, tel. 4/448-0482, cell tel. 320/788-4424, www.hotelacqua.com, COP$148,000 d) is a fairly good value, mostly because of its prime location in Provenza. There are 43 spotless rooms that are somewhat comfortable. You will be charged if you bring a guest to the room, though.

The **Hotel BH El Poblado** (Cra. 43 No. 9 Sur 35, tel. 4/604-3534, www.bhhoteles.com, COP$195,000 d) is across from the enormous Centro Comercial Santa Fe. This Colombian chain hotel with 70 rooms has huge, comfortable beds and modern rooms, and despite its location on a major street (Av. El Poblado), it's not that noisy. An included breakfast buffet is served in a pleasant open-air terrace. It also has a tiny hotel gym, with about three cardio machines.

Hotel Zona A (Cl. 10B No. 37-69, tel. 4/580-3800, www.hotelzonaa.com, COP$172,000 d) is a cute little hotel (19 rooms) with small rooms and a nice outdoor terrace where you can have breakfast. The location is perfect, in a surprisingly woodsy area of El Poblado, but that doesn't necessarily mean there will be no traffic noise.

A touch of rustic charm in happening El Poblado is on offer at **La Campana Hotel Boutique** (Cl. 11A No. 31A-70, tel. 4/312-2525, COP$180,000 d), a house with 13 rooms and pleasant common areas.

COP$200,000-500,000

Estelar Blue (Cra. 42 No. 1 Sur-74, tel. 4/369-8380, COP$245,000 d) is a Colombian business hotel chain. This location has spacious and no-surprises rooms and offers both breakfast and light dinner buffets.

For more privacy, consider an aparta-hotel such as **Orange Suites** (Cl. 8 No. 43C-37, tel. 1/216-9843, www.travelers.com.co/ciudades/medellin, COP$215,000 d). This high-rise in El Poblado has lots of space.

Yes, the ★ **Charlee Lifestyle Hotel** (Cl. 9A No. 37-16, tel. 4/444-4968, www.thecharlee.com, COP$485,000) is awesome: hot tubs on room balconies with a view to the Parque Lleras, a massive mini bar, a pool on the terrace, a spectacular gym, good food, and a disco.

Polished concrete floors, a gallery space in the lobby, and a rooftop terrace make the **Art Hotel Boutique** (Cra. 41 No. 9-31, tel. 4/369-7900, www.arthotel.com.co, COP$238,000 d) a swank choice. It's a bargain, considering how upscale it is. The gym and spa area in the basement is a little sad. This hotel is just a couple of blocks from the Parque Lleras.

OVER COP$500,000

Impeccable service awaits at **Park 10 Hotel** (Cra. 36 B No. 11-12, tel. 4/310-6060, www.hotelpark10.com.co, COP$520,000 d), located in a tree-lined area of El Poblado within walking distance of fine restaurants. Amenities include fantastic breakfasts and a small gym with modern machines and pilates studio. An English-speaking staff welcomes visitors to this classic property.

Centro
COP$70,000-COP$200,000

Hard-core city lovers will be the ones interested in staying in the Centro. The **Hotel Nutibara Conference Center** (Cl. 52A No. 50-46, tel. 4/511-5111, www.hotelnutibara.com, COP$127,000 d) is the area's best choice. It's a faded, grand old hotel located steps from the Museo de Antioquia, but the rooms are updated. With wide corridors and huge rooms with parquet floors, it retains mid-20th-century elegance and personality. There's a bar in the basement that hosts jazz performances, and there's a food court nearby. Many advise not to wander after dark in the area.

Hotel 61 Prado (Cl. 61 No. 50A-60, tel. 4/254-9743, www.61prado.com, COP$68,000 s, COP$91,000 d) is a charming guesthouse downtown, with large rooms and a rooftop terrace for breakfast at their 24-hour restaurant. Light sleepers may want to request a room in back to avoid street noise.

Laureles and the Stadium Area
UNDER COP$70,000

Located in a quiet residential neighborhood, but just behind a big Éxito department store, the ★ **Palm Tree Hostal** (Cra. 67 No. 48D-63, tel. 4/4447256, cell tel. 300/241-9209, www.palmtreemedellin.com, COP$28,000 dorm, COP$70,000 d with shared bath) is known for its friendly staff and similiarly laid-back guests. Despite having been around a long while, it remains a favorite. It's three blocks from the Suramericana Metro station. A basic breakfast is provided.

Wandering Paisa (Cl. 44 A No. 68A-76, www.wanderingpaisa-hostel.com, cell tel. 320/749-2073, tel. 4/436-6759, COP$27,000 dorm, COP$70,000 d) has a social vibe, with the on-site Paisa Bar and events like karaoke taking place often. It's close to the stadium. There are four dorm rooms, two with eight beds and two with four beds; it's more comfortable to be in a room with four. A metro station is a five-minute walk from the hostel.

In between bed-and-breakfast and hostel, the ★ **Yellow House Hostel** (Cra. 81A No. 47A-48, tel. 4/411-2873, www.yellowhouse.com.co, COP$25,000 dorm, COP$80,000 d) is a laid-back option on a quiet residential street in Floresta, a 10-minute walk to the Metro station. There are five private rooms (four with en suite bath) and one dorm room with six beds. Besides the relaxing and welcoming environs, guests love the breakfasts—and the fluffy canine residents.

COP$70,000-COP$200,000
The **Casa Hotel Asturias Medellín** (Circular 4 No. 73-124, tel. 4/260-2872, COP$145,000 d) is on a delightful corner of the tree-lined and quiet

Laureles neighborhood. That's the big selling point for this small hotel. Rooms are modern and comfortable, although not terribly huge. It's a good deal.

COP$200,000-500,000

Located across from the Atanasio Girardot sports complex, the **Hotel Tryp Medellín** (Cl. 50 No. 70-24, tel. 4/604-0686, www.tryphotels.com, COP$220,000 d) has 140 large, comfortable (if spartan) rooms and an excellent rooftop terrace with a whirlpool and steam room. Guests have access to an on-site gym. Restaurants are nonexistent in this area, except for street food, and hotel room service is iffy. The area revs up when Atlético Nacional is playing.

Ciudad del Río
COP$70,000-200,000

In contrast to many Colombian cities, Medellín has a fair variety of midrange hotels. Chain hotels tend to be best, holding few surprises.

French budget chain ★ **Hotel Ibis** (Cl. 20 No. 44-16, tel.4/444-1554, www.ibis.com, COP$99,000 d) has modern rooms with comfortable beds at great rates, and is in an interesting area of the Ciudad del Río, across the street from the Museo de Arte Moderno de Medellín. There's no gym, but the neighborhood is quiet, making a morning jog a possibility. The best views are on the hotel's south side. The hotel restaurant offers buffet meals for an additional price. On the weekends it's very quiet, and room rates may slide further.

It has a boring and unattractive location, but the standard-to-the-core **GHL Comfort Hotel San Diego** (Cl. 31, No. 43-90, www.ghlhoteles.com, COP$150,000 d) offers good prices and an attentive staff. A standard Colombian breakfast is served on the top-floor terrace (featuring an excellent view), and amenities include a sauna and small gym. It's close to a couple of malls and is between the Centro and El Poblado on a main road. The Ciclovía passes by on Sundays, making it a snap to get out and move.

INFORMATION AND SERVICES
Tourist Information

Medellín produces the most comprehensive tourist information of any city in Colombia. In addition to visitor information booths at the bus terminals and airports, there is a large office at the **Plaza Mayor** (Cl. 41 No. 55-80, tel. 4/261-7277, 8am-noon and 2pm-6pm Mon.-Sat.). The tourism office website (www.medellin.travel) maintains up-to-date information on what's going on in the city.

The main newspaper in Medellín is *El Colombiano* (www.elcolombiano. com). Another excellent resource is the website **Medellín Living** (www. medellinliving.com), which is run by expats. **Universo Centro** (www.universocentro.com) has a more urban focus: It's produced by and for folks living in Medellín's Centro.

Spanish-Language Courses
Universidad EAFIT Centro de Idiomas (Cra. 49 No. 7S-50, Bldg. 31, Of. 201, tel. 4/261-9399, www.eafit.edu.co/spanishprogram, COP$1,010,000 38-hr. course) offers intensive (20 hours per week) and semi-intensive (10 hours per week) Spanish classes.

TRANSPORTATION
Air
There are two airports serving Medellín. The main airport, with several international flights, is **Aeropuerto Internacional José María Córdova** (MDE, tel. 4/402-5110 or 4/562-2885) in the town of Rionegro, about 35 km (22 miles) from the city. Avianca, LATAM, and Viva Colombia operate domestic flights from MDE.

Taxis cost around COP$60,000 between the city and the airport; the drive takes about 45 minutes. To go to the airport in Rionegro, call the special **Rionegro airport taxi service** (tel. 4/261-1616, cell tel. 313/744-0680, http://acoataxiaeropuerto.com.co); these white cabs have a blue stripe on them.

There are also *busetas* (small buses) leaving the airport bound for the San Diego neighborhood, which is convenient to El Poblado. These can be found as you exit the terminal toward the right. Traveling to the airport from Medellin, there are buses (Conbuses, tel. 4/231-9681) that depart from a side street just behind the **Hotel Nutibara** (Cl. 52A No. 50-46, tel. 4/511-5111) in the Centro. These depart from about 4:30am until 8:30pm every day, and the trip costs COP$8,800. The buses are hard to miss: They're green and white with the word *aeropuerto* printed in all caps on the front window.

The **Aeropuerto Olaya Herrera** (EOH, Cra. 65A No. 13-157, tel. 4/403-6781, www.aeropuertoolayaherrera.gov.co) is the super-convenient in-town airport. It's especially useful for traveling to the Pacific coast and to Capurganá/Acandí. From EOH, **Satena** serves Bogotá, Quibdó, Apartadó, Bahía Solano, and Nuquí; **ADA** (Aerolínea de Antioquia) connects the city with towns such as Bahía Solano, Acandí, and Capurganá; and **EasyFly** serves cities in eastern Colombia like Cúcuta and Bucaramanga. The Olaya Herrera terminal was built in the 1930s and is an architectural gem—you'll love it.

Intercity Buses
Medellín has two bus terminals: the Sur and the Norte. The **Terminal del Sur** (Cra. 65 No. 8B-91, tel. 4/444-8020 or 4/361-1186) is across from the Aeropuerto Olaya Herrera, and it serves destinations in southern Antioquia and the coffee region. The **Terminal del Norte** (Cra. 64C No. 78-580, tel. 4/444-8020 or 4/230-9595) is connected to the Caribe Metro station. It serves Santa Fe de Antioquia and Guatapé, the Caribbean coast, and Bogotá.

Metro

Medellín's **Metro** (tel. 4/444-9598, www.metrodemedellin.gov.co) is the only urban train system in the country. It's a safe and super-clean system of two lines: Línea A, which runs from Niquía (north) to La Estrella (south), and Línea B, from San Antonio in the Centro west to San Javier. The Metro line A is useful for traveling between El Centro, El Poblado, and Envigado. Metro line B has a stop at the stadium. The current Metro fare is COP$1,800; however, if you think you may use the Metro, Metrocable, and Metroplús system on a regular basis, consider purchasing a refillable Tarjeta Cívica card that is valid on all three transportation networks. The cost per ride with the Tarjeta Cívica modestly drops to COP$1,600. The card can be purchased at Metro ticket booths.

Metrocable

The Metrocable public transportation system, consisting of gondola *(teleférico)* lines, was inaugurated in 2004 and consists of three lines, with two under construction. It has been internationally lauded as an innovative approach to solving the unique transportation needs of the isolated and poor *comunas* (residential sectors) built on the mountainsides of the city. The three Metrocable lines are: Línea J from the San Javier Metro station to La Aurora in the west, Línea K from the Acevedo Metro station in the north to Santo Domingo, and Línea L from Santo Domingo to the Parque Arví. The Metrocable runs 9am-10pm daily. The Metrocable Línea L from Santo Domingo to the Parque Arví operates 9am-6pm Tuesday-Sunday. When Monday is a holiday, the Línea L runs that day and does not operate the next day, Tuesday.

Metroplús Rapid Bus

The first line of the **Metroplús** (www.metroplus.gov.co) rapid bus system, with dedicated bus stops, debuted in 2013. There are two Metroplús lines: Línea 1 and Línea 2. Línea 1 connects the working-class neighborhood of Arjuanez in the north with the Universidad de Medellín in the southwest. Línea 2 connects the same two sectors but passes through the Centro and Plaza Mayor area. To access the system, you must use the Tarjeta Cívica, which can be purchased at any Metro station.

Taxis

Taxis are plentiful in Medellín. You can order them over the phone at 4/444-4444, or use an app like **Easy Taxi, Tappsi,** or **Uber.**

Northern and Eastern Antioquia

SANTA FE DE ANTIOQUIA

Living and breathing colonial charm, this pueblo 80 kilometers (50 miles) northwest of Medellín is the best of Antioquia. Set on the banks of the Río Cauca, Santa Fe was founded in 1541 by Jorge Robledo, a ruthless conquistador. It became an important center for gold mining, and the town was the capital of Antioquia until 1823, when it ceded that title to Medellín. Today its proximity to Medellín makes Santa Fe an easy trip for those interested in seeing a colonial-era jewel of a pueblo.

With the average temperature a sizzling 27°C (81°F), it can be a challenge to fully enjoy strolling the lovely streets of the pueblo during the heat of the day. If you can, plan to stay the night (one weekday night will do), arriving in late afternoon.

Sights

The town's narrow stone streets and compact center are adorned with charming plazas and parks and five historic churches. It's a delight to stroll the town in the late afternoon, after the heat of the day has subsided. Churches and historic buildings in Santa Fe are often built in the typical *calicanto* style, a mix of brick and stone construction materials. Historic colonial churches, with majestic facades, often face parks and are illuminated at night.

The "grandmother" of churches in Antioquia is the **Templo de Santa Bárbara** (Cl. 11 at Cra. 8, masses 7am and 6pm Mon.-Sat., 6am and 6pm Sun.). Built toward the end of the 18th century, it is characterized by its many baroque elements. Next to it, in what was a Jesuit college, is the **Museo de Arte Religioso** (Cl. 11 No. 8-12, tel. 4/311-3808, 10am-1pm and 2pm-5pm Fri.-Sun., COP$3,000), a museum that highlights paintings, sculptures, and gold and silver pieces from the Spanish New World colonies.

A nicely presented museum contained in a colonial-style house, the **Museo Juan del Corral** (Cl. 11 No. 9-77, tel. 4/853-4605, 9am-noon and 2pm-5:30pm Mon.-Tues. and Thurs.-Fri., 10am-5pm Sat.-Sun., free) has exhibits on the history of Santa Fe, including historical items from 1813 when Antioquia was declared free. The museum also puts on temporary exhibits of contemporary Colombian artists and hosts other cultural events.

Six kilometers (four miles) outside of town, on an old road that leads to the town of Sopetrán on the other side of the Río Cauca, is an architectural wonder: the **Puente de Occidente,** a suspension bridge made of iron and steel. It was built toward the end of the 19th century by José María Villa, an engineer who studied in New Jersey and worked on the Brooklyn Bridge. It's a narrow span and has been closed to vehicular traffic, for the most part. *Mototaxis* can take you there from town, cross the bridge, and return for COP$15,000. The bridge is easily reached by bike as well.

Festivals and Events

Semana Santa in Santa Fe (www.semanasantafe.org) means processions along the cobblestone streets and a Festival de Música Sacra y Religiosa that features concerts. Visitors from across the region converge on the town for this religious celebration.

The big event in Santa Fe is the weeklong **Festival de Cine de Antioquia** (www.festicineantioquia.com), a film festival held each year in early December. There is usually an international director or actor who is the guest of honor. Some free showings are held outdoors in the town's plazas and parks.

Recreation

Naturaventura (Hotel Mariscal Robledo, Cl. 10 No. 9-70, tel. 4/853-1946, cell tel. 313/667-8150, naturaventura1@hotmail.com) organizes nature walks, bike trips, horseback riding, and rafting excursions.

Shopping

Spaniards were once attracted to Santa Fe because of its gold. Today it is famous for its intricate filigree jewelry. To peruse some, visit **ORFOA** (Cl. 9 No. 6-02, tel. 4/853-2880, 9am-noon and 2pm-6pm daily) or **Dulces & Artesanías Clavellina** (Hotel Mariscal Robledo, Cl. 10 No. 9-70, tel. 4/853-2195, 9am-noon and 2pm-6pm daily).

Guarniélería y Marroquinería (Cl. 10 No. 7-66, cell tel. 314/847-8354, noon-7pm Mon.-Fri., 10am-7pm Sat.-Sun.) sells authentic Jericó *carrieles* (shoulder bags used by Paisa cowhands) and other locally made leather handicrafts. **La Casa Solariega** (Cl. de la Amargura No. 8-09, tel. 4/853-1530, 9am-noon and 2pm-6pm daily) has an eclectic collection of handicrafts, paintings, and antiques in a typical Santa Fe house.

Food

There are few places in Colombia where one can dine to the soft tones of classical or jazz music. The **Restaurante Bar La Comedia** (Parque Santa Bárbara, tel. 4/853-1243, noon-3pm and 6pm-10pm Wed.-Sun., COP$18,000) is one such place. Light dishes, sandwiches, and crepes dominate the small menu, and this is also an option for late-afternoon *onces,* tea time—or maybe an iced coffee. It's diagonal to the Santa Bárbara church.

Restaurante Portón del Parque (Cl. 10 No. 11-03, tel. 4/853-3207, noon-8pm Sun.-Thurs., noon-9:30pm Sat.-Sun., COP$20,000) is lavishly decorated with portraits and paintings by owner Olga Cecilia. In addition to typical Paisa specialties (lunch specials during the week go for less than COP$10,000), the extensive menu offers seafood and international cuisine.

The restaurant at the **Hotel Mariscal Robledo** (Cl. 10 No. 9-70, tel. 4/853-1111, cell tel. 313/760-0099, www.hotelmariscalrobledo.com, 8am-3pm and 7pm-10pm daily, COP$25,000) is a reliable choice serving a range of cuisines, from local Paisa specialties to pasta.

Accommodations

Medellín families converge on Santa Fe en masse on weekends, and for many the draw is the opportunity to lounge by the pool at one of the hotels lining the main road leading into town. Hotels in town, however, have more charm. Hotel prices can drop substantially during the week.

In town, the ★ **Hotel Mariscal Robledo** (Cl. 10 No. 9-70, tel. 4/853-1111, cell tel. 313/760-0099, www.hotelmariscalrobledo.com, COP$120,000-170,000 d) is far and away the most comfortable hotel, and one oozing personality. Antiques, especially with a cinematic theme, decorate the lobby and common areas. Rooms on the 2nd floor, which have not been given a 21st-century makeover, are nonetheless comfortable, and have far more character. The pool area is luxurious.

On the boutique side and just two blocks from the Parque Principal, the **Hotel Casa Tenerife** (Cra. 8 No. 9-50, tel. 4/853-2261, www.hotelcasatenerife.com.co, COP$162,000 d) has 12 rooms, is tastefully decorated, and has a nice pool and interior courtyard area adorned with a soothing fountain. It often caters to couples celebrating romantic getaways, with such details as rose petals on the bed. This house is over 200 years old.

The family-run **Hotel Caserón Plaza** (Cl. 9-41, Plaza Mayor, tel. 4/853-2040, www.hotelcaseronplaza.com.co, COP$145,000-208,000 d) has an excellent location but is overpriced for what you get. Some of the 33 rooms have air-conditioning, which is a plus in Santa Fe. There is also a pool in back, another plus. The pool is the major hangout area on weekends, and the area also has a nice deck with views.

Information and Services

A **tourist information office** on the Plaza Mayor (Cra. 9 and Cl. 9, tel. 4/853-1022) has maps and hotel information.

Transportation

There is regular bus service, several times a day, from the **Terminal de Transportes del Norte** (Cra. 64 No. 78-344, Medellín, tel. 4/267-7075, www.terminalesmmedellin.com) in Medellín to Santa Fe. The two-hour journey takes you through a feat of modern engineering: the **Túnel Fernando Gómez Martínez,** the longest tunnel in South America. To return from Santa Fe, walk a couple of blocks to the Turbo-Medellín highway near the market at Carrera 10 and flag down passing buses. Most of them are going to Medellín. The trip costs about COP$14,000 each way.

MAGDALENA MEDIO
★ Reserva Natural Río Claro

A visit to the spectacular, privately run **Reserva Natural Río Claro** (Medellín office tel. 4/268-8855, cell tel. 311/354-0119, www.rioclaroreservanatural.com, 8am-6pm daily) is a highlight for anyone visiting Colombia. In the steamy and remote Magdalena Medio region of Antioquia, about 200 kilometers toward the Río Magdalena to the east, the reserve encompasses

500 hectares (1,230 acres) along the Río Claro canyon, a babbling, crystal-clear river. This reserve is a place to enjoy the unspoiled beauty of the river and its jungle and to disconnect from the hectic pace of urban life.

The story behind the park begins with an oft-repeated tale about a pesky jaguar. It seems that the cat was blamed for killing some livestock of a campesino in the area. In a quest to track down the guilty party (the jaguar got away unharmed), the farmer followed its tracks through the jungle and to a spectacular canyon. When Juan Guillermo Garcés heard about the astonishing discovery, he had to see this undiscovered territory for himself. Garcés immediately knew that this was a special place, and he made a commitment to purchase the land to protect it from development, including a highway that was to pass through this pristine land.

Río Claro receives many weekend visitors. In addition to those staying at the reserve, many day visitors spend the afternoon at Río Claro. Don't go on a Saturday, Sunday, or holiday if you seek a peaceful commune with nature. If you visit the reserve midweek, you'll most likely have the place practically to yourself, which is heavenly.

RECREATION

Guides don't speak English, generally. There are two must-do activities at the reserve. The first is an easy rafting trip down the river (COP$25,000), during which you can see the karstic jungle, in which trees grow atop rocks. This excursion takes about two hours. The second activity is a combination swim/hike trip to the **Caverna de los Guácharos** (COP$20,000 pp). This guided walk has its challenging moments: wading across the swiftly flowing river, making your way through the dark cavern, climbing out of the cavern, and then making your way back across the river. *Guácharo* birds (oilbirds), living inside the cavern, act like they own the place (the cavern is, after all, named for them). They don't like it when humans invade their space, and they'll let you know that with their screeching. The cavern is made of

Reserva Natural Río Claro

marble; its stalactites and stalagmites are impressive. Waterproof shoes with good traction are recommended, as you'll be wading in water most of the time. Also, it's nice to have a headlamp so that you'll have hands free. You can take your camera, but at a certain point it will need to be kept in a water-repellent bag, which the guide will have. If you're up for both trips, go on the cavern tour in the morning and go rafting in the late afternoon.

Other activities at the reserve include rock climbing, a zip line, hanging out on the marble beach, self-guided nature walks, and tubing. These are all arranged by Río Claro staff.

ACCOMMODATIONS

The reserve has a variety of accommodation options. Contact the Río Claro office (tel. 4/268-8855, cell tel. 311/354-0119, www.rioclaroreservanatural.com) for all reservations and information. The **Bluemorpho Ecolodge** (COP$85,000) is above the reserve's reception and dining area, boasting comfortable all-wood construction. The best and most isolated lodging is at the far end near the canyon, a 15-minute walk from the main reception area in the **Cabañas El Refugio** (COP$95,000-200,000 pp). Rooms here are open-air and quite spectacular. You'll sleep well with the sounds of the rushing water to lull you asleep. Rooms are completely open, but there are no problems with mosquitoes.

The **Hotel Río Claro** (COP$95,000 pp) is across the highway from the rest of the reserve but still along the river, and it has a big pool. These are small concrete bungalows. The hotel is popular with student groups. All meals are included in the room rates. Tell staff when you make your reservation if you have any dietary needs or special requests, like fresh fruit.

GETTING THERE

The reserve is easily reached by bus from Medellín. All buses between Medellín and Bogotá pass in front of the Río Claro entrance, where there is a small security booth. From Medellín, it takes roughly three hours and costs around COP$24,000. Be sure to tell the driver you'd like to be dropped off at the *"entrada de la Reserva Río Claro."* ("the entrance to the Río Claro Reserve").

Hacienda Napoles

The **Hacienda Napoles** (Puerto Triunfo, tel. 4/444-2975, cell tel. 318/219-4553, www.haciendanapoles.com, 9am-5pm Tues.-Sun., COP$36,000) was a vacation home for the world's most infamous drug trafficker, Pablo Escobar, complete with an airstrip and exotic animals—including quite a few hippos, who apparently adapted nicely to the muggy climes of the Río Magdalena area. Today Hacienda Napoles is a theme park with giant dinosaur sculptures, some of which were built by Escobar for his children; two water parks (additional fees); hippopotami, zebras, and ostriches; an Africa museum; the remnants of Pablo Escobar's country house (now a museum); and his private airstrip.

Avoid the oppressive heat and intense sun of midday (and the crowds on weekends) by visiting early on a weekday morning. The park can easily be visited from Río Claro, which is about an hour away. When Monday is a holiday, the park closes on Tuesday rather than on Monday.

GUATAPÉ

The stone monolith La Piedra dominates the landscape here, but the Guatapé area is more than just a big rock: It's a weekend playground chockfull of recreational activities that keep the crowds from Medellín busy. While Guatapé is doable as a day trip, plenty of outdoorsy activities could keep one blissfully occupied for a day or two.

Sights

Guatapé is a resort town. Aside from La Piedra, it's known for its *zócalos*, the colorful friezes on the lower levels of the town's houses. Many of these honor the traditions of townspeople, such as farming and fishing; others have sheep or other animals; and still others hot rods or the occasional Pink Panther. A particularly colorful street is the **Calle del Recuerdos** near the Parque Principal.

On a serene mountainside near Guatapé, beyond El Encuentro hostel on the same road, is the **Monasterio Santa María de la Epifanía** (www.monjesbenedictinosguatape.org), home to around 30 Benedictine monks. Guests, up to eight at a time, are welcome to stay at the monastery. Every day of the week at the 5:15pm *visperas* (vespers) service, the public is invited to hear the monks sing Gregorian chants.

For a day at the park, head to the **Parque Recreativo COMFAMA Guatapé** (on main road toward Medellín, tel. 4/861-0840, www.comfama.com, 9am-5pm Tues.-Fri., COP$11,500). Run by an insurance company, this private park outside of Guatapé has nature paths and a lake where you can kayak or waterbike. Picnicking makes for a fine idea here; you're allowed to bring in food (but no alcohol).

LA PIEDRA PEÑOL

Known simply as La Piedra, **La Piedra Peñol** (8am-6pm daily, COP$15,000) is a giant rock monolith that soars 200 meters (650 feet) into the sky from the scenic Embalse Peñol-Guatapé, a reservoir covering some 64 square kilometers (25 square miles) that is an important source of hydroelectric energy for the country. There's been quite a rivalry between the towns of El Peñol and Guatapé over the years, with arguments over which town can claim La Piedra as its own. (The rock is located between the two, a tad closer to the Guatapé side.) Things digressed to a point where folks from Guatapé began to paint their town's name in large letters on one prominent side of the rock. People from El Peñol were not amused, and this giant marking of territory was halted by authorities. Today all that remains of that fierce brouhaha is what appear to be the letters "GI."

In front of La Piedra, there is a statue of Luis Villegas López, the man who first climbed the monolith in 1954. Inspired by a priest, López and two friends took five days to slowly climb up cracks in the rock. They had to deal with a beehive and a rainstorm along the way, adding to the challenge.

Today the rock is one of the top tourist attractions in Antioquia. La Piedra can be visited several ways. You can walk from Guatapé, which takes 45 minutes. (Sunscreen and water are essential.) You can bike it, although the road that winds its way up to the rock entrance is quite steep. You can take a *mototaxi* from your hotel (COP$10,000), or you can hop on a Jeep from the Parque Principal (between Cras. 28-29 and Clls. 31-32) in Guatapé. Visit during the early-morning hours or late in the afternoon.

Once you're at the bottom of the rock, look up and notice the hundreds of bromeliads growing along the sides of it. Then head to the top. The 360-degree views from the top of La Piedra over the Guatapé reservoir and Antioqiuan countryside are worth the toil of climbing the more than 600 steps of the ramshackle brick and concrete stairwell that is stuck to the rock. To celebrate your feat, you can have a drink at one of the snack bars at the top.

The town of El Peñol is surrounded by the reservoir, which is operated by Medellín utility company EPM. The reservoir was built in phases during the 1970s and was not without controversy, as the flooding of the area began without the full consent of the inhabitants. Finally, all families were resettled by EPM by 1979, and the town of El Peñol gradually was covered with rising waters, with only a church steeple remaining as a reminder of the town's past.

Tours

A popular excursion is to take a **boat tour** of the reservoir (Hotel Las Araucarias, cell tel. 313/646-7946). A standard stop on the tour is to (or rather, above) the submerged town of Viejo Peñol. It was flooded during the construction of the reservoir and nearby dam in 1978, and today the

the great view that comes from hiking La Piedra Peñol

only visible remnant of the town is a large cross rising out of the water. A small historical museum displays old photos and historical memorabilia from the town. These tours typically last 45 minutes to 1.5 hours.

Guatape Motos (Cl. 32 No. 22-09, cell tel. 313/788-9332, www.guatapemotos.com) does fun motorcycle and scooter tours of 1-3 days involving activities such as visits to old farms of Pablo Escobar (Hacienda Napoles and Finca Manuela), tubing, and people-watching at a refreshing waterfall; it can even throw in a paragliding adventure. Guatape Motos also rents scooters (COP$100,000 day), perfect for zipping around town and beyond.

Food

Fish such as massive carp and trout from the reservoir are the specialty in Guatapé. A reliable spot for fish and Colombian cuisine is **La Fogata** (Cra. 30 No. 31-32, tel. 4/861-1040, cell tel. 314/740-7282, 8am-8pm daily), on the waterfront.

For some healthy food, tilting toward the vegetarian persuasion, try the delightful sidewalk café ★ **Hecho con Amor Deli** (Cra. 27A No. 30-71, cell tel. 321/834-7979, noon-7pm Sat.-Tues.). The freshly baked bread is awesome, as are the desserts. The deli is across from the soccer field.

Bar Baroja (Plazoleta de Zócalos No. 30-48, cell tel. 323/523-5153) is the coolest place for a beer in Guatapé. It's run by Boris from Belgium, a fellow with a *barba roja* (red beard), hence the name: Bar Baroja. A gregarious mix of Colombians and foreigners sit on the colorful steps of Guatapé as they sip some refreshing cocktails. Twister competitions may take place.

Sometimes exceptional hospitality can give one a sugar headache. That's what happens at Gloria Elena's generous candy tastings at **Dulces de Guatapé** (Cl. 29 No. 23C-32, Barrio Villa del Carmen, tel. 4/861-0724, 7am-6pm). At this small candy factory, they make all kinds of sweets, many with *arequipe* (caramel) and some with fruits like the tart *uchuva* and guava. There are also some chocolate bonbons that have peanuts and almonds.

Accommodations

During the week, prices drop significantly at most hotels, especially if you pay in cash.

Tomate Café Hostel (Cra. 31 No. 30-41, tel. 4/861-1100, cell tel. 310/450-7981, www.tomatecafehostel.com, COP$18,000 dorm, COP$40,000 d) is run by a Paisa family and has four small private rooms and two dorm rooms in town. A strong cup of coffee is always on offer here, as well as healthy and vegetarian food in their restaurant.

At ★ **Mi Casa Guatape** (tel. 4/861-0632, cell tel. 301/457-5726, www.micasaguatape.com, COP$30,000 dorm, COP$70,000 d) guests wake up, step outside with a cup of coffee in hand, and greet their neighbor, La Piedra, with a warm *buenos días*. You can't get much closer to that big rock than from this small English-Colombian hostel. The hostel has five private rooms and one four-bed dorm as well as two kitchens for use. When not outdoors climbing La Piedra or taking the hostel's kayak for a spin, guests can laze in hammocks on the deck, watch movies, or bond with the owners' sweet dog. Mi Casa works closely with next-door neighbor **Adventure Activities** (cell tel. 301/411-4442), a group that organizes an intense-rock climbing excursion to one of dozens of routes up La Piedra (COP$90,000, 4-5 hours), as well as other outings. Owner Sean takes guests on a waterfall hike (6 km/4 miles round-trip, COP$15,000, 4 hours). It's easy to go into town from the hostel by catching a ride with a passing Jeep or with Mi Casa's preferred *mototaxi* driver. Mi Casa is about three kilometers before Guatapé on the main road (25-min. walk or COP$1,500 taxi ride) and is across the street from the landmark El Estadero La Mona.

There are a couple of upscale hotels in town. **Hotel Portobello** (Cl. 32 No. 28-29, tel. 4/861-0016, cell tel. 312/783-4050, www.hotelportobeloguatape.com, COP$215,000 d) has 16 rooms, and most of them have a view of the lake. You can obtain a 25 percent discount during the week if you pay in cash.

Transportation

There is frequent bus service from Medellín's north terminal to Guatapé. The trip takes about two hours and costs COP$13,000. Buses depart Guatapé at a waterfront bus terminal that was completed in 2013. It's just one block from the main plaza. Buses returning to Medellín often fill up in a hurry on Sundays, especially during holidays. If you are relying on public transportation, book your return bus trip early. The last bus for Medellín departs at 6:30pm.

Southern Antioquia

★ JARDÍN

Sometimes place-names fit perfectly. Such is the case with the picture-perfect Antioquian town of Jardín. The main park gushes year-round with trees and flowers that are always in bloom, and even the streets are corridors of color, lined with one brightly painted house after another.

The word is out about Jardín. Even still, if you arrive during the week, you'll feel like you've stumbled upon something special. On weekends, and especially holidays, a festive atmosphere fills the air, and the Plaza Principal buzzes with activity. The colorful town is an attraction in itself (especially for shutterbugs), but the cloud forests nearby—with caves, waterfalls, and birds aplenty—provide reasons for lacing up those hiking boots.

Sights

The **Parque Principal** is the center of life in Jardín. It's full of colorful wooden chairs, flower gardens, tall trees that provide welcome shade, and an endless cast of characters passing through, hanging out, or sipping a

Devils of Riosucio

Every two years in January, in the sleepy coffee- and plantain-growing town of Riosucio in northern Caldas near the Antioquian town of Jardín, residents (and a growing number of visitors) commune with the devil during the revelry of the **Carnaval de Riosucio.** This festival, one of the most beloved in the region, has an interesting story. It began out of a plea made by local priests for two feuding pueblos of Riosucio—the gold-mining village of Quiebralomo and La Montaña, home to a large indigenous population—to get along. In 1847 both communities were nudged to participate in that year's Three Kings Day commemoration and to set aside their differences, temporarily at least. If they didn't come together that year in peace, they would invite the wrath of the devil.

Over time, it was that last bit that resonated with the townspeople. From that 1847 onward, groups of families, friends, and neighbors would get together and create elaborate floats and costumes, seemingly in homage to the devil over this five-day celebration. The festival is run by the República del Carnaval, which reigns over the town during that time, and the culmination of the event is the ceremonial burning of an effigy of the devil. The festival gets going on the first Friday of January, with the most colorful activities taking place on Sunday.

---

coffee. Prominent on the east side of the park is the neo-gothic cathedral the **Basílica Menor de la Inmaculada Concepción** (Cra. 3 No. 10-71, mass daily 11am), a 20th-century construction with a striking interior painted in shades of turquoise.

The **Museo Clara Rojas** (Cra. 5 No. 9-31, tel. 6/845-5652, http://mcrpjardin.blogspot.com, 8am-noon and 2pm-6pm daily, COP$2,000) has 19th-century period furniture and relics from the *colonización antioqueña*, as well as a small collection of religious art, including a painting of Jesus as a child surrounded by lambs with medals hanging around their necks. The town's tourism office is behind the facility, operating the same hours as the museum.

Recreation

There's almost no better Jardín plan than taking a morning walk. You'll be enchanted by the scenery, reinvigorated by the fresh air, and perhaps get the heart rate up a little as you explore the countryside. There are two fairly easy walks that can be done in a couple of hours and are manageable without a guide; if you get lost, there's always a kind local to point you in the right direction. The first is the **Camino Herrera,** which begins at the sweets shop Dulces del Jardín (Cl. 13 No. 5-47), and leads to two waterfalls—Casacada del Amor and Cascada Escondida—a swimming hole, and the Garrucha gondola. The second walk is the **Camino La Salada,** which starts at the Liceo San Antonio (Cl. 16 with Cra. 5) and takes you to the 55-meter (174-foot) Cascada Escalera waterfall and Cristo Rey hill, from where you can return via mini chairlift.

Jardín has not one, but two mini chairlifts in town. The **Cable Aéreo** (8am-6pm daily, COP$5,000 round-trip) goes up to the Cristo Rey hill. The other, more rustic **La Garrucha** (8am-6pm daily, COP$4,000) goes across town. Although these are popular with tourists, they were built so that rural farmers would have an easier way to bring their coffee and other crops to market.

BIRDING

The mountainous countryside near Jardín is a fabulous habitat for birds, including the yellow-eared parrot *(Ognorhynchus icterotis),* which makes its nest in *palma de cera* (wax palm) trees. Both of these—the birds and the trees—are threatened. Dozens of bird species have been spotted here, as well as the next-to-impossible-to-glimpse pumas and famed *oso de anteojos* (an Andean bear), which live deep in the jungle.

It's easy to view birds in the area, and you don't have to join up with a flock of other tourists to go on a bird-watching expedition. On the road toward the town of Riosucio (Caldas) to the south of Jardín is an excellent spot to view birds—as well as hike, mountain bike, or wander. This area is called **Alto de Ventanas.** Many visitors head up here early in the morning and walk along the main road to observe birds. A good place to start is just a couple of kilometers beyond the highest peak on the right-hand side at **Lucia's farm.** For a small fee, Lucia will prepare breakfast for you; as you sip your locally grown coffee, you'll be treated to visits by hummingbirds, and more than likely, flocks of yellow-eared parrots will fly by. Rufous antpittas, chestnut-naped antpittas, Munchique wood wrens, tanagers, and the critically endangered dusky starfrontlet may also make cameos. Call Lucia (cell tel. 314/683-7549) or her son Octavio (cell tel. 313/686-1631 or 312/715-4711) in advance so they'll know to expect you and how you like your eggs; they'll also give you specific directions. To get to Ventanas, there is a bus that departs Jardín at 8am, which may arrive too late for optimal bird-watching. Alternatively, you can arrange for private transportation (COP$200,000 round-trip). Note that the area's high elevation (1,900-3,000 meters) means temperatures can dip as low as 4°C (39°F). Warm clothing and layers are essential; rubber boots, not so much.

La Esperanza (cell tel. 312/837-0782, US$80 pp all meals incl.) is a nonprofit nature reserve dedicated to habitat preservation, education, and research. It's set on a mountain ridge 15 minutes from town. Sunrises, with a view to Jardín, and sunsets, looking out toward the mountains of Los Farallones de Citará, cannot be beat. The facility is run by an American, Doug Knapp. A jack of many trades, birder Knapp built four comfortable cabins for birding enthusiasts complete with siesta-friendly decks and natural light pouring through the windows. He's also carved out some forest paths that meander through the property. Oh, and he cooks, too. At La Esperanza, you don't have to go far to catch a glimpse of some spectacular birds. Knapp's colleagues have documented the presence of eight special and endemic birds, including the Parker's antbird, whiskered wren, and

Colombian chachalaca. Of the close to 400 species estimated to live in the Jardín area, this site now has registered 175. Also present are numerous mammals: the newly discovered olinguito (a big deal), the tayra, two-toed tree-sloth, aquatic opossum, northern tamandua (a tree anteater), and western night monkey.

Another birding option is just a five-minute walk from the Parque Principal, at a site where you can observe the Andean cock-of-the-rock (*Rupicola peruvianus*). Flocks of 5-15 of these gorgeous birds, native to the cloud forest, can be seen here. Males of this species have bright orange plumage on their heads and put on a show, usually in the early morning and early evening, at this roosting site where they compete for the attention of females (lekking). To find out how to get to the site, go to **Las Margaritas restaurant** at the park and inquire about the *gallitos de roca,* as they are called, or contact Olga or Orlando at cell tel. 312/756-2650 so that they will open the gate and let you in to the observation deck they have built; you'll have to pay a fee for this, under COP$15,000.

TOURS

One of the most popular excursions in the area is to the **Cueva El Esplendor** (Vereda La Linda, COP$7,000 entrance fee, COP$70,000 tour incl. lunch and entrance), a cave through which waters cascade into a chilly natural pool. You can walk to the cave independently, but it'll be a long day; most choose to go by horseback. Groups typically meet in the Parque Principal at around 8am, then take a Jeep Willy about 20 minutes to the Alto de la Rosa farm, where they are paired with their companion horse. There are a couple of river crossings, so rubber boots will be needed (inquire about this). A country lunch is provided, and you may visit a farm where they make *panela* (brown sugar loaf). To organize a tour, contact Bernardo López (cell tel. 314/714-2021), who offers horseback riding excursions. Alternatively, you can go with **Original Travel** (Cra. 4 No. 8-64, cell tel. 301/286-1144) or **Condor de los Andes** (tel. 4/845-5374, cell tel. 311/746-1985, condordelosandes@colombia.com).

For a taste of campesino life, take the **Finca Los Ángeles Coffee Tour** (Vereda La Casiana, cell tel. 300/774-9395, COP$30,000 pp). At this family farm outside of town, you'll take part in a standard coffee tour, and then sit down together for a delicious home-cooked meal. To participate, you must reserve at least 24 hours beforehand.

Food

At **Las Margaritas** (Cra. 3 No. 9-68, tel. 4/845-6651, 7am-9pm daily, COP$15,000), the specialty is *pollo a la Margarita* (chicken fried with a Parmesan cheese breading). This back-to-Paisa-basics place is good for a hearty breakfast. Vegetarians will appreciate a generous morning serving of *calentado* (beans and rice). If you want to add some juice (not a part of the typical Paisa breakfast), there is a juice stall two doors down from Las Margaritas, as well as fruit vendors in the park. The *tienda* (store) next door often has fresh Colombian pastries, such as *almojabanas* (cheese rolls) and *pandebonos* (delicious pastries made of yuca flour and cheese).

It's a weekend ritual in Jardín: spend the afternoon with family and friends at one of the *trucheras* (trout farms). One of the largest and best known of these is **La Truchería** (Km. 5 Vía Riosucio, tel. 4/845-5159, noon-6pm daily, COP$18,000). Trout is served infinite ways here: *a la mostaza* (mustard), with fine herbs, and stuffed with vegetables, to name a few.

Soft candlelight and a little rare ambience—along with delish pizza and wine—are served up at ★ **Café Europa** (Cl. 8 No. 4-02, cell tel. 312/230-2842, 4pm-10pm daily). You'll want to settle in and get comfortable at this corner restaurant run by a German photographer and travel writer.

The menu at **Pastelatte** (Cra. 4 No. 8-45, cell tel. 301/482-3908, noon-8:30pm Wed.-Mon., COP$14,000) features crepes, cheesecakes, coffee, sandwiches, and pastas, and service is speedy and always with a smile. **Trigo y Centeno Crepes** (Cl. 9 No. 2-57, cell tel 315/258-3686) is a quaint café that specializes in French food—including rather massive crepes and drinks.

★ **Café Macanas** (Cra. 5 No. 9-43, cell tel. 313/657-5979) wins with its appealing decor and outdoor seating. It also has great pastries and light meals. After lunch you can buy a bag of coffee from Don Dario's farm.

Dulces del Jardín (Cl. 13 No. 5-47, tel. 4/845-6584, 8am-6pm Mon.-Sat.) is the candymaker in town. In addition to *arequipe* (caramel) sweets, they make all-natural jams and fruit spreads (COP$6,000) from pineapple, coconut, and papaya.

Accommodations

If you are planning to visit Jardín on a *puente* (long weekend) or during holidays, you will need to make a reservation at a hotel well in advance. On regular weekends, there is usually no problem in finding a hotel, although the best options do tend to fill up. During the week, the town is yours, and prices drop substantially (especially if you plan to pay in cash).

★ **Casa Selva y Café** (Cabaña La Isla-Vereda Quebrada Bonita, tel. 4/845-5430, cell tel. 318/518-7171, www.hostalselvaycafe.com, COP$40,000 dorm, COP$1000,000 d) is a cozy countryside spot, about a 30-minute walk away from the hustle and bustle of Jardín city life. Located behind a little pond surrounded by flowers and fruit trees, and with a backdrop of pastureland and mountains, it is pure peace here. This spot is simple: just a single wooden cabin with a dorm rooms (three beds) and four private rooms. Alexandra, the owner, is a yoga teacher, and when the weather cooperates, she may be up for holding a class outside. She also offers a day trip to some remote waterfalls called the Chorros de Tapartó to the northwest of town, near Andes.

Hotel Casa Grande (Cl. 8 No. 4-33, tel. 4/845-5487, cell tel. 311/340-2207, www.hotelcasagrande.co, COP$30,000 pp) features 12 rooms that have a capacity of 2-5 persons each. Most rooms have 2-4 beds to accommodate families. Breakfast is included in the price, and dinner can be arranged at the hotel as well. The friendly owner, a Jardín native, can supply tourist information for the area.

Want a front-row seat to park action? **Hotel Valdivia Plaza** (Parque Principal, next to the Museo Clara Rojas, tel. 4/845-5055, cell tel. 316/528-1047, COP$58,000 d) has 20 rooms and is clean, yet not bursting with personality. Splurge for a room with a private balcony and view. Across the park is **Hotel Jardín** (Cra. 3 No. 9-14, cell tel. 310/380-6724, COP$40,000 pp), with 11 spacious and modern apartments with a capacity of 4-8 persons each. It's a bargain. This is the most colorful house in this colorful town, with orange, yellow, red, and blue balconies, doors, and trim.

A comfortable, if conservative, choice is **Comfenalco Hotel Hacienda Balandú** (Km. 1 Vía Jardín Riosucio, tel. 4/845-5561, COP$158,000 d), a hotel with all the extras: restaurant, sauna, and heated swimming pool. It's a tranquil 15- to 20-minute walk from town.

Transportation

The bus company **Transportes Suroeste Antioqueño** (tel. 4/352-9049, COP$18,000) leaves Medellín each day bound for Jardín, leaving from the Terminal de Transportes Sur.

There is also one bus at 6:30am that departs for Manizales to the south from Jardín. This route goes through the town of Riosucio. From there you can board a *chiva* (rural bus) bound for Jardín. These depart at 8am and 3pm everyday except on Saturday, when there's one departure at noon. It's a bumpy three-hour journey from Riosucio to Jardín.

JERICÓ

Set on a gentle slope of a mountain overlooking a valley dotted with cattle ranches and coffee, tomato, plantain, and cardamom farms, Jericó is still a Paisa cowboy outpost. Colombians know Jericó for two very different reasons. The first is its unique handicraft, the *carriel,* a shoulder bag made from leather and cowhide that is a symbol of Paisa cowboy culture. The second is its homegrown saint, Laura Montoya, who was canonized in 2013. Jericó is a pleasant place to hang one's (cowboy) hat for a night or two, and its sleepy, sloping streets lined with brightly colored wooden balconies and doors are a playground for shutterbugs. Just don't visit Jericó on Wednesdays: Everything is closed.

Sights

The **Catedral de Nuestra Señora de las Mercedes** (Cl. 7 No. 4-34, Plaza de Bolívar, tel. 4/852-3494) is a brick construction that towers over the Parque Reyes. The cathedral is where Laura Montoya was officially declared a saint (Colombia's first) during a ceremony in 2013. Born into poverty in 1874 and raised by her grandmother, Montoya made her mark as a missionary to indigenous people. At the entrance to the cathedral, there is a bronze statue of the saint alongside an indigenous child, representing Montoya's devotion to assisting impoverished communities in remote areas. Locals are very proud of her, their favorite daughter.

Below the cathedral is the **Museo de Arte Religioso** (Cl. 7 No. 4-34, Plaza de Bolívar, tel. 4/852-3494, 8:30am-noon and 1:30pm-6pm Mon.-Fri., 8:30am-6pm Sat., 9am-noon and 1:30pm-5:30pm Sun., COP$2,000), in which religious art and ceremonial items from the colonial period onward are on display.

The **Museo de Jericó Antioquia** (MAJA, Cl. 7 between Cras. 5-6, tel. 4/852-4045, cell tel. 311/628-8325, 8am-noon and 1:30pm-6pm Mon.-Fri., 9am-5pm Sat.-Sun., COP$2,000) is mostly an archaeology museum, featuring ceramics and other items from the Emberá indigenous group of western Colombia, but there is also space devoted to contemporary Antioquian artists. The museum shows art films on Monday evenings and hosts occasional concerts.

The **Centro Historia de Jericó** (Cra. 4 No. 8-51, tel. 6/852-3481, www.centrodehistoriajerico.org, 8am-11am and 3pm-5pm Mon.-Tues. and Thurs.-Fri., donations accepted) has an art collection of around 130 works, along with exhibition spaces and a small library.

Shopping

To find your very own *carriel* shoulder bag or another leather souvenir from Jericó, walk down Carrera 5 around Calle 5. The classic *carriel* goes for about COP$130,000. *Carrieles* were used by *arrieros* (Paisa cowboys) for their horseback trips around Tierra Paisa. These bags are accordion-like, with several divisions in them for carrying items like money, a lock of hair, a knife, or a candle. Some suspect that the name *carriel* is derived from the English "carry all," while others say it comes from the French *cartier,* or handbag. It has been historically a masculine trade, but two young women are making names for themselves for their award-winning *carrieles* and other accessories. Their store is called **Carriel Arte Jerico** (Cra. 3 No. 7-03, tel. 4/852-4063, www.carrielarte.com).

Jericó is Colombia's cardamom capital—who knew? **Delicias del Cardamomo** (Cra. 5 No. 2-128, tel. 4/852-5289, 9am-6pm daily) pushes cardamom everything: candies, cookies, and plain old seeds.

Food

While tourist sights and most shops are closed on Wednesdays, many restaurants are open.

There are quite a few restaurant and café options along the east side of the Parque Principal. In the late afternoon, the entire length of one side of the plaza is full of folks enjoying a *tinto* (coffee) and watching the comings and goings of townspeople milling about the plaza. A meal with a view is the selling point of **El Balcón Restaurante** (Parque Principal, Cra. 4 No. 6-26, tel. 4/852-3191, cell tel. 311/784-4419, 8am-9pm daily, COP$15,000). From its perch on a balcony, you have front-row seats to the action below in the plaza and a nice vista of the mountains in the distance. The Colombian dishes are filling.

Other local favorites include **Montaña Parilla Burger** (Cra. 4 No. 6-20, 2nd Fl., tel. 4/ 852-3021) for hamburgers and grilled meats, and **Terra Santa** (Cl. 7 No. 5-22, tel. 4/ 852-3072), which has a little of everything.

On the Calle de los Poetas, **Café Saturia** (Cl. 5 No. 4-27, cell tel. 314/815-3437) features a variety of local coffees, and you can see the beans being roasted on-site (and delight in the aroma).

For dessert, enjoy a local delicacy: *postre Jericoano*. This very sweet treat has been enjoyed by locals for a century. It's a cake of seven creamy and cookie layers, doused in rum. The real deal takes two weeks to prepare. It is sold in stalls run by local women at Calle 6 with Carrera 6.

Accommodations

As in all Colombian pueblos, room rates tend to drop during the week.

★ **Hotel El Despertar** (Cra. 6 No. 8-29, tel. 4/852-4050, www.eldespertarhotel.com, COP$150,000 pp) is a boutique-ish option in which two old houses were meticulously refurbished and joined. A hot tub and views of the Río Piedras valley are included.

The best value in town is the **Casa Grande** (Cl. 7 No. 5-54, tel. 4/852-3229, cell tel. 311/329-2144, COP$40,000 pp). It's a nicely renovated old house with 15 simple rooms. Rooms facing the street are preferable. **Hotel Portón Plaza** (Cl. 7 No. 3-25, tel. 4/852-3009, cell tel. 313/732-3568, www.hotelportonplazajerico.com, COP$35,000 pp) runs a close second, although it's much larger. It is just off the plaza. Ask for room 209 for a good view, or a 2nd-floor room with a view over the street.

Hostal las Cometas (Cra. 5 No. 10-16, cell tel. 313/233-6786, www.lascometashostal.com, COP$20,000 pp dorm), diagonal from the hospital, is one of the first hostels in town geared toward international budget travelers. The main house is over 100 years old and is made in the traditional *bareque* construction method, with wooden floors and an interior courtyard with orange and guava trees. Some rooms are small, and decorated with kites on the walls. There are some private rooms with their own baths. It's a 10-minute walk from town.

Set in pure nature is the ★ **Centro Ecoturístic La Nohelia** (Vereda Buga, Vía Antigua Jericó, tel. 4/842-3567, cell tel. 310/384-5206, www.lanohelia.com, COP$30,000 pp), around four kilometers from town. Accommodations are generally in cabins almost entirely built with *guadua*. It offers a range of activities for guests and nonguests alike, such as a tour of a coffee farm (COP$50,000 pp), hikes to waterfalls, and Jeep trips to the Río Cauca canyon (COP$86,000 pp).

Information and Services

There is a small **tourist office** in the 1st floor of the Alcaldía Municipal building next to the cathedral. A recommended English-speaking guide is **Walter Montoya Suárez** (cell tel. 319/467-8320, walmontsur@hotmail.

com). **Turísmo Jericó** (Cl. 7 No. 3-31, tel. 4/852-3065, cell tel. 314/651-4030, www.turismojerico.com) is a locally run agency specializing in outdoor adventures in and around Jericó, as well as walking tours of town.

Transportation

From Medellín, there is regular bus service (Transportes Jericó) from the Terminal del Sur (COP$25,000), starting at 5am and going until 6pm. Buses arrive and depart Jericó from the **Parque Principal.**

To get to Jardín from Jericó, you must take a *chiva* (rural bus) to the town of Andes (two buses daily) or to the town of Peñalisa and transfer there to Jardín. It's easier to go to Peñalisa (COP$6,000), because you can just hop on a bus bound for Medellín that passes through there. The ride from Peñalisa to Jardín costs about COP$12,000.

The Coffee Region

Blessed with lush, tropical vegetation, meticulously manicured countryside dotted with beautiful haciendas and towns, spring-like weather, and a backdrop of massive, snowcapped mountains, Colombia's coffee region is almost Eden. Nature here is a thousand shades of green: bright green bamboo groves, emerald-colored forests with spots of white *yarumo* trees, dark green coffee groves, and green-blue mountains in the distance punctuated by brightly colored flowers and polychromatic butterflies and birds.

Though the main cities and many towns lack charm, dozens of well-preserved villages offer colorful balcony-clad buildings. Life in most of these towns remains untouched by tourism. A visit on market day, with bustling streets jammed with Jeeps and plentiful goods, is a memorable one.

And then there is coffee. It is true that Brazil and Vietnam are the world's top coffee producers, but arabica beans are grown throughout Colombia. Coffee grown in some parts of the country (such as Cauca and Nariño) is considered superior to that from this region, but here, more than anywhere else, coffee is an inseparable part of Paisa identity. While the extent of land devoted to coffee farming is diminishing, the numbers are still impressive: The department of Caldas contains over 80,000 hectares (200,000 acres) of coffee farms; Risaralda, 52,000 hectares (128,000 acres); and Quindío, 30,000 hectares (74,000 acres). Visit a coffee farm to understand the laborious production process or—even better—stay overnight.

In pre-Columbian times, this region was inhabited by the Quimbaya people. In 1537, Spanish conquistador Sebastián de Belalcázar conquered the region as he moved north from Ecuador toward the central Muisca region. Due to the sparse indigenous population and lack of precious metals, the region, which was governed from faraway Popayán, was largely uninhabited during most of the colonial period.

The Birth of the Coffee Economy

During the 19th century, demographic pressures spurred settlers from the northwestern province of Antioquia to migrate south, giving origin to what is known as the *colonización antioqueña*. For this reason, the coffee region is akin to Antioquia, with similar dialect, cuisine, and architecture. As the settlers made their way south, they founded towns and started farms: Salamina was established in 1825, Manizales in 1849, Filandia in 1878, and Armenia in 1889.

The region prospered enormously throughout the 20th century due to ideal conditions for producing coffee. The Colombian National Coffee Federation, owner of the Juan Valdez brand, provided technical assistance, developed infrastructure, and helped stabilize prices. High international coffee prices during the 1980s and 1990s made the region one of the most prosperous areas in the country.

The fall of global coffee prices in the past decade has forced the region to reinvent itself. Rather than produce a low-value commodity, many farmers have invested in producing high-quality strains that fetch much higher prices. Growers have also diversified, planting other crops, such as plantains, often interspersed through coffee plantations. Finally, agro- and ecotourism has provided a much-needed new source of revenue.

Planning Your Time

It's hard to go wrong as a tourist in the coffee region. No matter your starting point or home base, an immersion in coffee culture is easy, nearby, and rewarding. If you can, plan to spend about five days in this most pleasant part of Colombia. In that time you can stay at a coffee hacienda, visit a natural park, and tour a picture-perfect pueblo.

However, if time is short, a quick visit can be equally as rewarding. With easy transportation links to the major cities of the region and excellent tourism infrastructure to meet all budget needs, Salento has the trifecta of coffee region attractions: It's a cute pueblo, coffee farms are within minutes of the main plaza, and jungle hikes that lead through tropical forest to the Valle de Cocora are easy to organize. The town gets packed with visitors on weekends and during holidays, resulting in a more festive atmosphere, but also traffic jams.

Another option is to stay a couple of days at a hacienda. You can leisurely explore the farms and countryside, relax, and possibly go for a day trip or two to a nearby attraction. Many haciendas are high-end, like Hacienda Bambusa, Finca Villa Nora, and Hacienda San José. However, budget travelers can also enjoy the unique atmosphere of hacienda life at Hacienda Guayabal outside of Manizales and Finca El Ocaso in Salento. Meanwhile, Hacienda Venecia has something for travelers of all budgets.

For birders, the lush region offers many parks and gardens to marvel at the hundreds of species in the area. The Reserva del Río Blanco near Manizales, Jardín Botánico del Quindío near Armenia, and the Santuario de Flora y Fauna Otún-Quimbaya near Pereira are within minutes of the city, guided walks are regularly offered, and birdlife is abundant. Outside of metropolitan areas, the Parque Municipal Natural Planes de San Rafael, which adjoins the Parque Nacional Natural Tatamá, is less known, but is a natural paradise.

Day trips to natural parks, including the Parque Nacional Natural Los Nevados, are easily organized. PNN Los Nevados is home to *páramos* (highland moors), lunar landscapes, and snowcapped volcanoes. It can be accessed from many points, and it can even be visited by car. Multiple day treks offer challenges.

If there were a Cute Pueblo Region of Colombia, this might be it. While you'll have more flexibility driving your own vehicle, it's easy to check out a pueblo or two from the region's major cities traveling by public transportation. A night or two is enough to embrace village life.

MANIZALES

The capital of the Caldas department, pleasant and easygoing Manizales (pop. 393,200) is the region's mountain city. Instead of developing in a lowland valley like Armenia or Pereira, Manizales is set atop meandering mountain ridges. This location means that getting around town involves huffing and puffing up and down hills on foot, enduring roller coaster-like bus or taxi rides along curvy roads, or taking the scenic route on the city's expanding Cable Aéreo gondola network.

Perched above lush coffee farms below, at an altitude of 2,160 meters (7,085 feet), spectacular views abound in Manizales—but only when the sky is *despejado* (clear). On those days, you might see the peaks of the Parque Nacional Natural Los Nevados in the distance. It's easy to visit that park—as well as other natural sights—with Manizales as one's base.

Sights

The two main drags in Manizales—Avenida Santander (Carrera 23) and the Paralela (Carrera 25)—will take you to where you want to go in town. They connect the Zona Rosa/El Cable area with downtown and with Avenida 12 de October, which leads to Chipre and the Monumento a los Colonizadores.

CENTRO

Downtown Manizales is bustling with activity during weekdays but vacates in a hurry in the evenings. There aren't many sights of interest, save for some Republican-period architecture and some noteworthy churches.

The **Plaza de Bolívar** (Cras. 21-22 and Clls. 22-23) holds an odd sculpture to honor Simón Bolívar created by Antioqueño Rodrigo Arenas Betancourt. It's known as the *Condor-Bolívar,* portraying the Liberator with a body of a condor, the national bird. On the north side of the plaza is a **tourist office.**

On the south side of the plaza, the neo-gothic **Catedral Basílica de Manizales** (Cra. 22 No. 22-15, tel. 6/883-1880, open until 6:30pm daily) is imposing. Construction began in the late 1920s and was completed in

Manizales

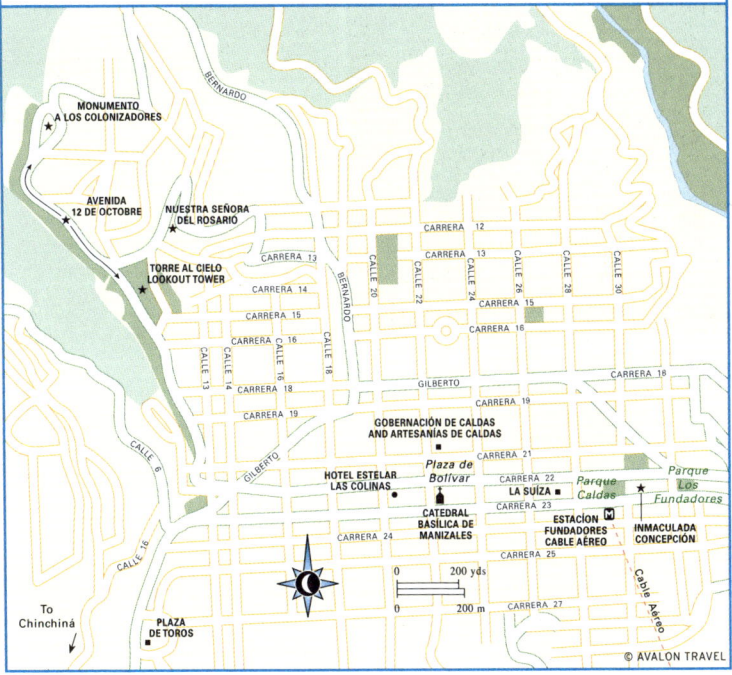

1936. It replaced the previous cathedral on the same spot, which had been damaged by earthquakes and had to be demolished. For 360-degree views of Manizales and beyond, climb the 500 steps of the spiral Corredor Polaco (the Polish corridor) in Colombia's tallest church tower. To climb the tower, a guide is required (COP$10,000), although it's hard to imagine getting lost inside. The tower is open 9am-noon and 2pm-5pm Thursday-Sunday. A cathedral café serves sadly mediocre coffee, but the view is nice.

Not as grandiose as the cathedral a couple of blocks away, the interior of the **Inmaculada Concepción** (Cl. 30 at Cra. 22, in the Parque Caldas, tel. 6/883-5474, 7am-noon and 2pm-6:30pm daily) is much more beautiful. The neo-gothic-style church, completed in 1909, was built with *bahareque* and *guadua,* natural materials used in construction across Colombia. The wooden rib vaulted ceiling is made of cedar, as are the columns and pews.

CHIPRE

This neighborhood to the west of downtown is known for its views and sunsets. Manizaleños like to boast how Chilean poet Pablo Neruda, when strolling on the promenade in Chipre along Avenida 12 de Octubre, marveled at this "sunset factory." You're guaranteed a nice vista from atop the

El Cable

Recinto del Pensamiento

futuristic lookout tower **La Torre al Cielo** (tel. 6/883-8311, 8am-8pm daily, COP$2,000).

At the far end of the walkway is the **Monumento a los Colonizadores** (Av. 12 de Octubre and Cra. 9, tel. 6/872-0420, ext. 22, 10am-6pm daily, free), designed by Luis Guillermo Vallejo. This monument honors the courage and sacrifice of Antioquian colonizers who settled the city. It depicts an Antioquian family on horseback and on foot forging ahead, with cattle in tow, to this part of Colombia during the *colonización antioqueña,* when hundreds of families migrated from Medellín to settle farms in the coffee region. Manizales residents played a role in building the monument by donating keys and the like to be melted and used in its construction. The sculpture stands atop 20 tons of *piedra de mani* (peanut stone), the namesake for the city. It was inaugurated in 2001. To get to this part of the city, look for a bus with a "Chipre" sign along Avenida Santander (Cra. 23).

EL CABLE

One of the city's icons is a soaring wooden tower known as **El Cable** (52 meters/171 feet tall) that once supported the unusual gondola system that transported coffee (10 tons per hour), other materials, and sometimes people from Manizales over the Central Cordillera. The system reached elevations of 3,700 meters (12,100 feet) and descended to the town of Mariquita (495 meters/1,625 feet). From there the coffee would be transported overland to Honda on the banks of the Río Magdalena. The rest of the journey in Colombia would take the coffee north to the port city of Barranquilla, where it would be transferred to big boats bound for North America and Europe. This system was developed in the 1920s and would last until the early 1960s.

Of the 376 towers that supported the line, this tower, which was in the town of Herveo, was the only one built out of wood (all the others were made of iron). They were all supposed to be made of iron, but the boat carrying one of them from Europe to Colombia was sunk by a German submarine in the Atlantic Ocean during World War I. An English engineer in Colombia, who also designed the neat **Estación del Cable,** the adjacent station for the cable transport system, designed this tower using wood found locally.

RESERVA DEL RÍO BLANCO

Nearly 400 species of birds have been spotted at the **Reserva del Río Blanco** (Vereda Las Palomas, tel. 6/887-9770, cell tel. 311/775-5159, reservariob-lanco@aguasdemanizales.com.co, 6am-6pm daily, COP$20,000 entrance), only three kilometers (two miles) outside of Manizales. From August to March the area receives many migratory birds from North America. This reserve is a must-do for serious international birders visiting the country.

An *oso anteojo andino* (Andean bear) that lived in captivity for most of his life was adopted and now lives in an enclosed field in the reserve near the cabins. It was decided that he would not be able to be released back into the wild.

It's a cumbersome process to obtain permission to visit the reserve and organize a birdwatching day trip—but not impossible. Most visitors ask front desk staff at hostels or hotels to set things up for them. A half-day guided hike costs COP$45,000 per person; some guides speak English. To see birds at their most active, consider staying overnight in one of the park's two **cabins** (tel. 6/870-3810, cell tel. 310/422-1883, COP$70,000 pp). These have a total of eight rooms, and meals are available as well. Hummingbird feeders dangle along the deck, and there are nearly always customers to be seen. Taxi transportation to the reserve entrance costs COP$30,000 from Manizales.

RECINTO DEL PENSAMIENTO

For a walk in the park, the **Recinto del Pensamiento** (Km. 11 Vía al Magdalena, tel. 6/889-7073, ext. 2990, www.recintodelpensamiento.com, 9am-4pm Tues.-Sun., COP$20,000 guided walk and chairlift) is a tranquil green space with guided nature walks, a chairlift, a two-hectare orchid forest with 12,000 orchids, a butterfly farm, and a Japanese bonsai garden. The centerpiece of the park is the **Pabellón de Madera,** a large open-air event space made of *guadua* (a type of bamboo) and built by a renowned Colombian architect. It's possible to get there by taking a blue public bus (that says Maltería) from downtown Manizales (Cra. 20) for about COP$2,000.

ECOPARQUE LOS YARUMOS

On undisturbed mountainsides throughout Colombia, you have undoubtedly noticed the silvery-white leaves of the *yarumo blanco* tree. Should you get a closer look, you'll see that the leaves of this tree are actually green; they have a fuzzy outer layer that only makes them appear white. The **Ecoparque Los Yarumos** (Cl. 61B No. 15A-01, Barrio Toscana, tel.

6/872-0420, ext. 22, 9am-6pm Tues.-Sun., free) is named for those tricky trees. A few *yarumos* can be seen in the more than 50 hectares (125 acres) of cloud forest and green space that make up this park. Geared toward families, the park has nature paths, a lookout tower, and activities such as jungle zip lines. Get there by taking a bus from the Manizales city center bound for Minitas. It's about a 7- to 10-minute walk from the bus stop to the entrance. The Cable Aéreo is scheduled to reopen its station here in 2017, which will make for the most scenic way to arrive.

HOT SPRINGS

Near Manizales are three popular *termales* (hot springs). Bring your own towel and sandals and visit on a weekday if you want to avoid the crowds.

Near the river, **Tierra Viva** (Km. 2 Vía Enea-Gallinazo, tel. 6/874-3089, www.termalestierraviva.com, 9am-midnight Mon.-Thurs., 9am-1am Fri.-Sun., COP$12,000-14,000) is closest to Manizales and less expensive. It consists of one pool, some bare-bones changing rooms, and a snack bar. A Gallinazo bus along Carrera 19 drops passengers off close to the springs for COP$2,000. You can also cab it for about COP$12,000.

With superior facilities to Tierra Viva, **Termales Otoño** (Km. 5 Vía Antigua El Nevado del Ruiz, tel. 6/874-0280, www.termaleselotono.com, 7am-midnight daily, day pass COP$40,000, hotel COP$107,000-356,000 d) is a hot spring-and-hotel complex a 25-minute ride (COP$15,000 taxi) southeast of the city. It's large, with four pools (though two of these are reserved exclusively for hotel guests).

One of the area's old mountain lodges has been given a much-needed facelift. The **Termales del Ruiz** (35 km south of Manizales, cell tel. 310/455-3588, www.termalesdelruiz.com, COP$18,000 day pass) is the most picturesque of the region's hot springs, set at 3,500 meters (11,500 feet) elevation on the edge of the Parque Nacional Natural Los Nevados, about 35 kilometers (22 miles) from Manizales and 10 kilometers (6 miles) from its source, the Nevado del Ruiz volcano. There is one large thermal pool, as well as a nature path, and many bird species can be spotted on the mountain slopes. Believe it or not, in the 1950s, this lodge was the headquarters for international ski competitions. Those days are long gone; the snow has bid *adíos*. Rooms at the hotel are chilly at night but have been completely revamped and are luxurious, and the restaurant is good too. Day-trippers to PNN Los Nevados often stop here for a soak on the way back down to Manizales. There is no public transportation here, but you can hire a taxi from Manizales (about COP$190,000) or have your hotel arrange for a hired car (about COP$165,000).

Festivals and Events

The Plaza de Toros (Cra. 27 10A-07, tel. 6/883-8124, www.cormanizales.com), or bullfighting ring, is the heart of the action during Manizales's biggest annual bacchanal, the **Feria de Manizales** (www.feriademanizales.gov.co, Jan.). The festivities also include concerts, a ballad festival (Festival de Trova), and a Miss Coffee beauty pageant. This citywide party is held in early January.

In June each year, jazz takes center stage at the Universidad de Caldas, the main university in town, during the **Temporada Internacional de Jazz** (June). Quartets from universities in the United States are often invited to perform in this event sponsored by the Centro Colombo Americano and the U.S. Embassy.

One of the country's top theater festivals is the **Festival Internacional de Teatro de Manizales** (www.festivaldemanizales.com, early Sept.). Theater troupes from Manizales and around Colombia, the Americas, and beyond perform in theaters throughout the city, and free performances are given in the Plaza de Bolívar, El Cable, and other public spaces.

Sports and Recreation

The **Ciclovía** in Manizales takes place every Sunday from 8am to noon along Avenida Santander (Carrera 23) and other main streets. The last Thursday evening of each month a **Ciclovía Nocturna** (7pm-10pm) is held.

Once Caldas (www.oncecaldas.com.co) is the Manizales soccer club, and their stadium, the **Estadio Palogrande** (Cra. 25 No. 65-00), is in the Zona Rosa within walking distance of many hostels and hotels. Tickets can be purchased in the Cable Plaza Mall (Cra. 23 No. 65-11, tel. 6/875-6595, 9am-9pm daily).

TOURS

Horseback riding through the countryside is what **Hato Caravana Club de Caballería** (Ecoparque Río Claro-Villamaría Occidental, cell tel. 311/739-2845, www.hatocaravana.com, COP$80,000) is all about. Excursions usually begin at around 9am and end with a hearty lunch.

A handful of recommended and professional tour agencies specialize in day trips and multiday adventures in Parque Nacional Natural Los Nevados. These are **Kumanday** (Cl. 66 No. 23B-40), **Ecosistemas** (Cra. 21 No. 20-45, tel. 6/880-8300, cell tel. 312/705-7007, www.ecosistemastravel.com.co), and **Asdeguías** (Cl. 25 No. 20-25, Of. 7, tel. 6/884-4525). Kumanday is famous for its downhill mountain bike day tours, but it also offers multiday excursions in the park out of Manizales. Ecosistemas focuses on treks to the Nevado del Ruiz and Santa Isabel (COP$170,000).

Food

For excellent down-home, regional cuisine, head to ★ **Don Juaco** (Cl. 65 No. 23A-44, tel. 6/885-0610, cell tel. 310/830-2218, noon-10pm daily, COP$15,000), which has been serving contented diners for decades. Try the Paisa hamburger: a hamburger sandwiched in between two arepas (cornmeal cakes). Enjoy it or the popular set lunch meals on the pleasant terrace.

For delectable grilled meat dishes, **Palogrande** (Cra. 23C No. 64-18, tel. 6/885-3177, 11am-10pm daily, COP$25,000) is the place you want. Located on a quiet street, it's a rather elegant, open-air place with a nice atmosphere.

For Italian fare, there are two decent options. **Spago** (Cl. 59 No. 24A-06, Local 1, tel. 6/885-3328, cell tel. 321/712-3860, noon-3pm and 6pm-10pm Mon.-Sat., noon-3pm Sun., COP$25,000), one of the upmarket restaurants in town, has tasty thin-crust pizzas. **Il Forno** (Cra. 23 No. 73-86, tel. 6/886-8515, noon-10pm Mon.-Sat., noon-3pm Sun., COP$22,000) is a family-style chain restaurant with a view of the city.

Vegetarian restaurants exist in Manizales, but it can be difficult to find them. **Orellana** (Cra. 24 No. 51-59, tel. 6/885-3907, noon-3pm Mon.-Sat., COP$10,000) serves healthy set lunches from its spot in the Versalles neighborhood. It's near the supermarket Confamiliares de la 50. Vegetarians should rush to the Palogrande area and to ★ **Rushi** (Cra. 23C No. 62-73, tel. 6/881-0326, cell tel. 310/538-8387, 11am-9pm Mon.-Sat., 11am-3pm Sun., COP$12,000), where they can find plant-based lunch specials and veggie burgers made with many organic ingredients.

A fantastic place for a late-afternoon cappuccino and snack is ★ **Juan Valdez Café** (Cra. 23B No. 64-55, tel. 6/885-9172, 10am-9pm daily). Yes, it's a chain, and there's one in any self-respecting mall in Colombia. But this one is different: Locals proudly boast that it is the largest Juan Valdez on the planet. But what truly sets this one apart is its great location, under the shadow of the huge wooden tower that once supported the coffee cable car line that ran from Manizales to Mariquita.

Tablecloths, stylish presentation, and an extensive menu of seafood dishes set **Vino y Pimienta** (Cl. 77 No. 21-74, tel. 6/886-5571) apart from the rest.

Accommodations

The El Cable area in Manizales is the best place to stay thanks to its large number of lodging options and its proximity to restaurants and shopping centers. It's a quiet neighborhood that bustles with international visitors, particularly on Calle 66.

One of the long-standing budget accommodations in Manizales is **Mountain Hostels** (Cl. 66 No. 23B-91, tel. 6/887-4736, cell tel. 300/521-6120, www.mountainhostels.com.co, COP$22,000 dorm, COP$60,000 d). Spread over two houses, it has a variety of room types and a small restaurant where you can order a healthy breakfast. It's also a fantastic source of information.

Hostal Kumanday (Cl. 66 No. 23B-40, tel. 6/887-2682, cell tel. 315/590-7294, www.kumanday.com, COP$25,000 dorm, COP$40,000 pp d) is a quiet and clean option on the same street as Mountain Hostels. There are 10 rooms and one small dorm room, and all options include breakfast. Kumanday has its own, highly recommended tour agency that specializes in hiking in and around the Parque Nacional Natural Los Nevados.

Casa Lassio Hostal (Cl. 66 No. 23B-56, tel. 6/887-6056, cell tel. 310/443-8917, COP$23,000 dorm, COP$35,000 private room pp) has six rooms, and they also organize bike tours.

The Colombian chain Estelar (www.hotelesestelar.com) has three hotels in the Manizales area. They are among the top hotels in the city, and all have spacious and clean rooms, as well as at least one room that is accessible for people with disabilities. Weekend rates tend to be significantly lower than during the week. There are few reasons for wanting to stay in downtown Manizales, but if you do, **Hotel Estelar Las Colinas** (Cra. 22 No. 20-20, tel. 6/884-2009, COP$188,080 d) is the best option (but only on weekends, when traffic, noise, and general urban stress is manageable). The hotel's 60-some rooms are large and clean, but the restaurant and bar area is a little gloomy. A breakfast buffet is available for an additional cost.

The ★ **Estelar El Cable** (Cra. 23C No. 64A-60, tel. 6/887-9690, COP$294,000 d) has 46 rooms over nine floors and is the upscale option in the El Cable/Zona Rosa area. Breakfast and a light dinner are often included in room rates. Rooms are spacious and clean, with pressed wood floors. A small gym offers modern cardio machines.

If you prefer birds and trees, check out Estelar's 32-room hotel at the **Recinto del Pensamiento** (Km. 11 Vía al Magdalena, tel. 6/889-7077, COP$210,000 d). Outside the city, surrounded by nature, this hotel feels a little isolated. It's a popular place for business conferences and events during the week. Rooms are spacious.

Information and Services

A **Punto de Información Turística** (Cra. 22 at Cl. 31, tel. 6/873-3901, 7am-7pm daily) can be of assistance in organizing excursions to parks and coffee farms throughout Caldas. A small **tourist office** is also located in the main hall of the Terminal de Transportes (Cra. 43 No. 65-100).

In case of an emergency, Manizales has a single emergency line: 123.

Transportation

Avianca and **ADA** serve **Aeropuerto La Nubia** (tel. 6/874-5451), about 10 kilometers (six miles) southeast of downtown. The runway is often shrouded in clouds; because of this, the airport is closed 35 percent of the time and always at night.

There is regular and speedy **bus service** to both Armenia (COP$17,500, 2 hours) and Pereira (COP$11,000, 70 mins.). **Empresas Arauca** (www.empresaarauca.com.co) runs buses to Pereira every 15 minutes. Buses bound for Cali and Medellín cost around COP$35,000-40,000 and take five hours each. Buses to Bogotá cost COP$50,000 and take about nine hours.

The **Terminal de Transportes** (Cra. 43 No. 65-100, tel. 6/878-5641, www.terminaldemanizales.com) is spacious, orderly, and clean. From there it is about a 15-minute taxi ride to the Zona Rosa area. The terminal adjoins the cable car **Cable Aéreo** station. The cable car route transports passengers from the terminal (Estación Cambulos) to the Fundadores station (Cra. 23 between Clls. 31-32) in the Centro.

Buses can get you where you want to go in Manizales, but you'll likely have to ask a local which one to take and where to flag it down. To get downtown from the Zona Rosa, take a bus bound for Chipre.

COFFEE FARMS

The Caldas countryside is home to coffee haciendas large and small. Hacienda Venecia and Hacienda Guayabal are two of the most highly recommended for coffee tours, as well as overnight stays. They are located near Chinchiná, only a 30-minute drive from Manizales. Many travelers comment that a day or two at one of these is the highlight of their trip to Colombia.

Hacienda Venecia

One of the most well-known, organized, and most visited coffee farms is **Hacienda Venecia** (Vereda El Rosario, Vía a Chinchiná, cell tel. 320/636-5719, www.haciendavenecia.com, coffee tour COP$50,000). This large working coffee plantation has been in the same family for four generations, and their coffee was the first in Colombia to receive UTZ certification for sustainable farming, in 2002. The farm is set far from the highway, providing a peaceful atmosphere; you're surrounded by coffee plants growing everywhere you look.

If you are day-tripping, organizing an excursion to the farm for a coffee tour is easy from Manizales. In fact, you won't have to do much at all except inform the hostel or hotel where you are staying that you'd like to go. The Hacienda Venecia makes a daily pickup at the main hostels in town at around 9am. Tours are given daily at 9:30am. The 2.5-hour tour begins with a comprehensive presentation of coffee-growing in Colombia and in the world, the many different aromas of coffee, and how to differentiate between a good bean and a bad bean. (And you'll be offered a knock-your-socks-off espresso to boot.) Later, the tour heads outside through the plantation, where you'll see coffee plants at all stages in the growing process. You'll also be able to observe the soaking and drying process. At the end, in the lovely original hacienda house, it's time to roast some beans and drink another freshly roasted cup of Venecia coffee. A typical and delicious lunch, such as *ajiaco* (chicken and potato soup), is offered as well (COP$15,000) at the end of the tour. A farm tour by Jeep and private tours can also be arranged, if requested in advance.

There are lodging options suitable for all budgets at Venecia: It's a big operation, attracting a United Nations of visitors every day. A hostel (COP$35,000 dorm), in the former quarters of coffee pickers, has three rooms, a social area, and a kitchen. Hostel guests can prepare their own breakfasts (ingredients provided) as well as other meals, or dine in the Casa de Huéspedes for an additional cost. In the Casa de Huéspedes (COP$135,000 d), which is the hub of activity at the farm, there are seven basic rooms, some with a private bath. And for those in search of charm, there is the Casa Principal (COP$400,000 d), the original house, dating back at least a century. It has six rooms, some with private bath, lovely common areas, and a beautiful *comedor* (dining room). It's not uncommon to see overlanding travelers drive up in their buses and campers. And, no matter where you stay, there's coffee on the house, all the time, and usually a hammock to sink into.

For those staying overnight, other activities at the farm include horseback riding (for an additional fee) or walks around the plantation on your own. A particularly pleasant activity in the early morning is to go on a self-guided birding walk, using the Venecia birding checklist. More than 117 species have been documented here. Guests are permitted to wander at their leisure on six trails.

Hacienda Guayabal

Hacienda Guayabal (Km. 3 Vía Chinchiná-Pereira, cell tel. 314/772-4856 or 315/540-7639, www.haciendaguayabal.com, tour COP$35,000, lodging COP$65,000 pp incl. breakfast) has a jaw-dropping setting, with mountains and valleys covered in coffee crops and *guadua* (bamboo) completely enveloping the hacienda. This hacienda has been in Doña María Teresa's family for over 50 years. This is a working coffee farm, and one of the pioneers in coffee farm tourism, but it's equally interesting to take a nature walk through the *guaduales* (forests of Colombia's bamboo) that tend to spring up along water sources.

If you come, you might as well stay, so that you can enjoy the peace and warm hospitality of this special place. While accommodations in the handful of rooms are not luxurious, they are more than adequate. There is a small cabin available as well, in the middle of nature. Meals are delicious, one of the things for which Guayabal is known. Tours around the *finca* (farm) take about two hours, and you learn about the coffee process as you maneuver along the orderly rows of coffee plants. In addition, you can hike up to a spectacular lookout on a mountainside for breathtaking views of the hills, the valleys, the forests, and the farms all around. Near the guesthouse just past the pool is a hut made from *guadua* with recycled floor tiles; it houses a small coffee bar where you can have a cup of coffee and wait for birds of every color and shape to fly up to nibble on a piece of banana. Tranquility is the watchword here, and it's no wonder Guayabal is occasionally host to meditation retreats. Ask about visiting the pueblo of Marsella from here; it makes a nice day trip.

To get to Guayabal, take an Autolujo bus (COP$3,000) or a shared taxi from Manizales to Chinchiná. From Chinchiná it's about COP$9,000 for a taxi to the hacienda. Regular cabs from Manizales are also an option.

★ SALAMINA

Designated as one of Colombia's most beautiful pueblos, Salamina features history, beauty, personality, and spectacular countryside; yet, for the most part, it remains off most tourists' radars. When you visit this historic town, you'll feel as if you have stumbled upon a hidden gem. The historic center of Salamina is marked by colorful and well-preserved two-story houses with their stunning woodwork, doors, and balconies. Salamina is often called the *pueblo madre* (mother town), as it was one of the first settlements of the Antioquian colonization. It's older than Manizales.

Sights

The **Plaza de Bolívar** (Clls. 4-5 between Cras. 6-7) is the center of activity in Salamina. It's an attractive plaza with a gazebo and large fountain brought over from Germany. Carried by mules over the mountains from the coast, it took a year to arrive, in several pieces, to its destination. The **Basílica Menor La Inmaculada Concepción** (Cl. 4 between Cras. 6-7) has an unusual architecture. The single-nave worship hall is rectangular and flat with wooden beams and no columns. The church was designed by an English architect, who is said to have been inspired by the First Temple in ancient Jerusalem.

The **Casa Rodrigo Jiménez Mejía** (Cl. 4 and Cra. 6) is the most photographed house in Salamina. The colors of this exceptionally preserved structure were chosen in an interesting way. An owner of the house called kids from the town to gather in the plaza and to give the owner their proposal on what colors to use for the house's exterior. The winner was a four-year-old girl, who chose bright orange, yellow, and green.

The **Casa de la Cultura** (Cra. 6 No. 6-06, tel. 6/859-5016, 8am-noon and 2pm-5pm Mon.-Fri., free) displays photos of old Salamina. It's often a hub of activity. It's also known as the Casa del Diablo, for the woodcarving of a jovial devil above the door that greets visitors as they enter.

For decades, the **Cementerio San Esteban** (Cra. 3 between Clls. 2-4, no phone), the town cemetery, was divided into three sections: one for the rich, one for the poor, and another for so-called "N.N." bodies (non-identified corpses, or "no names"). A wall was built to divide the rich from the poor, but it was knocked down at the behest of a priest in 1976. A skull and crossbones is displayed over the cemetery entrance. There is a small neo-gothic-style chapel (open occasionally) on the grounds.

In the village of **San Félix,** 30 kilometers (19 miles) east of Salamina, you can hike through serene countryside and admire a forest of 300-year-old *palmas de cera* (wax palms) from the hills above. It's as impressive as the Valle de Cocora, and without the crowds. Afterward, on the village plaza, ask at the stores for a refreshing *helado de salpicón* (ice cream made from chunks of fresh fruit in frozen watermelon juice). A bus makes the round-trip (COP$10,000 each way) to San Felix twice a day, once in the early morning and again in the afternoon. It leaves from the Plaza de Bolívar in Salamina.

Festivals and Events

Salamina's **Semana Santa** (Holy Week) celebrations, which fall in either March or April, are not that well known, but it is nonetheless a great time to get to know this cute town. Orchids and other flowers adorn the balconies of houses, adding even more color. In addition, free classical, religious, and jazz music concerts are held in churches, plazas, and even the cemetery.

San Felix is known for its **Exposición de Ganado Normando** in May, when local farmers show off their best Norman cows, with various competitions. It's an important event for ranchers throughout the region, and a chance to see an authentic display of Paisa culture.

Halloween is a big deal in Salamina. Here it's called the **Tarde de María La Parda,** named after a local woman who is said to have sold her soul to the devil to obtain riches. Her ghost supposedly causes mischief in the countryside every now and then. Events for Tarde de María La Parda take place in Plaza de Bolívar, and there are costume parties at night.

December 7 is a special day—or rather, night—to be in Salamina. That's when the lights are turned off in town, and the streets and balconies are illuminated with handmade lanterns made by locals. This beautiful celebration is called the **Noche de las Luces,** a night to stroll the streets and enjoy the special atmosphere. Locals greet each other serving sweets, snacks, or drinks. Music fills the air and the evening culminates in a fireworks show.

Food

One of the town's culinary specialties is *macana,* a hot drink made of milk, ground-up cookies, cinnamon, and sugar. The other is *huevos al vapor,* a boiled egg that is methodically steamed using giant coffee urns and served in a coffee cup.

Popular and atmospheric **Tierra Paisa** (no phone, 8am-9pm daily, COP$10,000), below the Hotel Colonial on the park, serves typical Colombian food, like *bandeja paisa* (a quintessential Paisa dish of beans, various meats, yuca, and potatoes), at incredibly low prices.

Accommodations

The best place to stay in Salamina by a long shot is the ★ **Casa de Lola Garcia** (Cl. 6 No. 7-54, tel. 6/859-5919, www.lacasadelolagarcia.com, COP$221,000 d, COP$84,000 dorm with breakfast), which opened its doors in 2012. The dream of a native Salamineño, musician Mauricio Cardona García, the carefully restored house was once the home of his grandmother, Lola García. Rooms are spacious and on the luxurious side. If you provide Mauricio with some notice, meals at the hotel can be arranged. Mauricio and his staff are the best resource there is on Salamina and things to do in the area, and the hotel can arrange a day trip to another beautiful town, Aguadas, known for its handicrafts. It's just a couple hours away to the north.

There are two other traditional hotels in town, that, while not fancy, will do the trick if you're sticking to a budget. Breakfast isn't included at these two. **Hospedaje Casa Real** (Cra. 6A No. 5-33, tel. 6/859-6355, cell tel. 311/784-2364, www.hospedajecasareal.wix.com, COP$70,000 d) has 24 rooms and is around the corner from the Plaza de Bolívar on a fairly busy street. The owners also have a *finca* with lodging facilities in the countryside. **Hotel Colonial** (Cl. 5 No. 6-74, tel. 6/859-5078, cell tel. 314/627-9124, hotelcolonial2011@hotmail.com, COP$55,000-95,000 d) is right on the square and has a variety of room options. In both hotels, ask to see the rooms before you check in, as their characteristics vary.

Want some cultural immersion? Manizales-based travel agency **Rosa de los Vientos** (Centro Comercial Parque Caldas Nivel 2, Local PB45, tel. 6/883-5940, www.turismorosadelosvientos.com) can set up a home stay (COP$35,000-50,000 pp) in one of the many historic homes in Salamina.

Transportation

There is frequent **shared taxi service** to Salamina from Manizales, costing COP$20,000. Taxis depart from the Terminal de Transportes (Cra. 43 No. 65-100) in Manizales.

One **bus** leaves Medellín at 7am daily bound for Salamina and other communities in the area. It departs from the **Terminal del Sur** (Cra. 65 No. 8B-91, tel. 4/444-8020 or 4/361-1186). The trip takes 4-6 hours on rural roads. The operator **T.P. Adventours** (cell tel. 312/864-1571) offers transportation from both Medellín and Manizales to Salamina.

★ PARQUE NACIONAL NATURAL LOS NEVADOS

This national park covers 583 square kilometers (225 miles) of rugged terrain along the Central Cordillera between the cities of Manizales to the north, Ibagué to the southeast, and Pereira to the northwest. Whether you do a day trip or a multiday trek, a visit to **Parque Nacional Natural Los Nevados** (www.parquesnacionales.gov.co) allows you to enjoy firsthand the stark beauty and intriguing flora and fauna of the upper reaches of the Andes, far above the forest line. Within the park are three snowcapped volcanoes: **Nevado del Ruiz** (5,325 meters/17,470 feet), **Nevado del Tolima** (5,215 meters/17,110 feet), and **Nevado Santa Isabel** (4,950 meters/16,240 feet), as well as myriad lakes, such as **Laguna del Otún.**

This rugged landscape was formed by volcanic activity and later sculpted by huge masses of glaciers. At their maximum extension, these glaciers covered an area of 860 square kilometers (332 square miles). They began to recede 14,000 years ago and, according to a 2013 study by the Colombian Institute of Hydrology, Meteorology, and Environmental Studies (IDEAM), will completely disappear by 2030.

Most of the park consists of *páramo,* a unique tropical high-altitude ecosystem, and super *páramo,* rocky terrain above the *páramo* and below the snow line. *Páramo* is a highland tropical ecosystem that thrives where UV radiation is higher, oxygen is scarcer, and where temperatures vary considerably from daytime to nighttime, when the mercury falls below freezing. It is the kingdom of the eerily beautiful *frailejones,* plants with statuesque tall trunks and thick greenish-yellow leaves. Other *páramo* vegetation includes shrubs, grasses, and cushion plants (*cojines*). The super *páramo* has a stark, moonlike landscape, with occasional dunes of volcanic ash. Though it's largely denuded of vegetation, bright yellow plants called *litamo real* and orange moss provide splashes of color. On a clear day, the

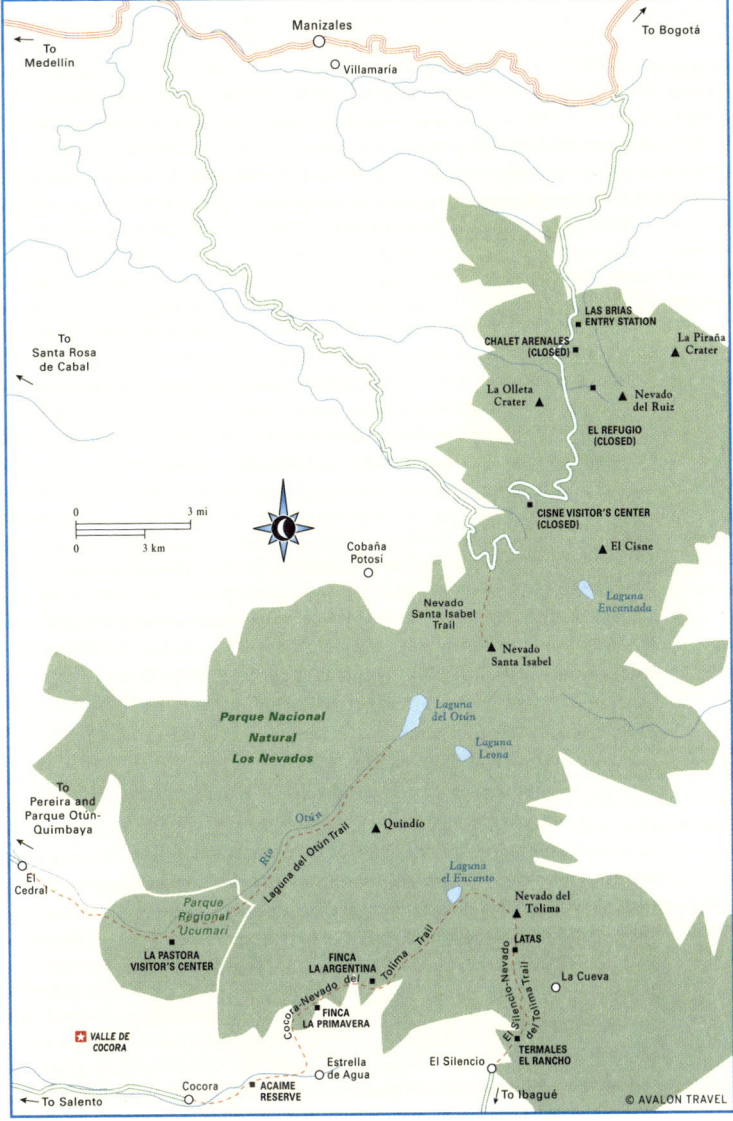

views from the *páramo* or super *páramo* of the snowcapped volcanoes and lakes are simply stunning.

The black-and-white Andean condor, *vultur gryphus*, with its wingspan of up to three meters (10 feet), can sometimes be spotted gliding along the high cliffs in the park. While it is estimated that there are over 10,000 of the birds on the continent (mostly in Argentina), there are few remaining in Colombia. Some estimates report that by the mid-1980s, there were no more than 15 left in Colombia, due in large part to poaching by cattle ranchers. To boost their numbers in Colombia, a reintroduction program was initiated in the park (and in other parts of the country) in the 1990s in conjunction with the San Diego Zoo, where newborns were hatched. Today it is estimated that there are 200-300 condors soaring above Colombia's Andean highlands. Numbers of the endangered birds in Los Nevados range 8-15. Other fauna includes spectacled bears *(oso de anteojos),* tapirs, weasels, squirrels, bats, and many species of birds.

The Nevado del Tolima and Nevado del Ruiz volcanoes are considered active, with the Ruiz presenting more activity. In 1985 it erupted, melting the glacier, which in turn created a massive mudslide that engulfed the town of Armero, burying an estimated 20,000 of the town's 29,000 residents.

Parques Nacionales has an office in Manizales (Cl. 69 No. 24-69, tel. 6/887-1611 or 6/887-2273, 8:30am-4pm Mon.-Fri.) for updated information on park conditions.

ORIENTATION

The Northern Sector of the park includes the Nevado del Ruiz, with its three craters (Arenales, La Piraña, and La Olleta), and extends south to the extinct Cisne volcano and Laguna Verde. Much of this sector can be accessed by vehicle.

The Southern Sector includes everything from the Nevado Santa Isabel south to the Quindío peak, as well as Nevado del Tolima, with Pereira, Salento, and Ibagué being the main points of entry into the park.

Northern Sector

The **Northern Sector** (turnoff to Las Brisas entry point at Km. 43 Vía Manizales-Honda, tel. 6/887-1611, www.parquesnacionales.gov.co, 8am-2pm daily, non-Colombians COP$38,000) is the most visited part of the park. Until relatively recently, day-trippers could drive from Manizales directly to El Refugio, a camp at the base of the Ruiz, and climb up to the main Arenales crater (5,325 meters/17,470 feet) in a strenuous three-hour hike. The Cisne visitors center provided lodging in this sector of the park and allowed easy access to the Nevado Santa Isabel and Laguna Verde. However, due to heightened volcanic activity at Ruiz, only a small section of the Northern Sector is open. A small area, from the **Las Brisas entry station** to the beautiful and eerie landscape of the **Valle de las Tumbas** (also known as Valle del Silencio), is open to visitors in organized tours and private vehicles. For current conditions at the Ruiz volcano, check the Colombian Geological Service website (www.sgc.gov.co/Manizales.aspx).

If you don't have a vehicle, the only way to visit this part of the park is on an organized day tour from Manizales. These tours leave early in the morning, drive to Las Brisas park entry station, and continue to the Valle de las Tumbas, making stops along the way to gaze at the landscape, particularly the Nevado del Ruiz and La Olleta crater (weather permitting), and to view birds and vegetation. On the way back to Manizales, the tour stops for an hour at some hot springs (often Termales de Otoño). You're back in Manizales by 5pm. This experience will be unsatisfying for people who want to move their legs, as you'll be in the car most of the day. **Asdeguias** (Cl. 25 No. 20-25, tel. 6/884-4525, cell tel. 314/507-4735, www.asdeguiascaldas.com) and **Ecosistemas** (Cra. 21 No. 23-21, tel. 6/880-8300, cell tel. 312/705-7007, www.ecosistemastravel.com.co) offer this day tour for around COP$140,000 for nonresidents. This excursion usually covers pickup in Manizales, transportation, meals, the park entrance fee, and a stop at hot springs.

If you have a vehicle (a car with 4WD is not necessary) you can drive the Brisas-Valle de las Tumbas segments but you will be required to take a guide in your vehicle and participate in a *charla* (chat) at the park entrance. The cost is COP$27,000 for nonresidents or COP$5,000 for students with valid student ID, COP$11,000 for obligatory guided tour per group, and COP$5,500 for the vehicle entry.

Nevado Santa Isabel Trek

A spectacular day trek from Manizales is up to the snow line of the **Nevado Santa Isabel.** It is a long day trip, starting with a bumpy 50-kilometer (31-mile) drive to the border of the park at Conejeras and then a three-hour (5.5-kilometer/3.4-mile) hike up the canyon of the Río Campo Alegre and then to the snow line. This hike requires good physical condition; it takes you from an elevation of 4,000 meters (13,100 feet) up to 4,750 meters (15,600 feet) through *páramo* and super *páramo*.

More serious mountaineers can extend the trek to the summit of the Nevado Santa Isabel (4,950 meters/16,240 feet) by camping past Conejeras and doing an early-morning ascent to the top. At sunrise, the views onto the surrounding high mountain landscape, with the Nevado del Ruiz and Nevado del Tolima in the background, are magnificent. The ascent to the top requires specialized gear.

Asdeguias (Cl. 25 No. 20-25, tel. 6/884-4525, cell tel. 314/507-4735, www.asdeguiascaldas.com), **Ecosistemas** (Cra. 21 No. 23-21, tel. 6/880-8300, cell tel. 312/705-7007, www.ecosistemastravel.com.co), and **Kumanday** (Cl. 66 No. 23B-40, tel. 6/887-2682, www.kumanday.com) each offer this tour out of Manizales. You'll have to get up with the chickens though: You'll be leaving town at 4am.

Laguna del Otún Trek

A popular three-day trek from Pereira is to the **Laguna del Otún.** The starting point is El Cedral, a *vereda* (settlement) 21 kilometers (13 miles) east of Pereira at an altitude of 2,100 meters (6,900 feet). The trek terminates at the lake at 3,950 meters (13,000 feet). This 19-kilometer (12-mile) hike provides an incredible close-up view of the transitions from humid tropical forest to higher-altitude tropical forests and the *páramo*. The trek

Parque Los Nevados

Río Otún

follows the valley of the crystalline Río Otún, first through the Parque Regional Natural Ucumarí and then into the Parque Nacional Natural Los Nevados. It's not too strenuous. Most trekkers split the climb into two segments, camping at El Bosque or Jordín on the way up and spending one night at the Laguna del Otún. The return hike can be done in one day. The path is easy to follow, though quite rocky and muddy. A guide is not necessary.

The only accommodation along this route is at the **Centro de Visitantes La Pastora** (6 km/4 mi from El Cedral toward Laguna del Otún, no phone, cell tel. 312/200-7711, COP$22,000 pp) in the Parque Regional Natural Ucumarí. The dormitory-style rooms are clean and comfortable in this cozy lodge. Meals (COP$6,000-9,000) by the fireplace are excellent. It is possible to buy snacks along the way, but there is no food at the *laguna,* so bring cooking equipment and food along with tents and sleeping bags.

To get to El Cedral from Pereira, take a *chiva* (rural bus) offered by **Transportes Florida** (tel. 6/331-0488, COP$5,000, 2 hrs.), which departs from Calle 12 and Carrera 9 in Pereira. On weekdays, the bus departs at 7am, 9am, and 3pm. On weekends there is an additional bus at noon. The buses return from El Cedral approximately at 11am, 2pm, and 5pm.

The Laguna del Otún can also be visited on an organized tour in a long day trip from Pereira. This involves leaving Pereira at 5am and driving 88 kilometers (55 miles) to Potosí (3,930 meters/12,895 feet) near the park border and then hiking two hours to the lake. This is not a strenuous walk. A recommended tour operator in Pereira for this excursion is **Ecoturismo Risaralda-Cattleya S.E.R.** (Cl. 99 No. 14-78, La Florida, tel. 6/314-4162, cell tel. 313/695-4305, grupocattleya@gmail.com, www.cattleyaser.com). The **Kolibrí Hostel** (tel. 6/331-3955, cell tel. 321/646-9275, www.kolibrihostel.com) in Pereira also offers guided treks to the laguna.

Nevado del Tolima and Paramillo del Quindío Treks

There are two ways to reach the classically cone-shaped Nevado del Tolima (5,215 meters/17,110 feet). The somewhat easier and more scenic route is from Vereda del Cocora near Salento, which takes four days. A more strenuous route is from Ibagué, which can be done in two days.

From **Vereda del Cocora** (2,200 meters/7,215 feet), you hike 7-8 hours (13.5 kilometers/8.4 miles) through the Valle del Cocora, up the Río Quindío canyon, and through the Páramo Romerales to the Finca La Primavera at 3,680 meters (12,075 feet). There you spend the night (COP$10,000 pp) and take a simple meal. On the second day you hike 6-7 hours (12 kilometers/7.5 miles) to a campsite at 4,400 meters (14,450 feet) near the edge of the super *páramo*. On the third day, you depart the campsite at 2am and climb 8 kilometers (5 miles) to reach the rim of the Tolima crater at 7am or 8am, when there are incredible views to the Quindío, Santa Isabel, Cisne, and Ruiz peaks. That evening you sleep again at the Finca La Primavera and return to Vereda del Cocora the following day. The path is not clearly marked and it is easy to lose your way (there's a reason why one part is called the Valle de los Perdidos, or Valley of the Lost), so it is best go with a guide. The ascent to the glacier requires specialized gear.

From Ibagué the starting point for the trek to Nevado del Tolima is **Juntas** (17 km/10.6 miles from Ibagué) in the beautiful Cañón de Combeima river canyon. There are two options for overnighting: a campground called **Finca Las Nieves,** which requires six hours of hiking on the first day, or the campground known as **Escuela El Salto/El Vergel,** which requires eight hours. On the second day, hikers arrive at **Termales de Cañón** (4,000m/13,123 ft.) after about four hours of hiking. There are again two options to reach the Tolima summit: via the **Ingeominas weather station,** leaving at 2am, or the **Helipuerto route,** which requires an additional overnight at 4,600 m (15,091 ft); the latter is the preferred route for those with less experience in high mountain climbing. Guide **Truman David Alfonso Bejarano** in Ibagué (cell tel. 315/292-7395, trumandavid01@gmail.com, www.truman.com.co) can organize excursions from Salento or Ibagué. His blog (www.truman-adventure.blogspot.com) has detailed information about the various routes up to Nevado del Tolima.

Another less traveled but beautiful hike is to the **Paramillo del Quindío** (4,750 meters/15,585 feet), an extinct volcano that once was covered by a glacier. The 17-kilometer (10.5-mile) ascent from Finca La Primavera takes eight hours and can be done in one long day. Alternatively, you can split the hike in two, camping so as to arrive at the top of the crater in the early morning when visibility is best. There are spectacular views of the Tolima, Santa Isabel, and Ruiz volcanoes. This is a strenuous but not technically difficult climb.

Recommended guides for the Tolima and Quindío treks are **Salento Trekking** (Cl. 4 No. 6-09, cell tel. 313/654-1619, www.salentotrekking.com) and **Páramo Trek** (Cl. 5 No. 1-37, cell tel. 311/745-3761, www.paramotrek.

com). Salento Trekking often prefers to stay at Finca La Argentina, which is less crowded with hikers than Finca La Primavera.

ARMENIA

The defining moment for Colombia's Ciudad Milagro (Miracle City) arrived uninvited on the afternoon of January 25, 1999, when an earthquake registering 6.4 on the Richter scale shook the city. One thousand people lost their lives, nearly half the city became instantly displaced, and thousands of nearby coffee farms were destroyed. The miracle of this coffee region city can be seen in how it rapidly rebuilt and began to thrive once more.

As is the case with sister cities Pereira and Manizales, Armenia was settled in the late 19th century by Antioquian colonizers. The city is not a tourist destination in itself, but you'll be astonished to see, within just a few blocks of the city center, a sea of green coffee farms. That lush countryside is the real attraction.

The city was founded in 1889 and initially named Villa Holguín to honor then-president Carlos Holguín Mallarino. It is widely believed that the city was renamed Armenia to honor victims of the 1894-1896 Hamidian massacres of ethnic Armenians living in the Ottoman Empire.

Armenia is a small city by Colombian standards, home to 294,000 residents. The downtown is compact and easy to traverse on foot. The northern areas of the city are where the hotels, malls, and restaurants are found. That part of town, around the Hotel Armenia, is also walkable.

Carreras run north-south and *calles* east-west. Main drags include Carreras 14 (Avenida Bolívar), 18, and 19, as well as Avenida Centenario, which runs parallel to the Río Quindío on the eastern side of the city. Carrera 14 is pedestrian-only downtown.

Sights

Standing in downtown Armenia's **Plaza de Bolívar** (between Cras. 12-13 and Clls. 20-21) is a sculpture of Simón Bolívar (northern side of the plaza) and the love-it-or-hate-it **Monumento Al Esfuerzo,** designed by Rodrigo Arenas Betancourt and built in the 1960s. This sculpture stands in remembrance of the sacrifices made and hardships faced by Antioquian settlers who arrived in the area seeking opportunity. The modern, triangular-shaped **Catedral de la Inmaculada Concepción** (Cra. 12 between Clls. 20-21, hours vary) is located on the plaza, which is on the stark side.

A stroll down the **pedestrian street** from the Plaza de Bolívar to the Parque Sucre is a pleasant way to see the modern downtown at its busiest.

MUSEO DEL ORO QUIMBAYA

It is worth the trek to Armenia just to visit the **Museo del Oro Quimbaya** (Av. Bolívar No. 40N-80, tel. 6/749-8433, www.banrepcultural.org, 10am-5pm Tues.-Sun., free) on the outskirts of town. The museum, designed by famed architect Rogelio Salmona, focuses exclusively on the Quimbaya nation, which predominated in the coffee region before the Spanish conquest.

Armenia

Much of the museum is devoted to ceramic and gold decorative and ceremonial items that were found in the area. Excellent explanations in English provide interesting background information on the history, ways of life, and traditions of the Quimbaya people.

Festivals and Events

Armenios celebrate their city's founding in October with the **Fiestas Cuyabras.** City parks and plazas are the stages for cultural events, a beauty pageant, and a fun Yipao (Jeep) parade. These U.S. military Jeeps (called Jeep Willys), a symbol of the region, began arriving in Colombia around 1946, after World War II.

Recreation

Several city parks and plazas are great places to enjoy the wonderful Armenia climate. These include the **Parque de la Vida** (Cra. 13 at Cl. 8N) and the **Parque Sucre** (Cra. 13 at Cl. 13) downtown, the latter of which is adjacent to a delightful pedestrian street. Locals and visitors gather in the late afternoon at the **Café Quindío** in the park for *onces* (tea time).

The **Parque El Bosque** (Cl. 21 No. 22-23) is a green space that has a bust of Abraham Lincoln that was donated to the city by the Armenian community of Fresno, California, to express their gratitude for naming the city in solidarity with the decimated Armenian nation in the early 20th century. The bullfighting ring is adjacent to the park.

Globos Colombia (cell tel. 320/667-7818, www.globoscolombia.com, COP$475,000) offers commanding views of the endless fields of coffee of this fertile region from a hot-air balloon. Flights (shared or private) usually lift off at 6am-6:30am and last 45 minutes, and breakfast is typically included. To paraglide over coffee fields, contact **Parapente Quindío Calarcá** (cell tel. 320/775-9888, COP$100,000). The price includes transportation and insurance.

Shopping

The **Centro Comercial Unicentro** (Cra. 14 No. 6-02, tel. 6/731-2667, 8am-9pm daily) along Avenida Bolívar has the usual array of Colombian mall stores, fast-food joints, an Éxito department store, a Cinemark movie theater, several ATMs, and food and coffee courts (with spectacular views of the bucolic valley). **El Portal del Quindío** (Av. Bolívar 19N No. 46-057, www.elportaldelquindio.com, 10am-8pm daily) is down the road from Unicentro and offers similar shops and a Cine Colombia movie theater.

Food

In the Centro, **Lucerna** (Cl. 20 No. 14-40, tel. 6/741-1005, 9am-7pm Mon.-Sat., 10am-7pm Sun.) is a retro-looking *salón de té* (tearoom) that specializes in sweets and pastries, but affordable lunches are on the menu, too. The original store is in Pereira and was started by a Swiss man in the 1950s.

If you have an appetite, head to **La Fogata** (Av. Bolívar No. 14N-39, tel. 6/749-5980, www.lafogata.com.co, noon-midnight daily, COP$28,000), a classic in Armenia. Their filet mignon ranks as the best in town.

Sitting smack-dab in the center of the coffee universe, you wouldn't think that finding a nice, hot brew in Armenia would have ever been a challenge. But it's a relatively recent phenomenon that fancy coffees and cafés have made it to the streets. **Café Quindío Gourmet** (Parque de la Vida, Cra. 14/Av. Bolívar 7N, tel. 6/745-4478, www.cafequindio.com.co, 11am-9:30pm Mon.-Sat., noon-4:30pm Sun.) is the most famous (and most commercial) of coffees around here, and this location has a very nice restaurant as well, with baby coffee plants on each table. Those in the know, however, will head to other cafés, appropriately hidden on back streets. Look for **Fika Café** (Cra. 13 No. 8N-16 #104, cell tel. 320/524-0373, 9am-12:30pm and 3pm-9pm daily), which is a pleasant spot to settle into on a late afternoon.

Natural Food Plaza (Cra. 14 No. 4-51, tel. 6/745-1597, 7:30am-6pm Mon.-Thurs., 7:30am-4pm Fri. and Sun., COP$10,000) always has a set lunch with soup, salad, a main, and a dessert, but you can also order Paisa dishes, like tamales and *bandeja paisa*—the quintessential dish of beans, various meats, yuca, and potatoes, reinvented vegetarian-style—all to the soothing sounds of elevator music. Check their Facebook page for the daily menu and information on one-day cooking classes.

Many of the best-known restaurants in Armenia are on the outskirts of town, like El Roble (Km. 12 Vía Armenia-Pereira, tel. 6/740-5120, 6:30am-9pm daily, COP$15,000), which is a sprawling family-style restaurant serving 100 percent Colombian cuisine.

Accommodations

The ★ Casa Quimbaya (Cl. 16N No. 14-92, tel. 6/732-3086, cell tel. 312/590-0066, www.casaquimbaya.com, COP$25,000 dorm, COP$80,000 d) is probably the best budget and hostel option in Armenia. Neighbor to the Universidad del Quindío, it can assist guests if they want to go to the library, swim in the pool, or check out some of the many free cultural events going on there. The busy café/restaurant draws students as well as tourists. The hostel has three dorm rooms with 4-5 beds each and three private rooms. It's in an ordinary-looking house on a quiet street, very close to the action of Carrera 14.

A midrange option downtown is Casa Hotel del Parque (Cra. 14 No. 12-26, tel. 6/731-3166, www.casahoteldelparque.com, COP$99,000 d). It has just five rooms and a great location on the Parque Sucre and a pedestrian street.

Isa Victory Hotel Boutique (Av. Bolívar No. 21N-47, cell tel. 320/770-7079, www.isavictoryhotelboutique.com, COP$150,000 d) lacks charm, but is a good midrange option along Avenida Bolívar. This modern business hotel has a terrace with hot tub on the top floor.

The top-end address in town is ★ Allure Aroma Mocawa (Cra. 14 No. 9N-00, tel. 6/735-9599, www.allurearomamocawahotel.com.co, COP$196,000 d), a 16-story high-rise with nearly 100 rooms, an awesome rooftop pool on the 17th floor with a view of the countryside, an ample breakfast buffet, and free parking. It's on Avenida Bolívar (Carrera 14) close to shopping malls.

The Armenia Hotel (Av. Bolívar and Cl. 8N, tel. 6/746-0099, cell tel. 320/696-9111, www.armeniahotel.com.co, COP$183,000 d) may have lost some of its allure to nearby Mocawa, but it remains a popular address, especially with Colombian business travelers. It has 129 rooms on nine floors, and a big atrium smells of eucalyptus emanating from the steam room. Rooms are furnished with locally made *guadua* bamboo furniture and have been updated. A spa, pool, and small gym are available on the premises, and guests also have privileges at a gym four blocks away.

Information and Services

Tourist offices are located at the bus station (Cl. 35 No. 20-68) and in the Edificio de la Gobernación (Plaza de Bolívar, tel. 6/741-7700, 8am-noon and 2pm-6pm Mon.-Sat.).

Transportation

There are few domestic flight options from **Aeropuerto Internacional El Eden** (Km. 10 Vía La Tebaida, tel. 6/747-9400). **Avianca** flies to Bogotá, while **Aerolíneas de Antioquia (ADA)** and **Air Panama** fly into Medellín. The airport is about 20 kilometers from town, and a taxi costs around COP$30,000. **Milano Rent A Car** (www.milanocar.com, cell tel. 300/800-1180) can set you up with wheels in Armenia. Before driving into Armenia, find out the days for *pico y placa*—vehicle restrictions in place during the workweek and based on the last digit of the license plate—in order to avoid fines.

The bus terminal, the **Terminal de Transportes** (Cl. 35 No. 20-68, tel. 6/747-3355, www.terminalarmenia.com) is just south of downtown, about 13 blocks from the Plaza de Bolívar. There is frequent service to Pereira (1 hour, COP$8,000), Salento (1 hour, COP$4,000), and Manizales (4 hours, COP$17,000). Buses bound for Medellín (6.5 hours, COP$38,000) leave all day from before dawn to around midnight. While short-distance buses depart until about 10pm or later, it's better to travel earlier if possible—for both safety reasons and so you can enjoy the scenery along the way.

The rapid bus system in Armenia is called the **Tinto** (www.tinto.com.co). A line on Avenida Bolívar connects the northern part of the city with downtown. The website can be confusing, so it's best to ask someone how to get around.

VICINITY OF ARMENIA
★ Jardín Botánico del Quindío

Just 10 minutes outside of town, the well-run **Jardín Botánico del Quindío** (Km. 3 Vía al Valle, tel. 6/742-7254, cell tel. 310/404-5223, www.jardinbotanicoquindio.org, 9am-4pm daily, English tour COP$30,000) is home to hundreds of tree and plant species, many of which are threatened. Knowledgeable volunteer guides, who are usually college students, lead visitors on a mandatory 2.5-hour tour along jungle paths, stopping every so often to point out flora that you would have overlooked had you walked through on your own. That might strike you as a major time commitment, but it really doesn't seem like it. In addition to palms (which aren't technically trees) and *guadua* (which is actually related to grass), look out for *matapalos*, a tree that wraps itself around other trees, strangling them as they fight for sunlight. It's been lovingly nicknamed the *abrazo de la suegra* (mother-in-law's hug).

In Colombia where there is tropical forest, there will be birds. The gardens are no exception, and they are home to at least 119 species. The birds are at their most active early in the morning. Some of the commonly seen species include tanagers, toucans, owls, woodpeckers, the multicolored *torito cabecirrojo* (red-headed barbet), and iconic *barranqueros* or *barranquillos* (blue-crowned motmots). These birds make their nests in the earth. Rodent residents who frequently make cameo appearances are *ardillas* (squirrels) and cute *guatines* (Central American agoutis). By far the most photographed sector of the park is the *mariposario* (enclosed butterfly garden) in the shape of a giant butterfly; it is home to thousands of the insects. The butterflies are livelier when the sun is out.

Guides are volunteers, and although the entry price is steep, it's good form to tip the guides after the tour. Call in advance to inquire about English-speaking tours. It's easy to get to the park using public transportation from Armenia. Just look for a bus from the Plaza de Bolívar or along Avenida Bolívar that says "Jardín Botánico."

Theme Parks

These parks are mobbed with families on weekends and holidays.

RECUCA (Km. 5 Vía La Y-Barcelona, Vereda Callelarga, tel. 6/749-8525, www.recuca.com, 9am-3pm daily, tour with lunch COP$30,000) is a theme park, but one without roller coasters or water rides. RECUCA stands for Recorrido de la Cultura Cafetera (Coffee Culture Experience). Upon arrival at the *finca* (farm), you'll be greeted by smiling employees dressed in traditional bean-picking garb. Then you'll explore a coffee farm, lend a hand by picking some ripe beans, and learn about the entire process. After that, you'll enjoy a big Paisa lunch (beans and rice for herbivores). If you prefer, you can just take part in a coffee-tasting session (COP$14,000). You can get to RECUCA by taking a bus bound for Barcelona from the Terminal de Transportes in Armenia (Cl. 35 No. 20-68). The bus drops you off at the park entrance. From there it is a 30-minute walk, or the guard at the entrance can order a Jeep for you (COP$5,000).

The **Parque Nacional del Café** (Km. 6 Vía Montenegro-Pueblo Tapao, tel. 6/741-7417, www.parquedelcafe.co, 8am-6pm daily, COP$25,000-59,000) is near the town of **Montenegro,** 12.5 kilometers (8 miles) west of Armenia. While part of the park is devoted to telling the story of coffee production in Colombia, it's mostly an amusement park with roller coasters, a chairlift, horseback rides, a coffee show, a water park, and other attractions.

Jardín Botánico del Quindío

PANACA (Km. 7 Vía Vereda Kerman, tel. 6/758-2830, cell tel. 313/721-9211, www.panaca.com.co, 9am-6pm daily, COP$45,000-62,000) is an agriculture-themed amusement park near the town of **Quimbaya,** where visitors can see and interact with all types of farm animals and watch the occasional pig race.

Festivals and Events

In June or sometimes July, **Calarcá** puts on an event to honor what made the coffee region what it is today. A number of the usual festival events take place during the **Fiesta Nacional del Café** (www.calarca.net), but it's the **Desfile de Yipao** that steals the show. That's when Jeep Willys—U.S. military Jeeps from World War II and the Korean War that were sold to farmers in the coffee region—are filled with people, animals, and furniture, and go on parade. There are competitions (essentially Willy beauty pageants) and a contest in which the Jeep Willys are loaded down with 1,800 kilos of cargo and race forward on two wheels only.

Accommodations

With more than a century's experience growing coffee, the **Hacienda Combia** (Km. 4 Vía al Valle-Vereda La Bella, tel. 6/746-8472, cell tel. 314/850-5695, www.combia.com.co, COP$152,000 d) has 33 rooms and an infinity pool that has a fantastic view, and there are coffee tours available through the nearby fields. This hotel is not far from a highway, but you can easily block out reminders of suburbia by focusing on the fertile lands that surround you and are home to colorful birds. Its proximity to the airport (airport pickups can be arranged) and easy access make it a popular event space for Colombian businesses.

Surrounded by 160 hectares of pineapple, cacao, banana, and citrus crops, it's hard to imagine a more relaxing place than ★ **Hacienda Bambusa** (off Vía Calarcá-Caicedonia south of Armenia, tel. 6/740-4935, cell tel. 300/778-8897 reservations, www.haciendabambusa.com, COP$490,000 d). Its isolation is a selling point, providing the perfect environment to disconnect. The house and much of the furniture are made of *guadua* and other traditional materials, and its seven rooms are luxurious and tastefully decorated, each with its own private balcony or terrace. The views from those balconies are spectacular, with endless farms punctuated by *guadua* forests and mountains in the distance. There are cacao tours to take, horses to ride, birds to watch, and massages to be enjoyed. The Armenia airport is about 40 minutes away; taking a cab from there costs COP$45,000, although the hotel can arrange all your transportation. Bambusa offers a range of packages, some including activities and excursions, transportation to and from the airport, and all meals.

Near the town of Quimbaya and off the road 800 meters past some ordinary-looking houses and apartments, a well-maintained hacienda awaits: ★ **Finca Villa Nora** (tel. 6/741-5472, cell tel. 310/422-6335, www.quindio-fincavillanora.com, COP$180,000 d with two meals). It's a 120-year-old red-and-white house that is charming and full of character. It's built in the typical Paisa style. Amid fruit trees, flowers, coffee fields, and a huge ficus tree, at Villa Nora the air is pure, sunsets are lovely, and drinks on the veranda is not a bad idea. There are only six rooms at this quiet refuge.

SALENTO

On the western edge of the Parque Nacional Natural Los Nevados, Salento (pop. 7,000) is one-stop shopping for those seeking a quintessential coffee region experience. The town, an enchanting pueblo that is home to coffee growers and cowboys, is adorned with the trademark colorful balconies and facades of Paisa architecture. It was one of the first settlements in the region during the 19th-century Antioquian colonization. In the nearby countryside, coffee farms dominate the landscape. Here you can be a Juan Valdez, the iconic personification of Colombian coffee, during a coffee tour in which you harvest coffee beans, learn about the bean-to-bag process, and sip the freshest coffee you've ever tasted.

Within minutes of town, to the east, is the Valle de Cocora, where you can play tree tag in forests of *palma de cera* (wax palm, the Colombian national tree), the skyscrapers of the palm family. Some of these can reach up to 60 meters (200 feet) high. For a more challenging hike, continue to the Reserva Acaime, a private nature reserve of tropical forest, babbling brooks, and not a few hummingbirds. From here adventurers can ascend into the *páramos* (highland moors) and, eventually, the snowcapped peaks of the Parque Natural Nacional Los Nevados.

Salento is easily accessed from between both Armenia and Pereira, and has become a destination for international backpackers. The town is loaded with hostels, hotels, and restaurants catering to visitors. To experience Salento with fewer crowds, go during the week. During high tourist season, such as around New Year's and during Semana Santa, it can be a nightmare with long traffic jams on the road into town. At times, authorities close the roads, not allowing any visitors into town.

Sights

The **Parque Bolívar,** or **Plaza Principal,** is the center of town and center of activity. The festive pedestrian **Calle Real** (between Cl. 1 and Cl. 5), lined by restaurants and shops painted in a rainbow of colors, is the most photogenic street in town. It starts at the Plaza Principal and leads up to the **Alto de la Cruz Mirador,** a scenic lookout atop the Calle Real from where you can catch a nice view of Salento. Farther on is another lookout with views over the surrounding jungles and valleys.

About a 10-minute walk southwest from the town center, near the cemetery, is the **Aldea Artesano** (cell tel. 315/436-6850 or 312/868-8633), a funky artists' commune where jewelers, weavers, painters, and musicians live and work. Browse their workshops and participate in a class. The artists enjoy sharing their craftsmanship with visitors. Aldea Artesano is in a peaceful setting, with a short nature path and a community garden.

Coffee Tours

In the outskirts of Salento are two very popular coffee tours. Your individual experience may vary, particularly depending on your guide and his or her English abilities (or your adeptness in Spanish). Tours typically last 1-1.5 hours. Tack on an hour or so if you plan on walking from Salento.

Finca El Ocaso (Km. 3.8, Vía Salento-Vereda Palestina, cell tel. 310/451-7329, cafeelocaso@hotmail.com, www.fincaelocasosalento.com, five tours in English 9am-4pm daily, tour COP$10,000) is a family-run farm with some 12 hectares (30 acres) of coffee crops. It produces coffee that has several international certifications, such as the German UTZ and the Rainforest Alliance. Elevation here is around 1,780 meters (5,800 feet), a good altitude for growing coffee. If you're doing the tour as a day trip and plan to walk, you can do a full loop, starting from the Puente Amarillo in Salento and returning along a river to Boquía, then taking a bus back to Salento. In addition, visitors can spend a night or two here in one of four cozy rooms.

The **Finca Don Eduardo coffee tour** (Plantation House, Alto de Coronel, Cl. 7 No. 1-04, cell tel. 316/285-2603, www.theplantationhousesalento.com, COP$20,000) is the most fun of the three tours (and the longest at more than two hours), and, being a London transplant, Tim's English isn't bad. He almost always gives the tours and, along with his Colombian partner, Cristina, runs the Don Eduardo coffee farm. This gorgeous land has been a working coffee farm for over 80 years. The farm grows four subvarieties of arabica coffee.

Recreation

For the real Paisa experience, **horseback riding** is a good way to enjoy the fresh air and birdsong of the hilly back roads near Salento and Boquía. In the Parque Bolívar there are usually horses at the ready, especially on

Horseback-riding is popular in Colombia's cowboy country.

weekends. **Don Álvaro** (cell tel. 311/375-1534, 3-hr. trip COP$40,000 pp) treats his horses well and is considered the best guide for this activity.

Most hostels can arrange bike rental. Additionally, **CicloSalento** (near Plantation Hostel, Alto de Coronel, Cl. 7 No. 1-04, cell tel. 318/872-9714, COP$10,000/hr., COP$35,000/day) rents out good-quality mountain bikes with helmets. Caution: The winding road leading into town from the Valle de Cocora does not have a shoulder for bikes. Vehicles tend to speed along this road, making this a dangerous stretch for cyclists and pedestrians. Another **bike place** is at Cra. 5N No. 9-06 (cell tel. 313/653-7622, COP$30,000 day).

A popular **day hike** takes you to **Cascada Santa Rita,** a 15-meter (50-foot) waterfall and swimming hole in the tropical jungles north of Salento. The starting point is near the Monteroca camping site in Boquía. There's a small fee to visit the waterfalls, as they are on the Santa Rita farm property. This could be done without a guide, if you get specific instructions, but it's best to contract an experienced local guide such as **Blaney Arisizabal of UMAYAKU** (cell tel. 314/885-3326, theblaney@gmail.com). Another option is **Salentour** (salentourcafetero@gmail.com). The cost of this guided day hike is around COP$80,000-100,000.

Food

With a fantastic location on the Parque Bolívar, ★ **Juan Esteban Parrilla y Vinos** (Cra. 7 No. 5-45, cell tel. 315/410-1059, 8am-11am and noon-3pm daily) is a popular place, with beautiful photography of the local scenery on its walls and a big menu of traditional Colombian dishes. It's a grilled meat place but it happily accommodates vegetarians.

It's a real treat to discover a restaurant like ★ **Casa La Eliana** (Cra. 2 No. 6-45, cell tel. 314/660-5987, http://casalaeliana.com, 10am-9pm daily, COP$20,000), where great service, a cozy atmosphere, and fantastic food are the norm. This Spanish-run spot a few blocks from the center of town is the only place in this part of the woods where you can find curry dishes and gourmet pizzas on the menu. And try as they might, the friendly cocker spaniels aren't allowed to mingle with diners.

The best place in town for pizzas is **Pizzería Piccola** (Cra. 6 No. 1-10, cell tel. 315/410-1059). Under the guidance of its Italian owner, it has a nice atmosphere with open-air seating. It also has a small attached guesthouse.

Brunch (Cl. 6 No. 3-25, cell tel. 311/757-8082, 6:30am-9:30pm daily, COP$15,000), a hip little joint with graffiti and messages from hundreds of visitors from around the globe decorating the walls, is another restaurant that operates with the international traveler in mind. They do serve brunch, but also breakfast, lunch, and dinner. The menu seems aimed squarely at Americans: hot wings, Philly cheesesteaks, black bean burgers, and peanut butter brownies.

On a quiet side street, **Café Bernabe** (Cl. 3 No. 6-3, cell tel. 318/393-3278) is the gourmet address in Salento, serving delicious coffee and desserts but also interesting main dishes like filet mignon with blackberry and coffee sauce. The outdoor terrace is perfect for a sunny Salento afternoon.

Swanky, with great views, fine drinks, and comfort food is ★ **Luciernaga** (Cra. 3 No. 9-19, cell tel. 310/425-0197, 7am-11:30pm daily). Sometimes it has live music, and this is the best place in Salento for a sundowner cocktail. **Mojitería** (Cl. 4 No. 5-54, cell tel. 310/409-2331, 2pm-11pm daily, COP$18,000) is a lively spot where you can grab a quick bite (appetizers, salads, soups, and pastas) or try one or two of the many mojitos on offer. At night it takes on a bar atmosphere, often with live music on the weekends and, of course, big, satisfying mojitos.

Hands down, the finest and fanciest café in this coffee region pueblo is ★ **Café Jesús Martín** (Cra. 6 No. 6-14, tel. 6/759-3282, www.cafejesusmartin.com, 8am-8pm daily), a family-run coffee producer. In addition, it runs excellent coffee tours, with transportation included, to the Finca Santana near the town of Quimbaya.

Ice cream, fruit salads, and the like draw visitors to **Sueño de Fresas** (Cl. 5 No. 6-35, cell tel. 310/892-6624, www.fresas.salento.com.co, noon-9pm daily).

Cheap local eats are on the menu at **Rincón de Lucy** (Cl. 4 with Cra. 6, 11am-2pm Mon.-Sat.), where the set lunch deal goes for a pittance: COP$6,000. Meanwhile, if you're hankering for a buttery arepa, look for **Luz Dary's stall** at the corner of Carrera 5 and Calle 7, near the bridge and a laundry place. She's usually up for a chat.

Accommodations

One of the best hostels in the area is ★ **Tralala** (Cra. 7 No. 6-45, cell tel. 314/850-5543, www.hostaltralalasalento.com, COP$18,000 dorm, COP$45,000 d). It's hard to miss this in-town option: It's a two-story white house with bright orange wooden trim, and the owner is from the Netherlands. At Tralala there are only seven rooms, including a dormitory that sleeps six, making for a chilled-out environment for guests. The hostel is spick-and-span and tastefully decorated. Its minimalist style provides a nice vacation for the eyes. Staff are friendly and knowledgeable, and the kitchen is a pleasant area to hang out and chitchat with others. There's a sundeck and garden area in case relaxation is needed. **Casa La Eliana** (Cra. 2 No. 6-45, cell tel. 314/660-5987, http://laelianasalento.com, COP$70,000 d) is more than just delicious food; it has nine comfortable, no-nonsense rooms as well.

Centrally located **Hostal Ciudad de Segorbe** (Cl. 5 No. 4-06, tel. 6/759-3794, www.hostalciudaddesegorbe.com, COP$145,000 d, COP$40,000 dorm) is a bed-and-breakfast-slash-hostel set in a nicely preserved centuries-old Paisa house. The hostel's seven rooms have high wooden ceilings with gorgeous original geometric designs and small balconies. One room is equipped for physically challenged visitors.

La Moraleja (Cra. 5 No. 7-4, cell tel. 321/632-8409, COP$65,000 pp) has 10 rooms, including two larger suites. It's an old house with antique furnishings and a pleasant garden.

Beta Town (Cl. 7 No. 3-45, cell tel. 321/218-7043, www.beta.com.co, COP$150,000 d) is a small hotel in town that boasts its own tejo court and even a small football field. It's one of the friendliest spots in town—and that also goes for its restaurant, which serves great breakfasts.

★ **Terrazas de Salento** (Cra. 4 No. 1-30, cell tel. 317/430-4637, COP$185,000-235,000) has seven rooms in gorgeous, understated Scandinavian style, a beautiful backyard garden area, and views of the pueblo. It's quiet, with tons of natural light, and furnishings are made of natural materials.

Londoner Tim was one of the first to help transform Salento from a sleepy Paisa pueblo into one of Colombia's top tourist destinations. His **Plantation House** (Alto de Coronel, Cl. 7 No. 1-04, cell tel. 316/285-2603, www.theplantationhousesalento.com, COP$22,000 dorm, COP$55,000 d), with 24 rooms total, remains one of the top places to get to know Salento and the surrounding areas. Catering to international visitors, this hostel has two houses, one of which is over 100 years old. It's quiet and green around the hostel, and, though you'll be bound to meet other travelers like yourself, there is plenty of space to find a little solitude. Plantation House can organize bike excursions, horseback riding, hikes to the Valle de Cocora, and more. Making life easier, it can also take care of airport transfer to Armenia and Pereira. It is an environmentally friendly hostel: Solar panels enable guests to have a hot shower, and a rainwater collection system provides water. Tim also runs coffee farm **Finca Don Eduardo.**

Another excellent hostel-type option is **La Serrana Eco-farm and Hostel** (Km. 1.5 Vía Palestina Finca, cell tel. 316/296-1890, www.laserrana.com.co, COP$22,000 dorm, COP$55,000 d). It's situated on a bluff with lovely views of coffee farms in every direction. The nine rooms, of various types and sizes, are comfortable, and there is also a women-only dorm room. Camping is also available for COP$12,000. It's a peaceful place where you can enjoy sunrises and sunsets, go for a walk into town, or just hang out. La Serrana is best known for its delicious (and nutritious) family-style dinners and other meals. Vegetarians always have options, and the cooks make an effort to buy local, fresh food. La Serrana has another, smaller lodging option, ★ **Las Camelias** (Km. 1.5 Vía Palestina Finca, cell tel. 316/296-1890, www.laserrana.com.co, COP$70,000 d), a colonial-style house you can see from the hostel. This is geared toward couples who want a little more privacy—there are only three rooms. Rooms, drenched with natural light, are spacious, with hardwood floors and fireplaces. Common space is ample with large windows, and there is a kitchen for guest use.

Between the Valle de Cocora and Salento is the fabulous ★ **Reserva El Cairo** (Km. 3 Vía Cocora, cell tel. 321/649-3439, www.reservaelcairo.com, COP$220,000 d), a meticulously maintained old farm with six rooms. Its almost 100 acres of cloud forest is now a nature reserve, and paths lead into the forests and mountains behind the house; you can even go to a swimming hole. A half-day bird-watching walk with an English-speaking guide can be arranged (COP$100,000, 4-person max.), or overnight guests can independently set out and take their bird checklist with them; about 100 bird species have been identified in the reserve. There are mammals in the reserve, as well, not to mention amphibians and reptiles: They can be spotted on a nighttime tour. Meals here use local organic ingredients, and the sitting area, full of books on birds and the natural world, is an inviting place to linger after dinner. Bikes are also available for use.

Kasaguadua (2.5 km south of town, cell tel. 313/889-8273, www.kasaguaduanaturalreserve.org, COP$38,000 dorm, COP$90,000 d) is a 12-hectare Andean rainforest nature reserve outside of town that has several trails that can be visited by nonguests for interesting guided walks. But the true Kasaguadua experience is to stay a few nights in one of the geodesic pods, called EcoHabs, that owners Nick and Carlos built themselves. There are private rooms and a dorm-style room. Meals are communal, taken with staff and fellow travelers. The very popular tours (requested donation COP$20,000-50,000), which generally last 3-3.5 hours, begin promptly at 9am. Over 82 species of birds inhabit the area, and birders will want to rise early to spot them. A Jeep Willy to Kasaguadua from the Parque Bolívar in Salento costs about COP$12,000. This reserve is on the road that leads to Palestina.

Located on the old Camino Nacional high up in the mountains is the lodge **El Rocio Eagle Nest** (Km. 16 Vía Toche, cell tel. 317/717-5714, www.elrocioeaglenest.com, COP$20,000 dorm, COP$50,000 d). There's just one private room and one dorm for eight sleepers. Without much nightlife around, activity centers on the warmth of the fireplace. Run by a community group, El Rocio offers day excursions including hikes to the cloud forest, reforestation activities, mountain biking, and birdwatching.

Four kilometers outside of Salento, on the banks of the Río Quindío, is **Camping Monteroca** (Valle del Río Quindío, cell tel. 315/413-6862, www.campingmonteroca.com, COP$70,000 cabin, COP$15,000 tent), a sprawling campground catering mostly to Colombian weekenders. The camp has 11 cabins, one of which is called the Hippie Hilton, and several of them have awesome waterbeds. There is a lot of space for tents here as well. Monteroca has a restaurant and two bars. Recreational activities such as horseback riding (COP$12,000 per hour), a three-hour hike to nearby waterfalls (COP$25,000), and yoga classes are on offer. To get there from Salento, take a Jeep bound for Las Veredas. They leave every 15 minutes from the Parque Bolívar during weekends.

Information and Services

Hostels usually provide the best tourist information, and most all have maps, but there is also a good city-run tourist kiosk, the **Punto de Información Turística** (10am-5pm Wed.-Mon.), in front of the Alcaldía (city offices) in the Parque Bolívar.

Transportation

There is frequent bus service from Pereira and Armenia to Salento. The last bus (COTRACIR) from Armenia leaves at 9pm (COP$4,000). From Pereira, there are four direct buses each weekday, costing under COP$6,500. There is more frequent service on weekends. Because Salento is well established on the tourist route, thieves are known to prey on foreigners on late-evening buses traveling from Pereira to Salento. Keep a vigilant eye on your possessions.

Buses to Armenia (every 20 mins. from 6am to 9pm, COP$4,000) depart from the Parque Bolívar. Buses to Pereira (COP$6,500) depart from the intersection of Carrera 2 and Calles 4-5, near the fire station, at 7:50am, 10am, 12:50pm, 2:50pm, and 5:50pm, with the last departure at 7:50pm daily. For Filandia you must first go to Armenia. Bus service to Medellín departs at 9:30am and at 4pm on Flota Occidental (call cell tel. 321/848-4158 to reserve, COP$44,000).

★ VALLE DE COCORA

The main attraction for most visitors to Salento is seeing the *palmas de cera* (wax palms) that shoot up toward the sky in the Valle de Cocora. These are some of the tallest palms in the world, reaching 50-60 meters high (200 feet), and they can live over 100 years. They have beautiful, smooth, cylindrical trunks with dark rings. In 1985, the species was declared the national tree of Colombia. **Día del Arbol Nacional** (National Tree Day) is celebrated on September 16 with gusto, with seed planting in the valleys and other events.

The Valle de Cocora is a 15-kilometer (9-mile) section of the lower Río Quindío valley. Much of it has been turned into pastureland, but, thankfully, the palms have been preserved. The palms look particularly stunning in the denuded landscape.

The gateway to the valley is the **Vereda de Cocora,** a stretch of restaurants specializing in trout. Most Colombian tourists come for a late lunch and take a stroll along the main road behind the *vereda* to view the palms.

From December until February, you'll get the best views, but it may be

the picturesque Valle de Cocora and its famous wax palms

dusty, and there will be less likelihood of seeing wildlife. High season is in early January. March and November tend to be wet months.

A 2016 census of endangered condors, symbols of Colombia, found seven of the birds living in the park. They, along with eagles, may be spotted with some luck, particularly near the area called Chispas. Pumas and *osos anteojos* (bears) also call the park home.

Hiking

If you have the time and energy, you can make a large loop of the valley on a four- to five-hour hike. The route goes up through the cloud forest and Reserva Acaime, backtracks a little, and then goes up to La Montaña—a ranger station for the local environment agency—before heading down through the main attraction: the palms.

The starting point for the loop is the blue gate after the last building in the Vereda de Cocora. There may be a sign for Acaime, which is what you want. After walking about four kilometers (2.5 miles) through pasture, you'll enter the dense cloud forest. The path crisscrosses the trickling Río Quindío. After three kilometers (two miles) you reach the **Reserva Acaime** (cell tel. 321/636-2818 or 320/788-1981, COP$5,000), a private reserve created to preserve the surrounding cloud forest. With the entrance fee, you can enjoy a complimentary cup of hot chocolate, *agua de panela* (a hot sugary drink), or coffee and watch throngs of hummingbirds of several varieties fly up to feeders. It's quite a show. You can also stay at Acaime, either in private rooms or a large dormitory (COP$40,000 pp including all meals).

After energizing and warming up a little at Acaime, backtrack a kilometer and then climb a steep path to **La Montaña** (about 3,000 meters/9,800 feet). Now for the delicious dessert: the valley of wax palms. You'll descend from La Montaña back to Vereda del Cocora through hills and valleys adorned with the trees.

Rubber or at least waterproof boots are recommended, as the path along the Río Quindío is muddy. Although authorities have been considering regulating visitors, at this point you do not need a guide for this wonderful hike.

TREK TO FINCA LA PRIMAVERA

If you would like to do a longer expedition, you can extend the Valle de Cocora hike beyond Reserva Acaime to the **Páramo de Romerales** on the border of the Parque Nacional Natural Los Nevados and to **Finca La Primavera,** a working farm located at an altitude of 3,680 meters (12,075 feet). All tour outfitters in Salento offer this trek, and typically this is accomplished in two days, with an overnight at Primavera. This excursion allows you to enjoy the transition from cloud forest to *páramo* (highland moor), the latter of which is dotted with the unusual Andean *frailejón* plants. The path from Acaime continues to **Estrella de Agua,** a research station, through the Páramo de Romerales and finally Finca La Primavera. The entire hike from Vereda de Cocora to Primavera is 16 kilometers (10 miles) and takes nine hours. On the way back, you'll pass through **Finca Argentina** (3,400 meters/11,155 feet) before descending to the Valle de Cocora. This family farm is cozy, and there are lots of birds flying around, including many varieties of hummingbirds and toucans. For a slower pace, this trek can be done in three days, with the first night spent at Finca Argentina and the second at Primavera.

From Finca La Primavera, you can continue into the **Parque Nacional Natural Los Nevados,** hiking to snowcapped volcano **Nevado del Tolima** (5,215 meters/17,110 feet). For this, hikers will need four days. Another option is the less visited **Paramillo del Quindío** (4,750 meters/15,585 feet), which no longer has snow. From here you can take in the views of the Nevado del Tolima, Santa Isabel, and Ruiz peaks. This trek requires three days.

Salento Trekking (Cl. 4 between Cras. 6-7, cell tel. 313/654-1619, www.salentotrekking.com) may be the most professional trekking outfit around, as the multilingual owners lead every hike. The company offers multiday hiking trips (2-5 days) for all fitness levels and takes care of everything. A three-day trek goes for COP$550,000 per person. **Páramo Trek** (cell tel. 311/745-3761, www.paramotrek.com) is also recommended.

Getting There

To get to Vereda del Cocora from Salento, take a Jeep Willy (COP$3,800), which leaves the Parque Bolívar at 6:10am, 7:30am, 9:30am, 11:30am, 2pm, and 4pm each day. More Willys ply the route on weekends. The last Willy back to town departs at about 5pm.

FILANDIA

As far as cute Paisa pueblos go, word among those in the know in the coffee region is that Filandia is the new Salento. This town, set halfway between Armenia and Pereira, offers charming coffee culture atmosphere and, although it attracts fewer visitors than Salento, has a burgeoning tourism infrastructure.

The focal point of the **Parque Central** (between Cras. 4-5 and Clls. 6-7) is the church, the **Templo María Inmaculada** (Cra. 7), which was built in the early 20th century. From the plaza you can branch out to explore the charming streets of the town, including the **Calle del Tiempo Detenido** (Cl. 7 between Cras. 5-6) and the **Calle del Empedrado,** two streets of two-story houses made of *bahareque* (a natural material) adorned by colorful doors and windows. Stop by the town's oldest construction, the **Droguería Bristol** (Cra. 6 No. 5-63), along the way. A nice view of the countryside can be had near the *clínica mental* (mental hospital; Cra. 8 No. 7-55).

Festivals and Events

The third Saturday of every month sees a **market** in the main square, with handicrafts—including the Filandia specialty of baskets, *cestería del bejuco*—fresh produce, and food.

Food and Accommodations

Accommodations and restaurants in Filandia are limited. In a traditional Paisa house, the **Hostal La Posada del Compadre** (Cra. 6 No. 8-06, tel. 6/758-3054, cell tel. 313/335-9771, www.laposadadelcompadre.com, COP$60,000 d) offers a handful of rooms and ample outdoor hangout space. Rooms are large, beds are adequate, breakfast is included, and the prices are reasonable.

The ★ **Hostal Colina de Lluvia** (Cl. 5 No. 4-08, COP$25,000 dorm, COP$60,000 d private) is a very friendly guesthouse with a range of options. Tastefully decorated rooms are spick-and-span with comfortable beds, and there is a small garden patio and several hammocks for late-afternoon snoozes.

Candlelit tables, lounge music, and art on the walls—you won't believe your eyes when you see ★ **Helena Adentro** (Cra. 7 No. 8-01, cell tel. 312/873-9825, noon-2am Sat.-Sun.). Started by a New Zealander and a Paisa, it's by far the coolest spot in Filandia, Quindío, and perhaps this side of Medellín. Cured meats and goat cheeses come from local farmers, as does the coffee. They have their own brand but also serve coffee from other regions of Colombia, using different brewing techniques. Locals keep coming back for the inventive libations here, such as the house cocktail, the Adentro Helena (aguardiente, *lulo* juice, and lime).

The popular place for a cappuccino is **Jahn Café** (Cl. 6A No. 5-45, 7:30am-midnight Mon.-Fri., 7:30am-2am Sat.-Sun.). For tea, go to its **Salón de Té** (Cl. 6 with Cra. 6), on the 2nd floor on the corner, which is also home to the **Hostal de Jahn** (cell tel. 317/435-3732, www.jahnquindio.com, COP$50,000d), a comfortable and colorful little guesthouse.

Orale's (Cl. 7 No. 7-58, cell tel. 311/795-0320, Mon.-Fri. 5pm-10pm, Sat. 2pm-10pm, Sun. noon-10pm) is a tiny spot serving authentic Mexican flavors, with fresh ingredients.

Information and Services

The Filandia tourist office is in the **Casa del Artesano** (Cra. 5 at Cl. 7, 2nd floor, tel. 6/758-2172, 7am-noon and 1:30pm-4:30pm Mon.-Fri.).

Transportation

Buses to Filandia leave from Armenia (COP$4,500, every 20 minutes) and Pereira (COP$5,600, hourly) all day long until around 8pm. These circulate the town picking up passengers, especially on Carrera 7. Travel to or from Salento involves a transfer at Las Flores.

PEREIRA AND VICINITY

Close to so much in the coffee region, Pereira (pop. 465,000), the capital of the Risaralda department, also makes a strong case for being the capital of the entire region, second only to Medellín in importance. Luring visitors just beyond the city are gorgeous hacienda hotels and natural parks such as Santuario de Flora y Fauna Otún-Quimbaya, and Pereira is also less than an hour's drive from Salento and other impossibly cute pueblos. A wide array of lodging, dining, and shopping options are here, but Pereira also has more to offer, including an abundant cultural life and a gritty-yet-not-unappealing old downtown area that feels like a step back in time.

Sights

The pulsing heart of the city is downtown, at the palm-lined **Plaza de Bolívar** (Clls. 19-20 and Cras. 7-8), where there stands a bronze sculpture by Rodrigo Arenas Betancourt depicting Simón Bolívar on horseback charging ahead to fight the Spaniards—naked. Facing the plaza is the beautiful **Nuestra Señora de la Pobreza Catedral** (Cl. 20 No. 7-30, tel. 6/335-6545, masses every hour 6am-noon and 5pm Mon.-Sat., 6am-noon and 5pm-8pm Sun.). The cathedral was built in 1890 using industrial-era building techniques; it was later damaged by an earthquake, needing to be almost completely reconstructed. It was rebuilt with a wooden ceiling and supports made from cumin laurel, a tree native to Colombia that is now endangered. The branch of **Banco de la República** (8:30am-6pm Mon.-Fri., 9am-1pm Sat., free) in Pereira, which has a public library and exhibition spaces with ever-changing shows, is located nearby. As interesting as these downtown highlights is the chance to brush shoulders with the locals and observe them going about their daily lives; the stretch between the Plaza de Bolívar and the **Parque El Lago** (Cl. 24 with Cra. 8) is particularly lively, with a couple of charming pedestrian alleys on Calles 18 and 22 between Carreras 7 and 8.

The **Museo de Arte de Pereira** (Av. Las Américas No. 19-88, tel. 6/317-2828, www.museoartepereira.org, 10am-7pm Tues.-Fri., 10am-5pm Sat.-Sun., COP$3,000) is one of the best art museums in the region, and deserving of a visit. It features temporary exhibitions of contemporary Latin American artists. There are often film showings on weekend evenings. It's south of downtown.

In the **Parque Olaya Herrera** (between Cras. 13-14 and Clls. 19-21) is the well-preserved **Antigua Estación del Tren,** a photogenic old train station. There is a Megabus station in the park, and the park is a nice place for a morning jog.

Amble along 11 paths lined by local plants and, of course, *guadua* bamboo, at the impressive **Jardín Botánico de la Universidad Tecnológica de Pereira** (Vereda La Julita, Vía Mundo Nuevo, tel. 6/321-2523, www.utp.edu.co/jardin, 8am-6pm Mon.-Fri., 9am-1pm Sat.-Sun., COP$20,000 1-3 persons). Residents in these 13 hectares of jungle include butterflies, tortoises, and 168 species of birds. This campus is south of the city, past the bus station.

Entertainment and Events

The city's website (www.pereiraculturayturismo.gov.co) is a resource for finding out what's happening in Pereira. If you're visiting on a **first Thursday,** then head to **La Cuadra** (Cra. 12 Bis with Cl. 12, 7pm-11pm

Pereira

first Thurs. of the month, free), a long-running open-air cultural space that hosts concerts, art exhibitions, theater performances, and more. The centrally located **Centro Cultural Lucy Tejada** (Cra. 10A No. 16-60, tel. 6/324-8749) is the city's major venue for concerts and events.

Recreation

For bike tours and rentals, contact **RetroCiclas Tours** (cell tel. 310/540-7327, www.retrociclas.co). One of the more popular tours is a trip to the village of Estación Pereira (COP$86,000), where in the town you'll take two different and exciting means of transportation: a *brujita,* a motorcycle-powered cart that zooms along old train tracks, and later a *garrucha,* which is a gondola-like metallic basket that transports passengers over the Río Cauca. Another trip on offer is along the Río Otún (COP$80,000) to the Santuario de Flora y Fauna Otún-Quimbaya.

On Sundays (8am-noon) Pereira celebrates the **Ciclovía,** during which the road from the Viaducto César Gaviria Trujillo to the Villa Olímpica is closed to traffic and open only to cyclists, joggers and walkers. Free bikes are available for rent at the Parque Olaya Herrera (between Cras. 13-14 and Clls. 19-21), but you'll need to leave ID (like a passport).

Food

★ **Ambar Diego Panesso** (Cra. 17 No. 9-50, tel. 6/344-7444, noon-3pm and 6pm-10pm Mon.-Sat., COP$30,000) serves the Pereira elite elaborate dishes like portobello mushrooms stuffed with apple puree and bacon bits. While vegetarian dishes are mostly nonexistent on the menu, the kitchen will gladly take on the challenge and whip up a pasta dish for you. It's in the upscale Pinares neighborhood. Another restaurant on the elegant side is **El Mirador** (Av. Circunvalar at Cl. 4, Colina, tel. 6/331-2141, noon-2am Mon.-Sat., COP$30,000), a steak house that has an incredible view of the city. There's an extensive list of Argentinian wines.

The menu at **El Meson Español** (Cl. 14 No. 25-57, tel. 6/321-5636, noon-3pm and 7pm-midnight daily, COP$22,000) runs the gamut from paella (the house specialty) to pad Thai.

For a hearty Colombian meal, like a big bowl of *ajiaco* (a filling potato-based stew), or to hang out and have a couple of beers at night, **La Ruana** (Av. Circunvalar No. 12-08, tel. 6/325-0115, 8am-2am Mon.-Sat., 8am-10pm Sun., COP$20,000) is the place to go on Avenida Circunvalar.

★ **Aly Torres** (Cl. 4 No. 16-45, tel. 6/331-3955, 8am-10:30pm daily, COP$20,000) is a cheerful restaurant at the Kolibrí Hostel, and it serves typical Colombian meals as well as backpacker favorites. It's worth a trip even if you're not staying at the hostel.

For a hamburger made from lentils, amaranth, cauliflower, or chicken, head to **Burger Green** (Cra. 12 No. 3-22, tel. 6/331-3236, www.burgergreen.co, 11am-10pm Tues.-Sun., COP$12,000).

Archie's (Centro Comercial Parque Arboleda, Circunvalar No. 5-20, tel. 6/317-0600, www.archiespizza.com, 8am-11pm daily, COP$22,000) has great pizzas (try the thin-crust *pizzas rústicas*) and salads. Its location on the top floor, with a breezy terrace, is a cool one. They also deliver.

Downtown, check out **Urbano** (C.C. Bolívar Plaza, Cra. 8 No. 19-41), a restaurant on the 2nd floor with a view to the Plaza de Bolívar. It has an extensive menu of international cuisine and happy hour specials. You may forget you're in a mall. On a quiet corner in the Centro, directly across from the Banco de la República library and cultural center is **Café Kahlua** (Cl. 18 Bis Peatonal with Cra. 9A, tel. 6/344-2144, 8am-8pm Mon.-Sat.). This open-air place on a pedestrian alley serves snacks, coffee, and beer.

Accommodations

Most visitors gravitate toward the Circunvalar area in Pereira, with malls and restaurants within walking distance. Otherwise, live it up at a nearby hacienda. The Centro has options, but prices are comparable to hotels on the Circunvalar, where you can walk without much concern at night.

Way better than any tourist information office is ★ **Kolibrí Hostel** (Cl. No. 16-35, tel. 6/331-3955, cell tel. 321/646-9275, www.kolibrihostel.com,

COP$25,000 dorm, COP$85,000 d), the first hostel to take hold in the city, run by a Dutch-Colombian couple who have traveled extensively in the region. The owners will keep you busy with loads of activity options including coffee, paragliding, and biking tours. The hostel is located just off the Circunvalar, within walking distance of the Arboleda mall and several restaurants. In addition to a mix of private rooms and dorms, Kolibrí has two extended-stay apartments that go for around COP$150,000 a night.

The **Hotel Movich** (Cra. 13 No. 15-73, tel. 6/311-3300, COP$333,000 d) is a good option if you like comfort and don't desire any surprises, yet want to be close to it all. The pool (usually open until 9pm) and gym (open 24 hours) are quite nice. A massive breakfast buffet is included in the room rate. It's across the street from the imposing neo-gothic Iglesia de Carmen.

The classic 77-room **Hotel Soratama** (Cra. 7 No. 19-20, COP$146,000 d) is right in the thick of things on the Plaza de Bolívar. It has a nice rooftop terrace area with a dipping pool, and the restaurant is all right.

Outside of town is the upscale **Sonesta Hotel** (Km. 7 Vía Cerritos, tel. 6/311-3600, www.sonesta.com, COP$260,000 d), with over 160 spacious rooms, good restaurants, and a huge outdoor pool area. It's particularly popular for business meetings during the workweek.

A restful sleep is assured at the **Hotel Don Alfonso** (Cra. 13 No. 12-37, tel. 6/333-0909, www.donalfonsohotel.com, COP$264,000 d), a small boutique-style hotel on the main nightlife and shopping drag of Avenida Circunvalar. It has 11 comfortable air-conditioned rooms, each with inviting beds covered by quilts.

Castilla Real Hotel (Cl. 15 No. 12B-15, tel. 6/333-2192, www.hotelcastillareal.com, COP$170,000 d) has 24 comfortable rooms and is located on a side street near the Circunvalar area.

HACIENDAS

Within minutes of Pereira's bright lights are some gorgeous and luxurious hacienda hotels. Some of them are popular places for special events, such as weekend weddings and corporate seminars during the week.

Hacienda Malabar (Km. 7 Vía a Cerritos, Entrada 6, tel. 6/337-9206, www.hotelmalabar.com, COP$257,500 d) is an authentic hacienda with seven rooms, ample gardens to wander, and a pool. The wooden ceilings with their geometric designs and tile floors with Spanish Mudejar designs throughout the house are spectacular.

★ **Castilla Casa de Huespedes** (Km. 10 Vía a Cerritos, tel. 6/337-9045, cell tel. 315/499-9545, www.haciendacastilla.com, COP$281,000 d), built in the 19th century, is set amid fruit trees and has a pool to boot. The nine rooms are lovely, and staff are friendly. They make their own jam at this serene spot, and a majestic cedar tree near the pool area looks even more regal when illuminated at night.

The **Hacienda San José** (Km. 4 Vía Pereira-Cerritos, Entrada 16, Cadena El Tigre, tel. 6/313-2612, www.haciendahotelsanjose.com, COP$275,000-310,000 d) was built in 1888 and has been in the Jaramillo family for generations. It's in the countryside, and the entrance to it, lined with palms, is a dramatic one. The home, with 11 rooms, is spectacular, and the lovely wooden floors make a satisfying creak when you step on the planks. Service is impeccable and the restaurant is excellent. The grounds make for a nice late-afternoon stroll, and you can admire an enormous and regal old *samán* tree, well into its second century of life, as you dine alfresco. Living Trips (www.livingtrips.com) manages this hotel, and they can arrange day-trip excursions for you. The restaurant is open to the public, and members of the public can also come for the day and enjoy the pool. The airport is only 10 minutes away.

Luxury hotel **Sazagua** (Km. 7 Vía Cerritos, Entrada 4, tel. 6/337-9895, www.sazagua.com, COP$446,000 d) is not technically a hacienda, as it is in a country club-type environment. But there's no need to be put off by that. Here attention to detail reigns. The 10 rooms are impeccable, the common space is inviting, the gardens are perfectly manicured (surrounded by elegant heliconia flowers, birds, and the occasional iguana), and you can lounge by the pool or enjoy a massage at the spa. Nonguests can enjoy the spa facilities for a separate charge.

Information and Services

There is a small **tourist information booth** in the lobby of the Centro Cultural Lucy Tejada (Cl. 10 No. 16-60, tel. 6/311-6544, www.pereiraculturayturismo.gov.co, 8am-noon and 2pm-6pm Mon.-Fri.).

Call 123 for any type of emergency.

Transportation

Excellent bus connections are available between Pereira and most major cities. The **Terminal de Transportes de Pereira** (Cl. 17 No. 23-157, tel. 6/315-2323, www.terminaldepereira.com) is relatively close to the Avenida Circunvalar area. It is clean.

The articulated bus rapid transit system, the **Megabus** (tel. 6/335-1010), has three routes and connects with 28 intracity buses. It's not terribly convenient for those staying near Avenida Circunvalar, unfortunately.

The **Aeropuerto Matecaña** (Av. 30 de Agosto, tel. 6/314-2765) is pint-sized and in need of some love, but it's only about a 10-minute ride east of the city. **Avianca, LATAM,** and **Viva Colombia** fly to Bogotá; **Viva Colombia** flies to Cartagena; **EasyFly** and **ADA** will take you to the heart of Medellín and the Olaya Herrera Airport; and **ADA** also serves Quibdó.

For those looking to rent a car, **Hertz** (airport tel. 6/314-2678, www.hertz.com, 8am-6pm Mon.-Fri., 8am-noon Sat.) has an office at the airport. **Milano Rent A Car** (cell tel. 300/800-1180, www.milanocar.com) is an alternative. Its office is nearby, but staff will meet you at the airport. If you do rent a car, find out the *pico y placa* days and hours (www.transitopereira.gov.co) before putting the key into the ignition; these are vehicle restrictions during the workweek based on the last digit of the license plate.

VALLE DEL RÍO OTÚN

A visit to the Valle del Río Otún between Pereira and the Laguna del Otún (located within Parque Nacional Natural Los Nevados) is an interesting, highly enjoyable, and easy-to-organize introduction to Andean cloud forests. There are many possibilities for visiting the valley, from day trips out of Pereira to multiday excursions utilizing some very pleasant lodging facilities in the Santuario de Flora y Fauna Otún-Quimbaya and Parque Regional Natural Ucumarí.

The Río Otún flows 78 kilometers (48 miles) from the Laguna del Otún to the Río Cauca and is the main source of water for Pereira. The conservation of the upper segment of the river, from Pereira to the Laguna del Otún, has been a success story, thanks to reforestation and land-protection efforts.

PLANNING YOUR TIME

The Santuario de Flora y Fauna Otún-Quimbaya is 14.4 kilometers (9 miles) southeast of Pereira along the Río Otún. The Parque Regional Natural Ucumarí is 6.6 kilometers (4 miles) upriver.

You can do day trips out of Pereira to either, but don't try to do both in one day. Santuario de Flora y Fauna Otún-Quimbaya is easily accessible by public transportation, and the main nature trails can be visited in one day. However, getting to Parque Regional Natural Ucumarí involves public transportation and a two-hour hike. It can be visited on a long day trip but it is much preferable to spend a night or two at the comfortable Pastora visitors center in the midst of the Andean forest. You can combine a visit to both, visiting Santuario de Flora y Fauna Otún-Quimbaya and then spending a day or two in Parque Regional Natural Ucumarí.

December and July-August are drier months, and are considered the best time for a hike to the Laguna del Otún. However, during mid-December through mid-January and Semana Santa (Holy Week) in March or April the trails can be packed with hikers, as this is high season for Colombians. The hike through Parque Regional Natural Ucumarí to the Laguna del Otún is very popular then, and there can be over a hundred hikers camping each night at that mountain lake.

Santuario de Fauna y Flora Otún-Quimbaya

It's a snap to trade the concrete jungle of Pereira for the real thing: make your way to the **Santuario de Fauna y Flora Otún-Quimbaya** (Km. 4.5 Vía Florida-El Cedral, Vereda La Suiza, cell tel. 313/695-4305, www.parquesnacionales.gov.co, COP$5,000) outside of town. Part of the national park system, Otún-Quimbaya covers 489 hectares (1,208 acres) of highly biodiverse Andean tropical forest at altitudes between 1,750 and 2,250 meters (5,740 and 7,380 feet). The vegetation is exuberant, and there are animal-viewing opportunities. The park is home to more than 200 species of birds, including endangered multicolored tanagers and the large *pava caucana* (Cauca guan). And, although you may not see them, you'll definitely hear the *mono aulladores* (howler monkeys). They make quite a brouhaha.

The main activities at the park are guided walks along three nature paths led by knowledgeable and enthusiastic guides from a local community ecotourism organization, the **Asociación Comunitaria Yarumo Blanco** (cell tel. 310/363-5001, www.yarumoblanco.co, reservas@yarumoblanco.co). Costs for the fairly easy walks (you must go with a guide) are around COP$50,000 per group, and generally take 1.5 hours.

Visitors can also bike along the main road that borders the crystalline Río Otún. **Yarumo Blanco** rents mountain bikes (COP$10,000 all day). The visitors center offers simple but comfortable lodging (COP$32,000-42,000 pp) and meals (COP$6,000-9,000).

To get to Otún-Quimbaya from Pereira, take a bus operated by **Transportes Florida** (tel. 6/331-0488, COP$4,000, 90 mins.) from Calle 12 and Carrera 9 in Pereira. On weekdays, the bus departs at 7am, 9am, and 3pm. On weekends there is an additional bus at noon.

Parque Regional Natural Ucumarí

The **Parque Regional Natural Ucumarí** is 6.6 kilometers (4 miles) southwest of Santuario Flora y Fauna Otún-Quimbaya. This regional park covers an area of 3,986 hectares (9,850 acres) of Andean tropical forest at altitudes between 1,800 and 2,600 meters (5,900 and 8,500 feet). The main path follows the Río Otún through lush cloud forests, with waterfalls feeding into the river. The park is a wonderful place to view nature, with more than 185 species of birds.

The starting point of the main path is **El Cedral,** a small *vereda* (settlement) southwest of Santuario Flora y Fauna Otún-Quimbaya. The path is a well-trod one (by humans and horses) and is often muddy and rocky. It is best to take rubber or waterproof boots. It takes about 2.5 hours to climb to the main La Pastora visitors center, six kilometers (3.73 miles) from El Cedral.

Day-trippers from Pereira can lunch at the **visitors center** (COP$7,000-10,000 pp) and set off independently on one of three nature hikes before returning to El Cedral to catch the last bus at 5pm. Better yet, consider overnighting in the clean and cozy **dormitory-style rooms** (COP$25,000 pp, COP$8,000 camping) there. That way, as the mercury begins to fall in the late afternoon, you'll be able to relax by the lodge's fireplace and sip hot chocolate and eat cheese (that's how they do it in Colombia). There is no electricity, making a stay at **La Pastora** truly restful. To make a reservation, contact the ecotourism organization **FECOMAR** (cell tel. 312/200-7711, fecomar.anp@hotmail.com). It can also arrange horses, if you would rather ride than hike up.

Beyond La Pastora, the path continues 13 kilometers (8 miles) to the Laguna del Otún in the Parque Nacional Natural Los Nevados.

To get to El Cedral, take the **Transportes Florida** bus (tel. 6/331-0488, COP$5,500, 2 hrs.) from Calle 12 and Carrera 9 in Pereira. On weekdays, the bus departs at 7am, 9am, and 3pm. On weekends there is an additional bus at noon. The buses return from El Cedral at noon and 6pm on weekdays and noon, 3pm, and 6pm on Sundays.

SANTA ROSA DE CABAL

Ready to soak up some atmosphere? Do as the Colombians do, and head to the hot springs of Santa Rosa de Cabal, near Pereira. To get there, you'll most likely pass through the town of Santa Rosa de Cabal. Start at the **Parque las Araucarias** (between Cras. 14-15 and Clls. 12-13), the main square, where there are juices to be drunk, *chorizo santarosano* sausages to be devoured (a specialty here), handicrafts to be bought, and people to be watched. Other points of interest are the **Santuario La Milagrosa** (Cl. 7 at Cra. 14, tel. 6/368-5201 or 6/368-5168), a modern church with fantastic stained glass windows, and the **Monumento al Machete** (Parque Gonzalo Echeverry, Cra. 16N No. 12-77, www.monumentoalmachete.blogspot.com.co), a small plaza with what are assumed to be the largest machetes in the world, at 4.5 meters (15 feet) long. There's food, beer, and souvenir stalls at this quirky homage to Paisa masculinity.

Hot Springs

There are two *termales* (hot springs) near Santa Rosa de Cabal: **Termales de Santa Rosa de Cabal** (Km. 9 Vía Termales, tel. 6/364-5500, www.termales.com.co, 9am-11:30pm daily, COP$22,000 in Feb. and Sep. and during the workweek, COP$36,000 weekends and high season) and **Termales San Vicente** (18 km east of Santa Rosa de Cabal, tel. 6/333-3433, www.sanvicente.com.co, 8am-midnight daily, COP$75,000 incl. transportation). Both can get packed with Colombian families on weekends and holidays. Go during the workweek, when it's less a scene and prices dip, too. Both springs offer bus transportation from Pereira, but it's ideal to have your own transportation so that you can take off when you wish.

Built in 1945, the Termales de Santa Rosa de Cabal hot springs are closer to Santa Rosa de Cabal. There are two areas in the complex. The first area, on the left as you enter the park, was recently built and is called the **Termales Balneario.** These consist of three large pools for adults and

Termales de Santa Rosa de Cabal

one for children. This area is the most popular for day-trip visitors, though it lacks natural beauty. The oldest part of the complex, called **Termales de Hotel** (COP$32,000 in Feb. and Sept. and during the workweek; COP$50,000 weekends and high season), is farther on at the base of some spectacular waterfalls of cool and pure mountain waters. The highest waterfall drops some 175 meters (575 feet). If you choose to stay the night, there are three options. **La Cabaña** (COP$360,000 d) is the newest and most comfortable place to stay and has 17 rooms. La Cabaña guests are allowed entry to the Termales Balneario, the Termales de Hotel, and their own small private pool. The advantage of staying at one of the hotels is that you can enjoy full use of the pools from 6am on, before the day-trip crowd begins arriving at 9am; the drawback is that the rooms are not luxurious, and the food doesn't receive raves either. At both Termales Balneario and Termales de Hotel, there are additional activities on offer, such as a guided nature walk (COP$14,000) to some waterfalls—wear shoes with traction for this, as the path is slippery—and spa treatments such as massages (COP$50,000, 30 mins.) and other services in a shabby-looking spa area.

The San Vicente hot springs are more remote, but the scenery of rolling hills, mountains in the distance, and farms is enchanting. Particularly scenic are the *pozos de amor,* small natural pools the size of whirlpools that perfectly fit two. Buses leave Pereira at 8am, returning at 5pm. San Vicente also offers various accommodation options, mostly cabins. A cabin for two people costs around COP$160,000 per person without meals.

Food and Accommodations

The bucolic countryside outside of Santa Rosa is home to many roadside, family-style restaurants and lodging facilities, good alternatives for hot springs day-trippers. The best two are run by the same owner. On the road toward the Termales de Santa Rosa, **Mamatina** (Km. 1 Vía Termales, La Leona, cell tel. 311/762-7624 or 314/767-2519, www.mamatinahotel.com, 9am-10pm daily, COP$18,000) specializes in trout covered with sausage, *sancocho* (a meaty stew), grilled meats, and beans and rice. Adjoining the restaurant is a hotel by the same name, which offers clean and comfortable rooms ranging in price from COP$40,000 per person to COP$140,000 for the suite with a hot tub. Horseback riding and walks through the countryside can be arranged here.

On the way toward Termales de San Vicente is the Mamatina owner's other, newer hotel. The ★ **Hospedaje Don Lolo** (Km. 5 Vía Termales San Vicente, cell tel. 316/698-6797, COP$50,000 pp d) is on a farm with cows, pigs, fish, horses, and dogs. If you're interested, you can lend a hand milking a cow or two. Some walks through the countryside are options as well, such as to an old Indian cemetery, to a big waterfall, and through jungle to see birds and butterflies. The countryside views and fresh air are delightful. If you're lucky, you may be able to see the Nevado del Ruiz in the distance in the early morning. The **Don Lolo** (Km. 5 Vía Termales San Vicente, cell tel. 316/698-6797) restaurant just down the road has a lot of personality and is a popular stop for those going to or returning from the Termales de San Vicente.

BELALCÁZAR

The coffee and plantain town of Belalcázar rests impossibly on a ridge, with fantastic views of the Valle de Cauca on one side and the Valle del Río Risaralda on the other. Besides the incredible views, Belalcázar, an agricultural town off the tourist map, offers the visitor pure coffee country authenticity. Belalcázar boasts distinct architecture, with its houses covered with colorful zinc sheets to protect against whipping winds.

Built in 1954 in hopes of preventing further bloodshed during the bloody Violencia period, the 45.5-meter-high (149-foot-high) **Monumento a Cristo Rey** (Km. 1 Vía Pereira-Belalcázar, COP$3,000) has become the symbol of this town. To get to the top of the statue of Jesus, you'll have to climb 154 steps. From atop, on a clear day, you can see six Colombian departments: Caldas, Risaralda, Quindío, Valle del Cauca, Tolima, and Chocó; and both the Central and Occidental mountain ranges. The other attraction in town is the **Eco Parque La Estampilla hike** (1.5 km, open daylight hours, free). It's on the northeast side of town, a 10-minute walk from the **Parque Bolívar** (Clls. 15-16 and Cras. 4-5), in which you can wander a winding path through forests of *guadua* (bamboo).

The best time to check out Belalcázar life at its most vibrant is on market day—Saturday—when farmers from the countryside converge on the town to sell coffee beans, plantains, pineapples, and other crops. The Parque Bolívar buzzes with activity as Jeep Willys, packed with farmers and marketgoers, come and go all day long. It's quite a carnival atmosphere.

The best hotel in town is the **Hotel Balcón Colonial** (Cra. 4A No. 12-10, tel. 6/860-2433, cell tel. 313/552-4652, COP$35,000 d). It's clean, cool, and basic, having just nine rooms.

Getting There

It is 54 kilometers from Pereira to Belalcázar. Buses depart from the Pereira Terminal de Transportes (Cl. 17 No. 23-157, Pereira, tel. 6/315-2323). **Flota Occidental** (tel. 6/321-1655, www.flotaoccidental.com) is the bus company that serves Belalcázar (COP$8,000, 2 hrs.) on an hourly basis from 6am until 6:30pm.

SANTUARIO

It's worth the arduous journey to this remote village on a mountaintop in the Cordillera Occidental (Western Mountains) just to take a photo of its famous **Calle Real,** dotted with stately Paisa houses that have been done up in a rainbow of colors. Calle Real is one of the most photographed streets in Colombia.

On Saturdays, campesinos converge on the town to sell their coffee, cacao, sugarcane, and other crops. There is so much activity on market day in the **Plaza de Bolívar** (between Clls. 6-7 and Cras. 5-6) that you'll be tempted to find a front-row seat in a café and take it all in: produce and coffee being unloaded and loaded, Jeep Willys filled with standing-room-only passengers arriving and departing, farmers drinking beer in taverns, women selling sweets in the park, and children being children. Many farmers, money in hand, whoop it up in town and stay the night.

Although Santuario is picture-perfect, it's far better to continue to the **Parque Nacional Natural Tatamá** than to spend the night in Santuario, even if you are not interested in doing any hiking: Hotels in town are not recommended.

There is regular bus transportation from the Terminal de Transportes de Pereira (Cl. 17 No. 23-157, Pereira, tel. 6/315-2323) to Santuario. **Flota Occidental** (tel. 6/321-1655, www.flotaoccidental.com) makes this two-hour trip (COP$8,000) three times a day: 6:55am, 11:45am, and 5:20pm.

PARQUE MUNICIPAL NATURAL PLANES DE SAN RAFAEL

Located in the remote, little visited Cordillera Occidental (Western Mountains), the Tatamá Massif contains one of the world's few remaining pristine *páramos* (highland moors). The topography of the mountain range is very broken, especially the jagged **Cerro Tatamá** (4,250 meters/13,945 feet), which is the highest point in the Cordillera Occidental. The range is highly biodiverse, with an estimated 564 species of orchids and 402 species of birds. It is also home to pumas, jaguars, and *osos anteojos,* the only breed of bear in Colombia. The central part of the massif is protected by the 15,900-hectare (39,300-acre) Parque Nacional Natural Tatamá.

Access to PNN Tatamá is through the Parque Municipal Natural Planes de San Rafael, which not only acts as a buffer zone on the eastern side of the national park near the town of Santuario, but is an attraction in itself.

The **Parque Municipal Natural Planes de San Rafael** (10 km from Santuario, cell tel. 311/719-1717, www.planesdesanrafael.blogspot.com, amorosa_santuario@hotmail.com) covers 11,796 hectares (29,149 acres) of cloud forest between the altitudes of 2,000 and 2,600 meters (6,562 and 8,530 feet), with significant patches of old-growth forest. Nature walks are conducted by friendly and knowledgeable guides from a local community organization, the **Asociación de Guías e Interpretes Ambientales (GAIA),** many of whom got their start through participation in groups of youth bird-watchers.

Within the park there are four paths. The shortest, called the **Lluvia de Semillas** (Rainfall of Seeds), allows visitors to see a forest in recuperation. It is a one-kilometer (0.6-mile) loop through land that was once used for cattle grazing and, over the past 15 years, has been slowly returning to a forest. The 9.6-kilometer (6-mile) round-trip **Cascadas** trail is a strenuous path to the border of the Parque Nacional Natural Tatamá at an elevation of 2,600 meters (8,530 feet). It crisscrosses the Río San Rafael and culminates at a group of waterfalls. Along the way you can see a great variety of birds and large patches of primary forest. The hike takes 3.5 hours up and 2.5

hours down. The 12-kilometer (7.5-mile) **Quebrada Risaralda** hike takes six hours and can be combined into a loop with the Laguna Encantada hike. The **Laguna Encantada** path is a nine-kilometer (5.5-mile) circuit that takes five hours and is especially good for bird-watching, with the possibility of viewing many hummingbirds. The best time for these hikes is early in the morning. Costs for these excursions are COP$25,000-50,000 per group of any size.

Parque Nacional Natural Tatamá

From Parque Municipal Natural Planes de San Rafael it is also possible to organize excursions into the **Parque Nacional Natural Tatamá** (tel. 6/368-7964, www.parquesnacionales.gov.co), located at the highest point of the Cordillera Occidental between the departments of Chocó, Risaralda, and Valle del Cauca. Though the park is not officially open to ecotourism, the folks at GAIA can organize an excursion that requires at least two nights of camping. The first day involves a 12-kilometer (7.5-mile), eight-hour hike to a campground at 3,200 meters (10,500 feet). The following day you explore the upper reaches of the Tatamá, with the unusual shrub-covered *páramo* (high tropical mountain ecosystem), craggy outcrops, and deep gorges. From the top you can see the Chocó lowlands. You return by nightfall to camp and return to Parque Municipal Natural Planes de San Rafael the following day. Contact **Parque Municipal Natural Planes de San Rafael** (cell tel. 311/719-1717) to organize.

Accommodations

The clean, comfortable, and cozy **lodge** (COP$25,000 pp or COP$52,000 with three meals) at the Parque Municipal Natural Planes de San Rafael visitors center accommodates 40 people. Meals (COP$7,000-10,000) are nothing short of delicious. To reserve lodging, contact the ecotourism organization **FECOMAR** (cell tel. 312/200-7711, fecomar.anp@hotmail.com) or call the park administrator (cell tel. 311/719-1717, amorosa_santuario@hotmail.com).

Bird-watching brings visitors to the **Rainforest Montezuma Ecolodge** (cell tel. 317/684-1034, www.montezuma-ecolodge.blogspot.com.co, COP$130,000 pp incl. all meals) at the fringes of the Tatamá park and the Cordillera Occidental near the town of Pueblo Rico (Risaralda). This lodge is a favorite among Colombian birding fanatics. There's a basic lodge, run by Leopoldina, which can accommodate 10. Visitors must contract a local guide to enter the national park (COP$80,000). Hiring a Jeep for the day to explore the area costs COP$300,000, although that is not essential.

Getting There

To get to the Parque Municipal Natural Planes de San Rafael visitors center and lodge, board one of the Jeeps that leave from the main square in Santuario each weekday at 7am and 3pm, or on Saturdays at 2pm and 5pm. If you miss those, no worries: You can take a *servicio express* (private car) for

COP$35,000. To get to Pueblo Rico (Rainforest Montezuma Ecolodge) from Pereira there are about 15 buses daily on Flota Occidental (COP$18,000, 3.5 hrs.), but any bus destined for Quibdó will also get you there. From Pueblo Rico to Montezuma hiring a Jeep costs COP$70,000.

IBAGUÉ

The bustling capital city of the Tolima department, Ibagué (pop. 600,000) is Colombia's "City of Music," hosting several music festivals each year. It's hard to believe, but just to the west of this tropical-fruit-producing region, and beyond the green folds of mountains and valleys, looms the snowy peak of the Nevado del Tolima in the Parque Nacional Natural Los Nevados. Ibagué is a great launch pad for the challenge of ascending to that mountain.

Sights

Should you have some time to spend in Ibagué, a handful of sights are worth a look. Shade is not an issue at the **Plaza de Bolívar** (between Cras. 2-3 and Clls. 9-10): The square is full of majestic, centuries-old trees, but it is the **Catedral Inmaculada Concepción** (Cl. 10 No. 1-129, tel. 8/263-3451, 7am-noon and 2:30pm-7:30pm daily) that steals attention. The **Banco de la República** (Cra. 3A No. 11-26, tel. 8/263-0721, www.banrepcultural.org, 8:30am-6pm Mon.-Fri., 8:30am-1pm Sat., free) always has an exhibit in its 2nd-floor exhibition hall. It's close to the **Calle Peatonal** (Cra. 3 between Clls. 10-15), which is refreshingly free from cars and motorbikes.

The **Conservatorio del Tolima** (Cra. 1 between Clls. 9-10, tel. 8/826-1852, www.conservatoriodeltolima.edu.co, open only for concerts) is one of the reasons Ibagué prides itself the "Capital Musical de Colombia." A few bars from the Colombian national anthem are painted on the exterior of the yellow Republican-era building.

Music festivals take place in the city year-round, including the **Festival Nacional de la Música Colombiana** (www.fundacionmusicaldecolombia.com, Mar.) and **Festival Folclórico Colombiano** (www.festivalfolclorico.com, June or July).

The **Museo de Arte del Tolima** (Cra. 7 No. 5-93, tel. 8/273-2840, www.museodeartedeltolima.org, 10am-12:30pm and 2pm-6:30pm daily, COP$3,500) is a small museum with a permanent collection and temporary exhibition space dedicated to contemporary Colombian artists. A leafy park in this pleasant part of town is the **Parque Centenario** (Cra. 6 between Clls. 8-10). Along with usual park goings-on, cultural events are often held in an amphitheater.

Food and Accommodations

The trendy dining and drinking spot in Ibagué is 15 stories high, with a superb bird's-eye view of the city and the Parque Nacional Natural Los Nevados. **Altavista** (Cra. 2 at Cl. 11, tel. 8/277-1381, noon-midnight Mon.-Wed., noon-3am Thurs.-Sat., noon-4pm Sun., COP$25,000) has a little bit of everything: Asian-inspired dishes, tapas, and vegetarian options. At night on weekends it becomes more of a lounge atmosphere, often with live shows.

The most luxurious hotel in town is the Colombian chain **Hotel Estelar Altamira** (Cra. 1A No. 45-50, tel. 8/266-6111, COP$203,000 d), located outside of the city center. In town choose the century-old **Hotel Lusitania** (Cra. 2 No. 15-55, tel. 8/261-9166, www.hotellusitania.com), a classic with comfortable rooms surrounding a nice-sized swimming pool.

For fresh air and birdsong galore, the welcoming ★ **Ukuku Rural Lodge** (www.ukuku.co, COP$42,000 dorm, COP$142,000 d) is the place to be. It's located in the beautiful Cañón del Combeima gorge, about 17 kilometers (10.6 miles) from Ibagué, and only about a 1.5-kilometer (0.9-mile) hike into the mountains. The ecolodge offers various types of rooms and specializes in a wealth of natural pursuits: bird-watching, canyoning, rock climbing, and especially trekking, to the Nevado del Tolima and a hike the lodge dubs the "Ruta de la Palma de Cera," which follows the path taken by European explorers and naturalists Alexander von Humboldt and Aimé Bonpland.

Transportation

The **Terminal de Transportes** (Cra. 2 No. 20-86, tel. 8/261-8122, www.terminalibague.com) is in a rough part of town, so you should take a cab to and from the bus station. For the most part, Ibagué is not a walkable city, except in the center of town. From the Ibagué airport there are nonstop flights to Bogotá and Medellín.

Background

The Landscape 112
Plants and Animals 118
History 123
Government and Economy 140
People and Culture 143

The Landscape

Colombia covers a land area of 1.14 million square kilometers (440,000 square miles), roughly the size of Texas and California combined, making it the fourth-largest South American country in area after Brazil, Argentina, and Peru. It is located in the northwest corner of South America, with seacoast on both the Pacific and the Atlantic, and it borders Venezuela, Brazil, Peru, Ecuador, and Panama. The Amazonian departments of Putumayo, Caquetá, Amazonas, and Vaupés in the south of the country straddle the equator.

For a country of its size, Colombia has an astonishing variety of landscapes, including the dense rainforests of the Amazon and the Pacific coast, the vast grassland plains of the Llanos, the lofty Andes Mountains, and the Caribbean islands of San Andrés and Providencia. Colombia's mountainous regions themselves hold a succession of vertically layered landscapes: tropical rainforests at their base, followed by cloud forests at higher elevations, topped by the unique tropical high mountain *páramo* (highland moor) above 3,500 meters (11,480 feet). The country boasts several peaks higher than 5,000 meters (16,400 feet), including Nevado del Ruiz (5,325 meters/17,470 feet) and Pico Cristóbal Colón (5,776 meters/18,950 feet).

GEOGRAPHY
Región Andina

This central part of Colombia is dominated by the Andes mountain range. This region, which is referred to as the Región Andina or simply *el interior* (the interior) is the heartland of the country. It covers roughly 25 percent of the surface of the country and is home to 60 percent of the Colombian population.

The Andes mountain range, 8,000 kilometers (5,000 miles) long, runs the entire length of South America. The Andes are relatively young mountains, and some of the loftiest in the world after the Himalayas, resulting from the collision of the westward-moving South American plate with the Nazca and Antarctic plates starting 145 million years ago. The heavier Nazca and Antarctic plates to the west subducted under the lighter and more rigid South American plate, propelling it upwards and forming the Andes. In Colombia, as a result of a complex pattern of tectonic collisions, three parallel ranges were formed. At the Masizo Colombiano (Colombian Massif), a mountain range 175 kilometers north of the border with Ecuador, the Andes split into the Cordillera Occidental (Western Range), Cordillera Central (Central Range), and Cordillera Oriental (Eastern Range).

The Cordillera Occidental is the lowest and least populated of the three ranges. It runs roughly 750 kilometers parallel to the Pacific coast and ends

Previous: campesino near Salamina; hot springs.

150 kilometers from the Caribbean Sea. Its highest point is the Cerro de Tatamá (4,250 meters/13,945 feet). Of Colombia's three ranges, it has the least human intervention and is home to some of the world's only pristine high mountain *páramos* ecosystems, notably that covering the Cerro de Tatamá.

The Central Cordillera is the highest of the three ranges and is the continuation in Colombia of the main Andes range. It runs roughly 800 kilometers and tapers off in the northern Caribbean plains, 200 kilometers from the Caribbean coast. Like the Andes in Ecuador, it is dotted with volcanoes. North of the Masizo Colombiano is the Serranía de los Coconucos (Coconucos Range), a range of 15 volcanoes including the Volcán del Puracé (Puracé Volcano, 4,580 meters/15,025 feet). Farther north, the Cordillera Central reaches its maximum elevation at the massive Nevado del Huila (5,750 meters/15,585 feet). Farther north is a large complex formed by the Nevado del Tolima (5,215 meters/17,110 feet), Nevado Santa Isabel (4,950 meters/16,240 feet), and Nevado del Ruiz (5,325 meters/17,470 feet). In its northern part, the Cordillera Central broadens to form the uneven highland that comprises the mountainous heartland of Antioquia with Medellín as its capital.

Several of the volcanoes of the Cordillera Central have seen recent activity, notably Volcán Galeras (4,276 meters/14,029 feet), near the southern city of Pasto, which last erupted in 2005, forcing evacuation of nearby settlements. Volcán Galeras is currently closed to visitors because of the threat of volcanic activity. In 1985, the Nevado del Ruiz erupted unexpectedly, creating a landslide that engulfed the town of Armero, killing more than 20,000 people. Since 2012, the Nevado del Ruiz has seen some activity, which has restricted access to the northern part of the Parque Nacional Natural Los Nevados.

The Cordillera Oriental, which like the Cordillera Occidental is nonvolcanic, extends more than 1,100 kilometers to the border with Venezuela. The range broadens to form a broad high plateau called the Altiplano Cundiboyacense, which extends 200 kilometers north of Bogotá. This is an area of broad valleys with the extremely rich soil of sedimentary deposits. The Sabana de Bogotá, or Bogotá High Plateau, where Bogotá is located, is one particularly broad valley. North of the altiplano is the soaring Sierra Nevada del Cocuy, a mountain range with 11 glacier-covered peaks, including Ritacuba Blanco (5,380 meters/17,650 feet). North of El Cocuy, the Cordillera Oriental loses altitude and splits in two: A smaller western segment forms the Serranía de Perijá on the border between Colombia and Venezuela, and a larger branch continues into Venezuela to form the Venezuelan Andes.

The 1,500-kilometer-long Río Magdalena flows along a broad valley that separates the Cordillera Central and the Cordillera Oriental, making it the main commercial waterway of Colombia. Due to heavy sedimentation, it is now only navigable when waters rise during the rainy seasons in the central part of the country (Apr.-May and Oct.-Nov.). The Río Cauca, which flows parallel to the Magdalena along the much narrower valley between the Cordillera Central and the Cordillera Occidental, is the main tributary of the Magdalena. They join in northern Colombia and flow into the Caribbean.

Andean Colombia is a seismically volatile area, and the country has suffered some major earthquakes in the past. The most deadly measured 7.5 on the Richter Scale and occurred in Cúcuta in 1875. It killed 10,000 and completely destroyed the city. In recent years, around 600 were killed in the Pacific port city of Tumaco during a quake and tsunami in 1979; 300 perished in the 1983 Holy Week earthquake in Popayán; and over 1,100 died in the Armenia quake of 1999.

Caribe

Colombia's Caribbean coast runs 1,760 kilometers (1,100 miles) from the border of Panama to Venezuela, just longer than the California coast. However, the term "Caribe" or "Región Caribe" refers to much more than the narrow strip of coast; it encompasses basically all of Colombia north of the Andes, including a vast area of plains. This region covers 15 percent of the surface of Colombia and is home to 20 percent of the population.

The terrain is mostly low-lying and undulating. Near the border with Panama, the land is covered by dense tropical forests, similar to those on the Pacific coast. Farther east is the Golfo de Urabá, a large, shallow bay. Between the Golfo de Urabá and Cartagena is the Golfo de Morrosquillo, a broad inlet that is 50 kilometers (31 miles) wide. Off the shore of the Golfo de Morrosquillo are two small archipelagos, the Islas de San Bernardo and the Islas del Rosario, with beautiful coral reefs. Inland to the south is a large savanna in the departments of Córdoba and Sucre largely devoted to cattle ranching. This area was once covered by dry tropical forests, which have been largely felled.

Bahía de Cartagena, farther east, is a magnificent deep bay that caught the attention of the early Spanish explorers. To the southeast of Cartagena is the lower valley of the Magdalena and Cauca Rivers, a vast expanse of low-lying lagoons and lands prone to seasonal flooding. The Río Magdalena flows into the Caribbean east of Cartagena at the port city of Barranquilla. Farther to the east along the coast is a major mountain range, the Sierra Nevada de Santa Marta. It was formed by the collision of the South American plate and the Caribbean plate to the north and is entirely independent of the Andes. This range is home to Colombia's two highest peaks, the twin Pico Cristóbal Colón and Pico Bolívar (5,776 meters/18,950 feet), and is considered the highest coastal mountain range in the world. The Sierra Nevada de Santa Marta contains the same range of vertically layered landscapes as the Andes, from low-lying tropical forest through cloud forest, Andean forests, *páramo,* and glaciers. There are eight peaks with elevations greater than 5,000 meters (16,400 feet).

Northeast of the Sierra Nevada de Santa Marta is La Guajira, an arid peninsula jutting into the Caribbean. Punta Gallinas, at the tip of La

Guajira, is the northernmost point in South America. There are a few low-lying mountain ranges in La Guajira, such as the Serranía de la Macuira (864 meters/2,835 feet), which is covered with rainforest. The Sierra Nevada de Santa Marta and Serranía de la Macuira are biological islands, and their upper reaches are home to numerous endemic species that evolved in isolation.

Pacífico

The Pacific coast of Colombia extends 1,329 kilometers from Ecuador to Panama, about the same length as the coast of California. The term Pacífico, as it relates to Colombia, designates all the land—jungle to be more accurate—that lies between the Pacific Ocean and the Cordillera Occidental. This region covers 6 percent of Colombia and is home to about 2 percent of the population.

The topography of this region is mostly flat, with the low-lying coastal Serranía del Baudó (1,810 meters/5,940 feet) providing a mountainous backdrop to the coastal plain and forming an inland basin that is drained by the mighty Río Atrato, which flows northwards into the Caribbean Sea. The coast has a number of bays and inlets, notably the Ensenada de Utría (Utría Inlet), visited by humpback whales traveling every winter from the Antarctic Sea to give birth in the warm waters of the Colombian Pacific. South of Buenaventura, the coast has extensive mangroves, much of which are well-preserved. Offshore are two islands: Isla Gorgona is 35 kilometers off the coast on the continental shelf, and tiny Malpelo is 490 kilometers off the coast. Both of these islands are likely of volcanic origin.

The Colombian Pacific region is one of the wettest places on Earth, with average annual rainfall of 10,000 millimeters (33 feet). Due to the enormous amount of precipitation, the region has a dense river network with dozens of major arteries, such as the Río Baudó, Río San Juan, and Río Patía.

Amazon

The Amazon region of Colombia comprises 400,000 million kilometers, or roughly 35 percent of Colombia's territory, including all the territory east of the Andes and south of the Río Guaviare. The Colombian portion covers only 10 percent of the entire Amazon drainage basin. Total population in the Amazon region is 1.1 million, or 2 percent of the country's population. It is the most sparsely populated area in the country.

Like the Llanos, the Amazon has an undulating terrain, interrupted occasionally with ancient, low-lying mountainous formations of the Guyana Shield, such as the Serranía de Chiribiquete, a series of highly eroded tabletop mountains. The Amazon consists of two distinct but intermingled areas: *terra firme*, the undulated lands that are above the highest flood point, and *varzea*, floodplains along the main rivers, which can extend 50 kilometers from the river.

There are two types of rivers in the Amazon: the predominant white rivers, which carry sediments down from the Andes; and the black rivers, which originate within the rainforest in the Guyana Shield formations that were long ago denuded of soil due to erosion. As these waters travel though the flooded forest, they pick up pigments that give them their characteristic black color. *Igapo* is the name given to jungles flooded by black water rivers. Most of the rivers of the Colombian Amazon are white, such as the massive Río Putumayo, Río Caquetá, Río Apaporis, and Río Vaupés, all of which are more than 1,000 kilometers long. The main black river in Colombia is the Río Guainía, which does originate in the Andes, and which is the headwater of the largest black river of the Amazon—the Río Negro—which flows into the milky Amazon at Manaus, in Brazil.

Los Llanos

The Llanos, Colombia's vast eastern plains, cover an area of 250,000 square kilometers, roughly 25 percent of Colombia's territory. The plains are hemmed in to the west by Cordillera Oriental and to the south by the Amazon rainforest, and extend far into Venezuela. Though the transition between the Amazon and the Llanos is gradual, the Río Guaviare, which flows from west to east at a longitude that is roughly midway between the northern and southern tips of Colombia, is considered the demarcation line between these two areas. The Llanos are home to about 1.5 million inhabitants, or about 3 percent of the population, making it the region with the second lowest population density—after the Amazon region—in the country.

After the genesis of the Andes, water flowing eastward down the mountains accumulated in a vast freshwater lake that was confined on the east by old mountainous formations (now the Guyana and Brazilian highlands). Large amounts of sediments were deposited, forming the basis for the Llanos' undulating topography. Near the Andes, elevations can reach 300 meters and, moving east, slowly decrease in altitude until they reach the north-flowing Río Orinoco, which forms the border between Colombia and Venezuela.

The only significant mountain range in Los Llanos is the Serranía de la Macarena (Macarena Range), a 120-kilometer-long, 30-kilometer-wide range that is 45 kilometers east of the Andes just of the Río Guayabero, a tributary of the Río Guaviare. This range is part of the Guyana Shield complex of ancient, highly eroded remnants of mountains that existed long before the formation of the Andes.

The Llanos are drained by a multitude of large rivers, such as the Río Guaviare, Río Vichada, and Río Meta, which flow down from the Andes and meander east. All the rivers of the Llanos are tributaries of the Orinoco—for this reason, this region is also often called La Orinoquía.

CLIMATE

Colombia has a typically tropical climate, with no change of seasons. Climate is related primarily to elevation, and there are defined annual precipitation patterns.

In the mountainous areas, temperature decreases approximately six

Colombia's National Parks

From undisturbed coral reefs to the Amazonian jungle to snow-covered mountain ranges, Colombia's national park system is a treasure, and making the effort to visit them is worthwhile for any visitor. The country's system of natural parks and protected areas covers more than 14 million hectares (34.6 million acres), around 13.4 percent of the country. It includes 43 Parques Nacionales Naturales (National Natural Parks), which are areas of major ecological interest that have remained largely untouched by human intervention, and 12 Santuarios de Flora y Fauna (Flora and Fauna Sanctuaries), areas that are devoted to the preservation of specific ecosystems. Of the 43 parks, 24 are open for tourism. The rest are officially off-limits, due to lack of infrastructure, security concerns, or in order to respect the territory of indigenous communities.

In 1960, PNN Cueva de los Guácharos, in the southwest, was the first park to be established. The number of parks steadily increased, especially from 1986 to 1990 when President Virgilio Barco doubled the park holdings from roughly 5 million hectares to 10 million hectares (12 million to 24 million acres). In the past few years, the government has again been increasing the number and extension of parks. In 2013 President Juan Manuel Santos doubled the size of the PNN Serranía de Chiribiquete to its present 2.8 million hectares (7 million acres), or three times the size of Yellowstone National Park.

Charged with the considerable task of administering this huge system are a mere 430 rangers—roughly one person for every 33,000 hectares (82,000 acres). Rangers face a great challenge in protecting the parks against threats related to human encroachment, particularly cattle ranching and the planting of illicit crops. There are other threats as well, such as illegal mining and logging. Paradoxically, what has preserved many of the parks until now has been the lack of security due to Colombia's internal conflict. As security conditions improve, there will be increasing pressure on these natural habitats. The Parks Service is actively engaging with the communities that live near the parks and is transferring the operation of much of the ecotourism infrastructure to community-based organizations as part of an effort to enlist local communities in the preservation of the land.

Entry permits and entry fees are only required in a handful of highly visited parks, such as PNN Tayrona, PNN Gorgona, PNN Cocuy, and PNN Los Nevados. At these, you will automatically be charged if you book lodging in advance, or if not, upon arrival. If you want to be meticulous, you can obtain the entry permit and pay entry fees in advance by contacting the **Parques Nacionales** (tel. 1/353-2400, www.parquesnacionales.gov.co) in Bogotá.

---

degrees Celsius per every 1,000 meters (3,280 feet) of elevation (or three degrees Fahrenheit per every 1,000 feet). The common designations for the altitudinal zones are as follows: *tierra caliente* (hot lands) is anywhere below 1,000 meters of elevation; *tierra templada* (temperate lands) is anywhere between 1,000 and 2,000 meters; and *tierra fría* (cold land) is anywhere above 2,000 meters. Roughly 80 percent of the country is *tierra caliente*, 10 percent is *tierra templada*, and 7 percent is *tierra fría*.

Cartagena, which is at sea level, has an average temperature of 27.5°C (81.5°F); Medellín, which is at 1,600 meters (5,250 feet), has an average temperature of 22°C (71.5°F); and the capital city of Bogotá, which is built at 2,625 meters (8,612 feet), has an average temperature of 13.5°C (56°F).

Precipitation patterns vary throughout the country. In the Andean region, there are generally two periods of *verano* (dry season, literally "summer"), from December to March and from June to September, and two periods of *invierno* (rainy season, literally "winter"), in April and May and from October to November. On the Caribbean coast, the dry period is from December to April and the rainy season is from May to November. In the Pacific it rains almost the entire year, but there is a slight dry spell from December to March. In the Llanos, there are two very marked seasons: a very dry *verano* from November to March and a very wet *invierno* from April to October. In the Amazon, it rains almost the entire year, but there is a slight dry spell from August to October.

Extreme weather in Colombia is rare, but the country is susceptible to weather phenomena such as El Niño or La Niña, when temperatures in the Pacific Ocean rise or fall, respectively. In 2015-2016, the country was affected by a strong El Niño, which brought prolonged drought.

San Andrés and Providencia are occasionally, and the Caribbean mainland of Colombia rarely, in the path of Atlantic hurricanes from August through October. The last storm of significance was Hurricane Beta in 2005. It caused considerable damage in Providencia.

Plants and Animals

When it comes to biodiversity, Colombia is a place of superlatives. Though representing only 0.2 percent of the planet's surface, it is home to about 10 percent of all the species in the world. The country has an estimated 55,000 plant species, including 3,500 species of orchids. Only Brazil, with seven times the land surface, has as many plant species. Colombia is the country with the greatest number of bird species in the world—about 1,800. It's also home to about 3,200 fish, 750 amphibian species, 500 reptile species, and 450 mammal species. No wonder Colombia was designated as one of 17 so-called megadiverse countries, a select club of countries that are home to an outsized proportion of the world's biodiversity. Other megadiverse countries include Australia, Brazil, China, Democratic Republic of Congo, Indonesia, Madagascar, Mexico, the United States, and South Africa.

This enormous biodiversity is the result of Colombia's location in the tropics, where year-round sunlight and high precipitation are conducive to plant growth, plus the country's mountainous topography with numerous climatic zones and microclimates that have created biological islands where species have evolved in relative isolation. Furthermore, the recent ice ages were not as severe in this part of the world, and as a result many ancient species were preserved. Finally, Colombia's location at the crossroads of Central and South America has further enriched the country's biodiversity.

Colombian Fruits

Colombia is a land bursting with exotic fruit. Sold from the back of pickup trucks by farmers on the roadside, overflowing at stalls in colorful markets in every town and village, lined up in neat rows in the produce section at fancy grocery stores and at juice stands—just about anywhere you go, delicious fruit is in reach.

You know pineapple, papaya, mangoes, and bananas, but be sure to try these tropical delights that you may not have encountered outside of Colombia.

- *Pitahaya* **(dragon fruit):** Looking like a yellow grenade, *pitahayas* have a sweet white meat inside.

- *Guanábana* **(soursop):** By far the strangest-looking fruit, soursop resemble prehistoric dinosaur eggs. Inside the large green spiky fruit is a milky and slimy flesh. *Guanábana* is great in juices and desserts.

- *Granadilla:* Crack open this orangey-yellow fruit and slurp down the slimy gray contents, seeds and all. It's delicious.

- *Higo* **(prickly pear):** This green fruit comes from cactus plants and has sweet, if tough, orange-colored meat.

- *Chirimoya* **(cherimoya):** This green fruit that resembles a smooth artichoke is covered with a smooth, silky skin and filled with delectable, sweet pulp.

- *Níspero* **(sapodilla):** A fruit with a deep brown color that tastes like a prepared sweet.

- *Mangostino* **(mangosteen):** Crack open a deep-purple mangosteen and enjoy the sweet segments inside. They're full of antioxidants.

- *Uchuva* **(Cape gooseberry):** Known in English as Cape gooseberries, these tart yellow berries are a cousin of the tomato and are tasty on their own or in salads, but are often used in jams and sweets.

- *Mamoncillo:* Tough-skinned grapes (don't eat the skin), *mamoncillos* are usually sold only at street markets.

RAINFOREST

Rainforests are among the most complex ecosystems on Earth. They have a layered structure with towering trees that soar 30-40 meters high (100-130 feet) to form the forest's canopy. Some of the most common rainforest trees are the ceiba, mahogany, myrtle, laurel, acacia, and rubber trees. Occasionally, particularly high trees known as *emergentes* pierce the canopy, reaching as high up as 60 meters (200 feet). Below the canopy is the *sotobosque*, a middle layer of smaller trees and palms that vie for the sunlight filtering in through the canopy. In the canopy and *sotobosque* there are many epiphytes (plants such as orchids and bromeliads) that have adapted to live on top of trees so as to be nearer to the sunlight. Near the ground live plants that require little sunlight, including ferns, grasses, and many types of fungi. The two main rainforests in Colombia, the Amazon and the Chocó, have the same layered structure, though they have some differences in their flora and fauna.

The Amazon rainforest is home to an impressive array of vertebrates. Over millennia, a large number of canopy-dwelling species evolved. Monkeys, such as the large and extremely agile spider monkey, the woolly monkey, and the howler monkey, evolved prehensile tails that allowed them to move easily from branch to branch. Anteaters, such as the tamandua and the *oso mielero* (giant anteater) and the incredibly cute *kinkajú* (kinkajou), also developed prehensile tails. Other inhabitants of the canopy include sloths, such as the adorable three-toed sloth, whose strategy is not agility but passivity: It eats tree vegetation and is covered with algae that gradually turns the animal green to allow for good camouflage. The canopy is also home to myriad bats and many birds, including exotic eagles, curassows, toucans, woodpeckers, cotingas, and macaws.

Notable is the majestic harpy eagle, with powerful claws and the ability to fly unencumbered through the canopy. It preys on monkeys and sloths, which it kills with the force of its claws. The *tigrillo* (tiger cat) is a small and extremely endangered species. It has a long tail that helps with its balance as it moves from tree to tree.

On the ground, large vertebrates include the extremely endangered tapir, an ancient mammal species that can grow two meters long (over six feet) and weigh 300 kilograms (660 pounds). It is equally at ease on land as in the water. Other land mammals include the giant armadillo, giant anteater, deer, and boars, such as the *saíno* and *pecarí*. Smaller mammals include the *guatín* and *borugo*, both rodents. These animals are often prey to the puma and jaguar, both of which inhabit the Amazon but are difficult to observe in the wild.

The rivers of the Amazon are home to more than 1,500 species of fish, including endangered pirarucu, one of the largest freshwater fishes on Earth. There are also dolphins, both pink and gray. The former evolved separately from the oceangoing dolphins when the Amazon was an inland sea. The Amazonian gray dolphins are sea dolphins that adapted to living in freshwater. Other aquatic mammals include the highly endangered manatee and otters.

The Chocó Rainforest is particularly rich in palms, of which 120 species have been identified. In fact, it is sometimes referred to as the "Land of the Palms." The forest also abounds in cycads, ancient plants that have a stout trunk and crowns of hard, stiff leaves. Chocó is also notable for more than 40 species of brightly colored poisonous frogs, known locally as *ranas kokois*. These small frogs are covered with a deadly poison and have evolved stunning coloration, from bright orange to red, gold, and blue. They are active in the day and therefore relatively easy to spot. Of Colombia's 1,800 species of birds, more than 1,000 have been identified in the Chocó, including a large number of hummingbirds.

Offshore, the Pacific Ocean welcomes the annual migration of Antarctic humpback whales. The beaches of the Pacific coast are popular nesting areas for sea turtles, in particular the *tortuga golfina* (olive ridley) and *tortuga carey* (hawksbill) sea turtles.

CLOUD FOREST

Rainforests that grow at higher altitudes on the flanks of the Andes are known as montane rainforests or cloud forests because they are often enveloped in mist that results from the condensation of warm air against chillier mountain currents. Unlike the lowland rainforest, cloud forests only have two layers, the canopy and ground layer. Generally, the vegetation is less dense than that in the lowland rainforest. However, it is home to many palms, ferns, and epiphytes, particularly orchids.

The type of cloud forest vegetation is dictated by altitude. *Selva subandina* (sub-Andean forest) vegetation grows between the altitudes of 1,000 and 2,300 meters (3,300-7,500 feet), where temperature varies 16-23°C (61-73°F). Plant species include the distinctive Seussian white *yarumo* with its oversized leaves, as well as cedar, oak, and mahogany trees. Many palms grow here, including the svelte wax palm and *tagua*, which produces a nut that resembles ivory. Ferns include the striking *palma boba* or tree fern. Colombia's premier crop, coffee, is grown at this elevation.

At elevations between 2,300 and 3,600 meters (7,500-12,000 feet), the vegetation is described as *selva Andina* (Andean forest). This vegetation is even less dense and at higher elevations the trees are smaller. *Selva Andina* includes many oak, *encenillo*, *sietecuero* (glory bush), and pine trees.

Mammals include the spectacled or Andean bear, the only species of bear in South America, the mountain (or woolly) tapir, anteaters, armadillos, sloths, boars, foxes, and *olingos,* small arboreal carnivores of the raccoon family. In 2013, the *olinguito* (small *olingo*), an incredibly cute animal, was declared a new species. Other unusual animals include the slow-moving *guagua loba* and *guatín,* both of which are rodents. In addition, numerous species of monkeys inhabit the cloud forest, including noisy troops of howler monkeys. Birds include many types of *barranqueros* (motmots), including the spectacular blue-crowned motmot. Other common birds include *tángaras* (tanagers), woodpeckers, warblers, parrots, owls, and ducks, including the beautiful white-and-black torrent duck.

PÁRAMOS

Páramos are unique tropical highland ecosystems that thrive above 3,500 meters (11,500 feet), where UV radiation is higher, oxygen is scarcer, and where temperatures vary from minus-2 to 10 degrees Celsius (28-50°F). Due to frequent mist and precipitation, *páramos* are often saturated with water and have many lakes. They are true "water factories" that provide water to many of Colombia's cities, notably Bogotá. Though *páramos* exist throughout the New World tropics, most are located in Colombia. The Parque Nacional Natural Sumapaz, south of Bogotá, is the world's largest *páramo*.

Páramo vegetation includes more than 50 species of *frailejón* (genus *Espeletia*), eerily beautiful plants that have imposing tall trunks and thick yellow-greenish leaves. Other *páramo* vegetation includes shrubs, grasses, and *cojines* (cushion plants). Mammals include the spectacled bear, *páramo* tapir, weasels, squirrels, and bats. The *páramo* is the realm of the majestic black-and-white Andean condor, which has a wingspan of up to three meters (10 feet). The condor, whose numbers had declined almost to the point of extinction, is found in the national parks of the Sierra Nevada de Santa Marta, Sierra Nevada del Cocuy, and Los Nevados. The *páramo* lakes welcome many types of ducks, including the Andean duck, as well as smaller birds.

TROPICAL DRY FORESTS

Tropical dry forests exist in areas where there is a prolonged dry season. The vegetation includes deciduous trees that lose their leaves during the dry season, allowing them to conserve water. Trees on moister sites and those with access to groundwater tend to be evergreen. Before Columbus, this ecosystem covered much of the Colombian Caribbean coast. However, much of it has since been cut down for cattle ranching. Pockets still exist east of the Golfo de Morrosquillo and at the base of the Sierra Nevada de Santa Marta. Tropical dry forests are the most endangered tropical ecosystem in the world.

Though less biologically diverse than rainforests, tropical dry forests are home to a wide variety of wildlife. They were once the stomping ground of the now highly endangered *marimonda*, or white-fronted spider monkey.

TROPICAL GRASSLANDS

Los Llanos (The Plains) of Colombia are covered with lush tropical grasslands. Vegetation includes long-stemmed and carpet grasses in the drier areas and swamp grasses in low-lying humid areas. There are also thick patches of forest throughout the plains and along the rivers (known as gallery forests). These plains are teeming with wildlife, including deer, anteaters, armadillos, tapirs, otters, jaguars, pumas, and *chigüiros* (also known as capybaras), the world's largest rodent. The Llanos are also home to the giant anaconda and to one of the most endangered species on Earth, the Orinoco crocodile, which reaches up to seven meters (23 feet) long.

History

BEFORE COLUMBUS

Located at the juncture of Central and South America, what is now Colombia was a necessary transit point for the migration of people who settled South America. However, because these peoples left few physical traces of their passage, little is known of them. The oldest human objects found in Colombia, utensils discovered near Bogotá, are dated from 14,000 BC. With the expansion of agriculture and sedentary life throughout the territory of present-day Colombia around 1000 BC, various indigenous cultures started producing stunning ceramic and gold work, as well as some monumental remains. These remains provide rich material evidence of their development. Nonetheless, there are significant gaps in the understanding of the history of these early peoples.

From around 700 BC, the area of San Agustín, near the origin of the Río Magdalena in southern Colombia, was settled by people who practiced agriculture and produced pottery. Starting in the 1st century AD, the people of San Agustín created hundreds of monumental stone statues set on large platforms, which comprise the largest pre-Columbian archaeological site extant between Mesoamerica and Peru. By AD 800, this society had disappeared.

In the northwestern plains of Colombia, south of present-day Cartagena, starting in the 1st century AD, the Sinú people constructed a large complex of mounds in the shape of fish bones. These mounds regulated flooding, allowing cultivation in both rainy and dry seasons. During rainy seasons, the water flooded the lower cavities, allowing for cultivation on the mounds; during dry season, cultivation took place in the cavities that had been enriched by the flood waters. These monumental formations are still visible from overhead. By the time of the Spanish conquest, these people no longer inhabited the area.

From AD 500 to 900, the area of Tierradentro, west of San Agustín, was settled by an agricultural society that dug magnificent decorated underground tombs, produced large stone statues, and built oval-shaped buildings on artificial terraces. As in the case of the San Agustín and the Sinú people, it is not known what happened to these people.

At the time of the conquest, present-day Colombia was populated by a large number of distinct agricultural societies that often maintained peaceful trading relations among themselves. The two largest groups were the Muisca people, who lived in the altiplano (highlands) of the Cordillera Oriental, and the Tayrona, who lived on the slopes of the Sierra Nevada de Santa Marta. Other groups included the Quimbaya, who settled the area of the present-day Coffee Region; the Calima, in present-day Valle del Cauca; and the Nariños, in the mountainous areas of southwest Colombia.

These indigenous societies were mostly organized at the village level with loose association with other villages. Only the Muisca and the Tayrona had a more developed political organization. Though these were all agricultural societies, they also engaged in hunting, fishing, and mining and produced sophisticated ceramics and goldwork. Each group specialized in what their environment had to offer and engaged in overland trade. For example, the Muiscas produced textiles and salt, which they traded for gold, cotton, tobacco, and shells from other groups.

The Muiscas, a Chibcha-speaking people, were the largest group, with an estimated 600,000 inhabitants at the time of the Spanish conquest. They settled the Cordillera Oriental in AD 300 and occupied a large territory that comprises most of the highland areas of the present-day departments of Cundinamarca and Boyacá. At the time of the conquest, they were organized into two large confederations: one in the south headed by the Zipa, whose capital was Bacatá near present-day Bogotá, and another headed by the Zaque, whose capital was at Hunza, the location of present-day Tunja. The Muiscas had a highly homogeneous culture, and were skilled in weaving, ceramics, and goldwork. Their cosmography placed significant importance on high Andean lakes, several of which were sacred, including Guatavita, Siecha, and Iguaque.

The Tayrona, who settled the slopes of the Sierra Nevada de Santa Marta, were also a Chibcha-speaking people. They had a more urban society, with towns that included temples and ceremonial plazas built on stone terraces, and practiced farming on terraces carved out of the mountains. There are an estimated 200 Tayrona sites, of which Ciudad Perdida (Lost City), built at 1,100 meters (3,600 feet) in the Sierra Nevada de Santa Marta, is the largest and best known. Many of these towns, including El Pueblito in the Parque Nacional Natural Tayrona, were occupied at the time of the Spanish conquest. The Kogis, Arhuacos, Kankuamos, and Wiwas, current inhabitants of the sierra, are their descendants and consider many places in the sierra sacred.

THE SPANISH CONQUEST (1499-1550)

As elsewhere in the New World, the arrival of Europeans was an unmitigated disaster for the Native American societies. Though there were pockets of resistance, on the whole the indigenous people were unable to push back the small number of armed Spanish conquistadores. Harsh conditions after the conquest and the spread of European diseases, such as measles and smallpox, to which the indigenous people had no immunity, killed off millions of natives. The Spanish conquest of present-day Colombia took about 50 years and was largely completed by the 1550s.

In 1499, the first European set foot on present-day Colombia in the northern Guajira Peninsula. In 1510, a first, unsuccessful colony was established in the Golfo de Urabá near the current border with Panama. In 1526, the Spanish established Santa Marta, their first permanent foothold, from where they tried, unsuccessfully, to subdue the Tayronas. In 1533, they established Cartagena, which was to become a major colonial port.

In 1536, Gonzalo Jiménez de Quesada set off south from Santa Marta to conquer the fabled lands of El Dorado in the Andean heartland. After a year of grueling travel up the swampy Río Magdalena valley, 200 surviving members of Jiménez de Quesada's 800 original troops arrived in the Muisca lands near present-day Bogotá. After a short interlude of courteous relations, the Spaniards' greed led them to obliterate the Muisca towns and temples. They found significant amounts of gold, especially in the town of Hunza, but they were, by and large, disappointed. In 1538, Jiménez de Quesada founded Santa Fe de Bogotá as the capital of this new territory, which he called Nueva Granada—New Granada—after his birthplace.

Sebastián de Belalcázar, a lieutenant of Francisco Pizarro, led a second major expedition that arrived in the Muisca lands from the south. Having conquered the Inca city of Quito, Belalcázar and his army traveled north, conquering a vast swath of land from present-day Ecuador to the *sábana* (high plateau) of Bogotá. Along the way, he founded several cities, including Popayán and Cali in 1536. He arrived shortly after Quesada had founded Bogotá. Incredibly, a third conquistador, the German Nikolaus Federmann, arrived in Bogotá at the same time, having traveled from Venezuela via the Llanos. Rather than fight for supremacy, the three conquistadores decided to take their rival claims to arbitration at the Spanish court. In an unexpected turn of events, none of the three obtained title to the Muisca lands: When Bogotá became the administrative capital of New Granada, they came under the sway of the Spanish crown. Other expeditions swept across the Caribbean coast, through current-day Antioquia and the Santanderes.

COLONIAL NUEVA GRANADA (1550-1810)

For most of its colonial history, Nueva Granada, as colonial Colombia was called, was an appendage of the Viceroyalty of Peru. In 1717, Spain decided to establish a viceroyalty in Nueva Granada but changed its mind six years later because the benefits did not justify the cost. In 1739, the viceroyalty was reestablished, with Santa Fe de Bogotá as its capital. It was an unwieldy territory, encompassing present-day Colombia, Venezuela, Ecuador, and Panama. To make it more manageable, Venezuela and Panama were ruled by captain-generals and Ecuador by a president. At the local level, the viceroyalty was divided into *provincias* (provinces), each with a local assembly called a *cabildo*.

Settlement in Nueva Granada occurred primarily in three areas: where there were significant indigenous populations to exploit, as in the case of Tunja in the former Muisca territory; where there were gold deposits, as in Cauca, Antioquia, and Santander; and along trade routes, for example at Honda and Mompox on the Río Magdalena. Cartagena was the main port of call for the biennial convoys of gold and silver sent to Spain. Bogotá lived off of the official bureaucracy and sustained a fair number of artisans. Present-day Antioquia and Santander supported small-scale farming to provide provisions to the gold mining camps. Nueva Granada was one of the least economically dynamic of Spain's New World possessions. The mountainous topography and high transportation costs meant that agricultural production was primarily for local consumption and gold was the only significant export.

Colonial society was composed of a small Spanish and Creole (descendants of Spanish settlers) elite class that governed a large mestizo (mixed indigenous-white) population. The Spanish had initially preserved indigenous communal lands known as *resguardos*, but the demographic collapse of the native population and intermarriage meant that, unlike in Peru or Mexico, there were relatively few people who were fully indigenous. There were also black slaves who were forced mostly to work in the mines and haciendas (plantations). Society was overwhelmingly Catholic and Spanish-speaking.

Culturally, Nueva Granada was also somewhat of a backwater. Though there was a modest flourishing of the arts, Bogotá could not compete with the magnificent architectural and artistic production of Quito, Lima, or Mexico City. The only truly notable event of learning that took place was the late 18th-century Expedición Botánica (Botanical Expedition), headed by Spanish naturalist José Celestino Mutis, the personal doctor to one of the viceroys. The aim of the expedition was to survey all the species of Nueva Granada—a rather tall order given that Colombia is home to 10 percent of the world's species. However, the expedition did some remarkable research and produced beautiful prints of the fauna and flora.

The late colonial period saw unrest in Nueva Granada. Starting in 1781, a revolt known as the Rebelión de los Comuneros took place in the province of Socorro (north of Bogotá) in present-day Santander as a result of an attempt by colonial authorities to levy higher taxes. It was not an antiroyalist movement, however, as its slogan indicates: ¡*Viva el Rey, Muera el Mal Gobierno!* ("Long live the king, down with bad government!"). Rather it was a protest against unfair taxes, not much different from the Boston Tea Party. However, it gave the Spanish government a fright. A rebel army, led by José Antonio Galán, marched on Bogotá. Negotiations put an end to the assault, and later the authorities ruthlessly persecuted the leaders of the revolt.

STRUGGLE FOR INDEPENDENCE (1810-1821)

Though there was some ill feeling against the colonial government, as the Rebelión de los Comuneros attests, as well as rivalry between the Spanish- and American-born elites, it was an external event, the Napoleonic invasion of Spain, that set off the chain of events that led to independence of Nueva Granada and the rest of the Spanish dominion in the New World.

In 1808, Napoleon invaded Spain, took King Ferdinand VII prisoner, and tried to impose his own brother, Joseph, as king of Spain. The Spaniards revolted, establishing a Central Junta in Seville to govern during the king's temporary absence from power. Faced with the issue of whether to recognize the new Central Junta in Spain, the colonial elites decided to take matters in their own hands and establish juntas of their own. The first such junta in Nueva Granada was established in Caracas in April 1810. Cartagena followed suit in May and Bogotá on July 20, 1810. According to popular myth, the revolt in Bogotá was the result of the failure of a prominent Spaniard merchant to lend a flower vase to a pair of Creoles.

Though they pledged alliance to Ferdinand VII, once the local elites had tasted power, there was no going back. Spanish authorities were expelled, and in 1811, a government of sorts, under the loose mantle of the Provincias Unidas de Nueva Granada (United Provinces of New Granada), was established with its capital at Tunja. Bogotá and the adjoining province of Cundinamarca stayed aloof from the confederation, arguing that it was too weak to resist the Spanish. Subsequently, various provinces of Nueva Granada declared outright independence, starting with Venezuela and Cartagena in 1811 and Cundinamarca in 1813.

Several cities remained loyal to the crown, namely Santa Marta and deeply conservative Pasto in the south. From 1812 to 1814 there was a senseless civil war between the Provincias Unidas and Cundinamarca—that is why this period is called the Patria Boba, or Foolish Fatherland. Ultimately, the Provincias Unidas prevailed with the help of a young Venezuelan captain by the name of Simón Bolívar.

After the restoration of Ferdinand VII, Spain attempted to retake its wayward colonies, with a military expedition and reign of terror known as the Reconquista—the Reconquest. The Spanish forces took Cartagena by siege in 1815 and took control of Bogotá in May 1816. However, in 1819, a revolutionary army composed of Venezuelans, Nueva Granadans, and European mercenaries headed by Bolívar arrived across the Llanos from Venezuela and decisively defeated the Spanish army in the Batalla del Puente de Boyacá—the Battle of the Boyacá Bridge—on August 7, near Tunja. The rest of the country fell quickly to the revolutionary army. With support from Nueva Granada, Bolívar defeated the Spanish in Venezuela in 1821. Panama, which had remained under Spanish control, declared independence in 1821. Finally, Bolívar dispatched Antonio José de Sucre to take Quito in 1822, bringing an end to the Spanish rule of Nueva Granada.

GRAN COLOMBIA: A FLAWED UNION (1821-1830)

Shortly after the Battle of Boyacá, the Congress of Angostura, a city on the Río Orinoco in Venezuela, proclaimed the union of Nueva Granada, Venezuela, and Ecuador under the name of the República de Colombia. Historians refer to this entity as Gran Colombia. In 1821, while the fight for independence was still raging in parts of Venezuela and Ecuador, a constitutional congress met in Cúcuta. An ongoing debate about whether a centralist or federalist scheme was preferable resulted in a curious compromise: the República de Colombia assumed a highly centralist form, considered necessary to finish the battle for independence, but left the issue of federalism open to review after 10 years. The document was generally liberal, enshrining individual liberties and providing for the manumission of slaves, meaning that the children of slaves were born free.

Bolívar, who was born in Venezuela, was named president. Francisco de Paula Santander, who was born near Cúcuta in Nueva Granada, was named vice president. Santander had fought alongside Bolívar in the battles for independence of Nueva Granada and was seen as an able administrator. While Bolívar continued south to liberate Ecuador and Peru, Santander assumed the reins of power in Bogotá. He charted a generally liberal course, instituting public education and a curriculum that included avant-garde thinkers such as Jeremy Bentham. However, the highly centralist structure was unsavory to elites in Venezuela and Ecuador, who disliked rule from Bogotá. Shortly after the Congress of Cúcuta, revolt broke out in Venezuela and Ecuador. In 1826, Bolívar returned from Bolivia and Peru, hoping for the adoption in Gran Colombia of the Bolivian Constitution, an unusual document he drafted that called for a presidency for life.

There had been a growing distance between Bolívar and Santander: Bolívar saw Santander as an overzealous liberal reformer while Santander disliked Bolívar's authoritarian tendencies. In 1828, after a failed constitutional congress that met in Ocaña in eastern Colombia, Bolívar assumed dictatorial powers. He rolled back many of Santander's liberal reforms. In September 1828 there was an attempt on Bolívar's life in Bogotá. This was famously foiled by his companion, Manuela Sáenz. The last years of Gran Colombia were marked by revolts in various parts of the country and a war with Peru. In 1830, a further constitutional assembly was convened in Bogotá, but by that point Gran Colombia had ceased to exist: Venezuela and Ecuador had seceded. In March 1830, a physically ill Bolívar decided to leave for voluntary exile in Europe and died on his way in Santa Marta.

CIVIL WARS AND CONSTITUTIONS (1830-1902)

After the separation of Venezuela and Ecuador, what is now Colombia adopted the name República de Nueva Granada. In 1832, it adopted a new constitution that corrected many of the errors of the excessively centralist constitution of Gran Colombia. There was a semblance of stability with the orderly succession of elected presidents. The elimination of some monasteries in Pasto sparked a short civil conflict known as the Guerra de los Supremos, which lasted 1839-1842. During this war, Conservative and Liberal factions coalesced for the first time, establishing the foundation of Colombia's two-party system. Generally, the Conservative Party supported the Catholic Church, favored centralization, and followed the ideas of Bolívar. The Liberal Party supported federalism and free trade and identified with the ideas of Santander.

The country's rugged topography meant that Nueva Granada was not very integrated into the world economy. Gold, extracted mostly in Antioquia, was the main export. Most of the country eked out its subsistence from agriculture, with trade restricted within regions. This period saw some economic development, such as steam navigation on the Magdalena and Cauca Rivers, and a contract for the construction of the trans-isthmian railroad in Panama, which had yet to secede.

Midcentury saw the rise of a new class of leaders who had grown up wholly under Republican governments. They ushered in a period of liberal reform. In 1851, Congress abolished slavery. In 1853, a new constitution established universal male suffrage, religious tolerance, and direct election of provincial governors. The government reduced tariffs and Nueva Granada experienced a short export-oriented tobacco boom.

Conflicts between radical reformers within the Liberal Party, moderates, and Conservatives led to unrest in various provinces. In 1859, discontented Liberals under Tomás Cipriano de Mosquera revolted, leading to generalized civil war in which the Liberals were ultimately victorious. Once in power, they pushed radical reform. Mosquera expropriated all nonreligious church property, partly in vengeance for church support of the Conservatives in the previous civil war.

The 1863 constitution was one of the world's most audacious federalist experiments. The country was renamed the Estados Unidos de Colombia (United States of Colombia), comprising nine states. The president had a two-year term and was not immediately reelectable. All powers that were not explicitly assigned to the central government were the responsibility of the states. Many of the states engaged in true progressive policies, such as establishing public education and promoting the construction of railroads. This period coincided with agricultural booms in quinine, cotton, and indigo that, for the first time, brought limited prosperity. This period saw the establishment of the Universidad Nacional (National University) and the country's first bank.

In 1880 and then in 1884, a coalition of Conservatives and moderate Liberals, who were dissatisfied with radical policies, elected Rafael Núñez as president. Núñez tried to strengthen the power of the central government, sparking a Liberal revolt. The Conservatives were ultimately victorious and, in 1886, enacted a new centralist constitution that lasted through most of the 20th century. The country was rechristened República de Colombia, the name it has conserved since then. During the period from 1886 through 1904, known as the Regeneración, the Conservative Party held sway, rolling back many of the previous reforms, especially anticlerical measures and unrestricted male suffrage. The Liberal Party, excluded from power, revolted in 1899. The ensuing Guerra de los Mil Días (Thousand Days' War), which raged through 1902, was a terribly bloody conflict. It is not clear how many died in the war, but some historians put the figure as high as 100,000, or an incredible 2.5 percent of the country's population of four million at the time.

One year after the end of the war, Panama seceded. During the late 19th century, there had been resentment in Panama about the distribution of revenues from the transit trade that mostly were sent to Bogotá. However, in 1902 the local Panamanian elites had become alarmed at the lackadaisical attitude of the government in Bogotá regarding the construction of an interoceanic canal. After the failure of the French to build a canal, Colombia had entered into negotiations with the United States. In the closing days of the Guerra de los Mil Días, Colombia and the United States signed the Hay-Terran Treaty, which called for the construction of the canal, surrendering control over a strip of land on either side of the canal to the United States. The Americans threatened that if the treaty were not ratified, they would dig the canal in Nicaragua. Arguing that the treaty undermined Colombian sovereignty, the congress in Bogotá unanimously rejected it in August 1903. That was a big mistake: A few months later, Panama seceded with the support of the United States.

PEACE AND REFORM (1902-1946)

Under the leadership of moderate Conservative Rafael Reyes, who was president 1904-1909, Colombia entered a period of peace and stability. Reyes focused on creating a professional, nonpartisan army. He gave representation to Liberals in government, enacted a protective tariff to spur domestic industry, and pushed public works. During his administration, Bogotá was finally connected by railway to the Río Magdalena. He reestablished relations with the United States, signing a treaty that provided Colombia with an indemnity for the loss of Panama. During the 1920s and 1930s, Colombia was governed by a succession of Conservative Party presidents. Though there was often electoral fraud, constitutional reform that guaranteed minority representation ensured peace.

Expanding world demand for coffee spurred production across Colombia, especially in southern Antioquia and what is now known as the Coffee Region, creating a new class of independent farmers. Improved transportation, especially the completion of the railways from Cali to Buenaventura on the Pacific coast and from Medellín to the Río Magdalena, was key to the growth of coffee exports. In the Magdalena Medio region and in Norte de Santander, U.S. companies explored and started producing petroleum. Medellín became a center of textile manufacturing. With the country's broken geography, air transportation developed rapidly. The Sociedad Colombo Alemana de Transportes Aéreos (Colombian German Air Transportation Society) or SCADTA, the predecessor of Avianca, was founded in Barranquilla in 1919, and is reputedly the second-oldest commercial aviation company in the world (the oldest is KLM).

In 1930, a split Conservative ticket allowed the Liberals to win the elections. After being out of power for 50 years, the Liberal Party was happy to regain control of the state apparatus. This led to strife with Conservatives long accustomed to power—presaging the intense interparty violence that was to erupt 14 years later.

From 1932 to 1933, Colombia and Peru fought a brief war in the Amazon over the control of the port city of Leticia. The League of Nations brokered a truce, the first time that this body, which was a precursor to the United Nations, actively intervened in a dispute between two countries.

Starting in 1934, Liberal president Alfonso López Pumarejo undertook major social and labor reforms, with some similarities to Roosevelt's New Deal. His policies included agrarian reform, encouragement and protection of labor unions, and increased spending on education. He reduced the Catholic Church's sway over education and eliminated the literacy requirement for male voters. Many of these reforms simply returned the country to policies that had been enacted by Liberals in the 1850s, 80 years prior. In opposition to these policies, a new radical right, with a confrontational style and strains of fascism and anti-Semitism, arose under the leadership of Laureano Gómez.

During World War II, Colombia closely allied itself with the United States and eventually declared war on the Axis powers in retaliation for German attacks on Colombian merchant ships in the Caribbean Sea. The government concentrated those of German descent in a hotel in Fusagasugá near Bogotá and removed all German influence from SCADTA.

LA VIOLENCIA (1946-1953)

In the 1946 elections, the Liberal Party split its ticket between establishment-backed Gabriel Turbay and newcomer Jorge Eliécer Gaitán. Gaitán was a self-made man who had scaled the ladders of power within the Liberal Party despite the opposition of the traditional Liberal elite. He had a vaguely populist platform and much charisma. The moderate Conservative Mariano Ospina won a plurality of votes and was elected to the presidency. As in 1930, the transfer of power from Liberals to Conservatives and bureaucratic reaccommodation led to outbursts of violence.

On April 9, 1948, a deranged youth killed former presidential candidate Gaitán as he left his office in downtown Bogotá. His assassination sparked riots and bloodshed throughout the country, with severe destruction in the capital. The disturbance in Bogotá, known as El Bogotazo, occurred during the 9th Inter-American Conference, which had brought together leaders from all over the hemisphere. Young Fidel Castro happened to be in Bogotá that day, though he had no part in the upheaval.

The assassination of Gaitán further incited the violence that had started in 1946. Over the course of 10 years, an estimated 100,000-200,000 people died in what was laconically labeled La Violencia (The Violence). This conflict was comparable in destruction of human life with the Guerra de los Mil Días, the last civil war of the 19th century. The killing took place throughout the country, often in small towns and rural areas. Mostly it involved loyalists of the predominant party settling scores or intimidating members of the opposite party in order to extract land or secure economic gain. In some cases, the violence was sheer banditry. Numerous, horrific mass murders took place. The police often took sides with the Conservatives or simply turned a blind eye. In response, some Liberals resorted to armed resistance, giving birth to Colombia's first guerrilla armies. The Liberal Party boycotted the 1950 elections, and radical Conservative Laureano Gómez was elected president. His

DICTATORSHIP (1953-1957)

In 1953, with the purported aim of bringing an end to fighting between Liberals and Conservatives, the Colombian army, under the command of General Gustavo Rojas Pinilla, staged a coup. Rojas was able to reduce, but not halt, the violence, by curtailing police support of the Conservatives and by negotiating an amnesty with Liberal guerrillas. In 1954, Rojas was elected for a four-term period by a handpicked assembly. Incidentally, it was this, nondemocratically elected assembly that finally got around to extending suffrage to women, making Colombia one of the last countries in Latin America to do so. Rojas tried to build a populist regime with the support of organized labor, modeled after Perón in Argentina. His daughter, María Eugenia Rojas, though no Evita, was put in charge of social welfare programs. Though a majority of Colombians supported Rojas at first, his repressive policies and press censorship ended up alienating the political elites.

THE NATIONAL FRONT (1957-1974)

In May 1957, under the leadership of a coalition of Liberals and Conservatives, the country went on an extended general strike to oppose the dictatorship. Remarkably, Rojas voluntarily surrendered power and went into exile in Spain. As a way to put an end to La Violencia, Liberal and Conservative Party leaders proposed alternating presidential power for four consecutive terms while divvying up the bureaucracy on a 50-50 basis. The proposal, labeled the National Front, was ratified by a nationwide referendum and was in effect 1958-1974.

The National Front dramatically reduced the level of violence. After years of fighting, both factions were ready to give up their arms. During this period, thanks to competent economic management, the economy prospered and incomes rose. The government adopted import substitution policies that gave rise to a number of new industries, including automobiles.

By institutionalizing the power of the two traditional parties, the National Front had the unintended consequence of squeezing out other political movements, especially from the left. As a result, during the 1960s a number of leftist guerrilla groups appeared. Some were simply the continuation, under a new name, of the guerrilla groups formed during La Violencia. The Fuerzas Armadas Revolucionarias de Colombia (FARC) was a rural, peasant-based group espousing Soviet Marxism. The Ejército de Liberación Nacional (ELN) was a smaller group inspired by the Cuban revolution. The even smaller Ejército Popular de Liberación (EPL) was a Maoist-inspired group. The Movimiento 19 de Abril (M-19) was a more urban group formed by middle-class intellectuals after alleged electoral fraud deprived the populist ANAPO Party (Alianza Nacional Popular; created by ex-dictator Rojas) of power. During the 1970s and 1980s, the M-19 staged flashy coups, such as stealing Bolívar's sword (and promising to return it once the revolution had been achieved) in 1974 and seizing control of the embassy of the Dominican Republic in Bogotá in 1980.

UNDER SIEGE (1974-1991)
The Drug Trade and the Rise of Illegal Armed Groups

Due to its relative proximity to the United States, treacherous geography, and weak government institutions, Colombia has been an ideal place for cultivation, production, and shipment of illegal drugs, primarily to the United States. During the 1970s, Colombia experienced a short-lived marijuana boom centered on the Sierra Nevada de Santa Marta. Eradication efforts by Colombian authorities and competition from homegrown marijuana produced in the United States quickly brought this boom to an end.

During the late 1970s, cocaine replaced marijuana as the main illegal drug. Though most of the coca cultivation at the time was in Peru and Bolivia, Colombian drug dealers based in Medellín started the business of picking up coca paste in Peru and Bolivia, processing it into cocaine in Colombia, and exporting the drug to the United States, where they even controlled some distribution at the local level. At its heyday in the mid-1980s, Pablo Escobar's Medellín Cartel controlled 80 percent of the world's cocaine trade. The rival Cali Cartel, controlled by the Rodríguez brothers, emerged in the 1980s and started to contest the supremacy of the Medellín Cartel, leading to a bloody feud.

During the 1980s and 1990s, coca cultivation shifted from Peru and Bolivia to Colombia, mainly to the Amazon regions of Putumayo, Caquetá, Meta, and Guaviare. Initially, leftist guerrillas such as the FARC protected the fields from the authorities in return for payment from the cartels. Eventually, they started processing and trafficking the drugs themselves. Though the guerrillas had other sources of income, such as kidnapping and extortion, especially of oil companies operating in the Llanos, the drug trade was a key factor in their growth. With these sources of income, they no longer needed popular support and morphed into criminal organizations. By the mid-1980s, the FARC had grown into a 4,000-person-strong army that controlled large portions of territory, especially in the south of the country.

During the 1980s and 1990s, the price of land was depressed as a result of the threat posed by the guerrillas. Using their vast wealth and power of intimidation, drug traffickers purchased vast swaths of land, mostly along the Caribbean coast of Colombia, at bargain prices. To defend their properties from extortion, they allied themselves with traditional landowners to create paramilitary groups. These groups often operated with the direct or tacit support of the army.

Colombian campesinos (small farmers), caught in the middle of the conflict between guerrillas and paramilitaries, suffered disproportionately. They were accused by both guerrillas and paramilitaries of sympathizing with the enemy, and the government was not there to protect them. The paramilitaries were particularly ruthless, often ordering entire villages to abandon their lands or massacring the population. The conflict between guerrillas and paramilitaries is at the source of the mass displacement of people in Colombia. According to the Office of the United Nations High Commissioner for Refugees, the number of displaced people in Colombia ranges 3.9-5.3 million, making it the country with the most internal refugees in the world.

Peace Negotiations with the FARC and M-19

In 1982, President Belisario Betancur was elected with the promise of negotiating peace with the guerrillas. The negotiations with the guerrillas got nowhere, but the FARC did establish a political party, the Unión Patriótica (UP), which successfully participated in the 1986 presidential elections and 1988 local elections, managing to win some mayoralties. The paramilitaries and local elites did not want the political arm of the FARC to wield local power. As a result, the UP was subjected to a brutal persecution by the paramilitaries, who killed more than 1,000 party members. In the midst of this violence, Colombia suffered one of its worst natural disasters: the eruption of the Nevado del Ruiz in November 1985, which produced a massive mudslide that engulfed the town of Armero, killing more than 20,000 people.

In 1985, the M-19 brazenly seized the Palacio de Justicia in Bogotá. The Colombian army responded with a heavy hand, and in the ensuing battle, half of Colombia's Supreme Court justices were killed. Many people, including many cafeteria employees, disappeared in the army takeover, and there is speculation that they were executed and buried in a mass grave in the south of Bogotá. Weakened by this fiasco, leaders of the M-19 took up President Virgilio Barco's offer to negotiate peace. The government set down clear rules, including a cease-fire on the part of the M-19, before talks could proceed. Unlike the FARC, the M-19 was still an ideological movement. The leaders of the M-19 saw that by participating in civil life they could probably gain more than by fighting. And they were right: In 2011 the people of Bogotá elected Gustavo Petro, a former M-19 guerrilla, as their mayor. On March 19, 1990, Barco and the M-19's young leader, Carlos Pizarro, signed a peace agreement, the only major successful peace agreement to date between the authorities and a major guerrilla group.

The Rise and Fall of the Medellín Cartel

Initially, the Colombian establishment turned a blind eye to the rise of the drug cartels and even took a favorable view of the paramilitaries, who were seen as an antidote to the scourge of the guerrillas. For a time, Escobar was active in politics and cultivated a Robin Hood image, funding public works such as parks and housing projects. Rather than stick to his business, as the Cali Cartel did, Escobar started to threaten any official who tried to check his power. In 1984, he had Rodrigo Lara Bonilla, the minister of justice, assassinated. When the government subsequently cracked down, Escobar declared outright war. He assassinated judges and political leaders, set off car bombs to intimidate public opinion, and paid a reward for every policeman that was murdered in Medellín—a total of 657. To take out an enemy, he planted a bomb in an Avianca flight from Bogotá to Cali, killing all passengers on board. The Medellín Cartel planted dozens of massive bombs in Bogotá and throughout the country, terrorizing the country's population. The cartel is allegedly responsible for the assassination of three presidential candidates in 1990: Luis Carlos Galán, the staunchly anti-mafia candidate of the Liberal Party; Carlos Pizarro, the candidate of the newly demobilized M-19; and Bernardo Jaramillo, candidate of the Unión Patriótica.

There was really only one thing that Escobar feared—extradition to the United States. Through bribery and intimidation, he managed to get extradition outlawed, and he negotiated a lopsided deal with the government of César Gaviria: In return for his surrender, he was allowed to control the jail where he was locked up. From the luxurious confines of La Catedral, as the prison was named, he continued to run his empire. In 1992 there was an outcry when it became known that he had interrogated and executed enemies within the jail. When he got wind that the government planned to transfer him to another prison, he fled. In December 1993, government intelligence intercepted a phone call he made to his family, located him in Medellín, and killed him on a rooftop as he attempted to flee. It is widely believed that the Cali Cartel actively aided the authorities in the manhunt.

A New Constitution

The 1990s started on a positive footing with the enactment of a new constitution in 1991. The Constitutional Assembly that drafted the charter was drawn from all segments of the political spectrum, including the recently demobilized M-19. The new constitution was very progressive, devolving considerable power to local communities and recognizing the rights of indigenous and Afro-Colombian communities to govern their communities and ancestral lands. The charter created a powerful new Constitutional Court, which has become a stalwart defender of basic rights, as well as an independent accusatory justice system, headed by a powerful attorney general, which was created to reduce impunity.

COLOMBIA ON THE BRINK (1992-2002)
New Cartels, Paramilitaries, and Guerrillas

Drug cultivation and production increased significantly during the 1990s. The overall land dedicated to coca cultivation rose from 60,000 hectares (148,300 acres) in 1992 to 165,000 hectares (407,700 acres) in 2002. As a result of the government's successful crackdown first on the Medellín Cartel and then on the Cali Cartel, drug production split into smaller, more nimble criminal organizations. During the 1990s, the paramilitaries became stand-alone organizations that engaged in drug trafficking, expanding to more than 30,000 men in 2002. They created a national structure called the Autodefensas Unidas de Colombia, or AUC, under the leadership of Carlos

Castaño. The AUC coordinated activities with local military commanders and committed atrocious crimes, often massacring scores of so-called sympathizers of guerrillas.

At the same time, the guerrillas expanded significantly during the 1990s. Strengthened by hefty revenues from kidnapping, extortion, and drug trafficking, they grew to more than 50,000 mostly peasant fighters in 2002. Their strategy was dictated primarily by military and economic considerations and they had little to no public support. At their heyday, the FARC covered the entire country, attacking military garrisons and even threatening major urban centers such as Cali. They performed increasingly large operations, such as attacking Mitú, the capital of the department of Vaupés, in 1998 or kidnapping 12 members of the Assembly of Valle del Cauca in Cali in 2002. The FARC commanders moved around the countryside unchecked. In the territories they controlled, they ruled over civilians, often committing heinous crimes. In 2002, they attacked a church in the town of Bojayá in Chocó, killing more than 100 unarmed civilians, including many children, who had sought refuge there.

Plan Colombia

The increasing growth of drug exports from Colombia to the United States in the 1990s became a source of concern for the U.S. government. From 1994 to 1998, the United States was reluctant to provide support to Colombia because the president at the time, Ernesto Samper, was tainted by accusations of having received campaign money from drug traffickers and because of evidence about human rights abuses by the Colombian army. When Andrés Pastrana was elected president in 1998, the Colombian and U.S. administrations designed a strategy to curb drug production and counteract the insurgency called Plan Colombia. This strategy had both military and social components, and was to be financed jointly by the United States and Colombia. Ultimately, the United States provided Colombia, which was becoming one of its strongest and most loyal allies in Latin America, with more than US$7 billion, heavily weighted toward military aid, especially for training and for providing aerial mobility to Colombian troops. While the impact of Plan Colombia was not immediately visible, over time it changed the balance of power in favor of the government, allowing the Colombian army to regain the upper hand in the following years.

Flawed Peace Negotiations with the FARC

President Pastrana embarked on what is now widely believed to have been an ill-conceived, hurried peace process with the FARC. He had met Manuel Marulanda, the head of the FARC, before his inauguration in 1998 and was convinced that he could bring about a quick peace. Without a clear framework, in November 1998 he acceded to the FARC's request to grant them a demilitarized zone the size of Switzerland in the eastern departments of Meta and Caquetá. In hindsight, it seems clear that the FARC had no interest or need to negotiate as they were at the peak of their military power. Rather, the FARC commanders saw the grant of the demilitarized zone as an opportunity to strengthen their organization.

From the beginning, it became clear that the FARC did not take the peace process seriously. Marulanda failed to show up at the inaugural ceremony of the peace process, leaving a forlorn Pastrana sitting alone on the stage next to a now famous *silla vacilla* (empty seat). They ran the demilitarized zone as a mini-state, nicknamed Farclandia, using it to smuggle arms, hold kidnapped prisoners, and process cocaine. During the peace negotiations, the FARC continued their attacks on the military and civilians. In February 2002, after the FARC kidnapped Eduardo Gechem, senator and president of the Senate Peace Commission, Pastrana declared the end of this ill-advised demilitarized zone and sent in the Colombian army.

A Failed State?

In 2002, the Colombian army was battling more than 50,000 guerrillas and 30,000 paramilitaries, with an estimated 6,000 child soldiers among those groups. The insurgents controlled approximately 75 percent of the country's territory. An estimated 100,000 antipersonnel mines covered 30 of 32 departments. More than 2.5 million people had been internally displaced between 1985 and 2003, with 300,000 people displaced in 2002 alone. Not surprisingly, prestigious publications such as *Foreign Policy* described Colombia at the time as failed state.

REGAINING ITS FOOTING (2002-PRESENT)

Álvaro Uribe's Assault on the Guerrillas

In the 2002 elections, fed-up Colombians overwhelmingly elected Álvaro Uribe, a former governor of Antioquia who promised to take the fight to the guerrillas. Uribe had a real grudge against the FARC, who had assassinated his father. The FARC were not fans of his, either. In a brazen show of defiance, during Uribe's inauguration ceremony in Bogotá on August 7, 2002, the guerrilla group fired various rockets aimed at the presidential palace during a post-swearing-in reception. Several rockets struck the exterior of the palace, causing minor damage (attendees were unaware of the attack), but many more fell on the humble dwellings in barrios nearby, killing 21.

During his first term, Uribe embarked on a policy of Seguridad Democrática, or Democratic Security, based on strengthening the army, eradicating illicit crops to deprive the guerrillas of revenues, and creating a controversial network of civilian collaborators who were paid for providing tips that led to successful operations against the insurgents. The government increased military expenditure and decreed taxes on the rich totaling US$4 billion to finance the cost of the war. Colombian military personnel grew from 300,000 in 2002 to 400,000 in 2007.

From 2002 to 2003, the army evicted the FARC from the central part of the country around Bogotá and Medellín, although that did not prevent them from causing terror in the cities. In February 2003, a car bomb attributed to the FARC exploded in the parking lot of the exclusive social club El Nogal, killing more than 30 people—mostly employees. From 2004 to 2006, the army pressed the FARC in its stronghold in the southern part of the country. Aerial spraying of coca crops brought down cultivated areas from 165,000 hectares (407,700 acres) in 2002 to 76,000 hectares (187,800 acres) in 2006.

In 2006, Uribe was reelected by a landslide, after Congress amended the constitution to allow for immediate presidential reelection. There is clear evidence that the government effectively bribed two congressmen whose votes were necessary for passage of the measure. Uribe interpreted the election results as a mandate to continue single-mindedly pursuing the guerrillas. The FARC came under severe stress, with thousands of guerrillas deserting, and for the first time, the FARC was subjected to effective strikes against top commanders. No longer safe in their traditional jungle strongholds in Colombia, many FARC operatives crossed the border into Venezuela and Ecuador, causing tension between Colombia and the governments of those countries.

In early 2008, the Colombian military bombed and killed leading FARC commander Raúl Reyes in a camp in Ecuador, causing a diplomatic crisis with that country. Later that year, the military executed Operación Jaque (Operation Checkmate), a dramatic rescue operation in which they duped the FARC into handing over their most important hostages. The hostages released included three U.S. defense contractors and Ingrid Betancur, a French-Colombian independent presidential candidate who was kidnapped by the FARC during the 2002 presidential election as she proceeded by land, against the advice of the military, toward the capital of the former FARC demilitarized zone. In 2008, Manuel Marulanda, founder of the FARC, died a natural death. At that time, it was estimated that the FARC forces had plummeted to about 9,000 fighters, half of what they had been eight years before.

The Colombian army has been implicated in serious human rights abuses. Pressure from top brass to show results in the war against the guerrillas and the possibility of obtaining extended vacation time led several garrisons to execute civilians and present them as guerrillas killed in combat. In 2008, it was discovered that numerous young poor men from the city of Soacha, duped by false promises of work, had been taken to rural areas, assassinated by the army, and presented as guerrillas killed in anti-insurgency operations. This macabre episode—referred to as the scandal of *falsos positives* (false positives)—was done under the watch of Minister of Defense Juan Manuel Santos, who was later elected president of Colombia.

Peace Process with the AUC

From 2003 to 2008, the Uribe government pursued a controversial peace process with the right-wing paramilitaries, the Autodefensas Unidas de Colombia. As part of that process, an estimated 28,000 paramilitary fighters demobilized, including most of the high-level commanders. In 2005, the Colombian Congress passed the Justice and Peace Law to provide a legal framework for the process. Unlike previous peace laws that simply granted an amnesty to the insurgents, this law provided for reduced sentences for paramilitaries who had committed serious crimes in exchange for full confessions and reparation of victims. Domestic and international observers were extremely skeptical about the process, worrying that the paramilitaries would use their power to pressure for lenient terms. These misgivings were justified by evidence that they used their power of coercion to influence the results of the 2006 parliamentary elections, a scandal referred to as *parapolítica*. Many congresspersons, including a first cousin of Uribe, ended up in prison.

It soon became clear that the paramilitary commanders were not sincere in their commitment to peace. Many refused to confess crimes and transferred their assets to front men. Covertly, they continued their drug-trafficking operations. The government placed scant importance on the truth and reparation elements of the Justice and Peace Law, severely underfunding the effort to redress crimes committed against more than 150,000 victims who had signed up as part of the process. Through 2008, the paramilitaries had confessed to a mere 2,700 crimes, a fraction of the estimated total, and refused to hand over assets. Fed up with their lack of cooperation, in 2008 Uribe extradited 14 top-ranking paramilitary commanders to the United States, where they were likely to face long sentences. However, the extradition severely hampered the effort to obtain truth and reparation for the victims of their crimes.

The difficulty in redressing the crimes against victims has been further troubled by the growth of the dozens of small *bacrim (bandas criminals,* or illegal armed groups) who have taken territorial control of former paramilitary areas, intimidating victims who have returned to their rightful lands under the peace process. Many of these *bacrim* inherited the structures of the former AUC groups and employed former paramilitaries.

Social and Economic Transformation

During the past decade, Colombia has made some remarkable strides in improving social and economic conditions. Due to improved security conditions, investment, both domestic and international, has boomed, totaling almost US$80 billion from 2003 to 2012. Economic growth averaged 4.8 percent 2010-2014, a significant increase over the prior decades. The number of people below poverty, as measured by the ability to buy a wide basket of basic goods and services, has declined from 59.7 percent in 2002 to 27.8 percent in 2015. In Colombia's 13 largest cities, which represent 45 percent of the population, poverty has fallen to 18.9 percent. In terms of basic needs, most urban areas are well served in terms of education, health, electricity, water, and sewage. However, there is a wide gap between the cities and rural areas, where 30 percent of the country's population lives. As of 2013, rural poverty stood at 43 percent. Though income inequality has been slowly falling, Colombia still has one of the most unequal distributions of income in the world.

Peace with the FARC

In the 2010 elections, Uribe's former minister of defense, Juan Manuel Santos, was elected president by a large majority. Santos continued to pursue an aggressive strategy against the FARC. Army operations killed Alfonso Cano, the new leader of the FARC, as well as Víctor Julio Suárez Rojas, the guerrillas' military strategist. As evidenced in the diary of Dutch FARC member Tanya Nijmeijer, found by the Colombian army after an attack on a rebel camp, morale within the FARC had sunk to an all-time low.

At the same time, Santos recognized the need to address nonmilitary facets of the violence. In 2011, Congress passed the comprehensive Victims and Land Restitutions Law, meant to rectify Uribe's Justice and Peace Law. This law provides a framework to redress the crimes committed against all victims of violence since 1985.

After a year of secret negotiations, Santos announced the start of peace dialogues with the FARC in October 2012, first in Oslo, Norway, and then in Havana, Cuba. These have proceeded at a slow pace and have covered a large number of topics, including agrarian development and drug trafficking. Former president Uribe and his allies are against this initiative, claiming that a military defeat of the FARC is the best path forward.

In 2016, after four years of arduous negotiations, the government and the FARC agreed to comprehensive terms, which covered rural development, political participation, illegal drugs, justice for victims, and ending the armed conflict, among other topics. On September 26, 2016, the government and the FARC signed the agreement, only to have it rejected by a slim majority in a national vote. The government and the guerillas renegotiated the agreement, which was ratified on November 30, 2016, by Congress. Demobilization began in December 2016 and the guerillas are expected to hand over their weapons to the UN during the first half of 2017. President Juan Manuel Santos won the 2016 Nobel Peace Prize in honor of his efforts.

Government and Economy

Under the 1991 constitution, Colombia is organized as a republic, with three branches of power—the executive, the legislative, and the judicial. The country is divided into 32 *departamentos* (departments or provinces) and the Distrito Capital (Capital District), where Bogotá is located. The departments are in turn divided into *municipios* (municipalities). These *municipios* include towns and rural areas.

The president of the republic, who is both head of state and head of government, is elected for a four-year term. With the exception of the military dictatorship of Gen. Gustavo Rojas Pinilla from 1953 to 1957, presidents have been elected by the people since 1914. In 2005, then-president

Álvaro Uribe succeeded in changing the constitution to allow for one immediate presidential reelection. In 2009, he attempted to get the constitution changed once more to allow for a second reelection but was thwarted by the powerful Constitutional Court, which decreed that this change would break the necessary checks and balances of the constitutional framework.

Presidential elections are held every four years in May. If no candidate receives more than 50 percent of the votes, there will be a runoff election. Inauguration of the president takes place on August 7, the anniversary of the Batalla del Puente de Boyacá, which sealed Colombia's independence from Spain.

The legislative branch is made up of a bicameral legislature: the Senado (102 members) and the Cámara de Representantes (162 members). These representatives are elected every four years. Senators are voted for on a nationwide basis, while representatives are chosen for each department and the Distrito Capital. In addition, two seats in the Senate are reserved for indigenous representation. In the Cámara de Representantes, there are seats reserved for indigenous and Afro-Colombian communities as well as for Colombians who live abroad. As negotiated in 2016, the FARC will be assured 10 seats in Congress until 2022: 5 in the Senado and 5 in the Cámara de Representantes.

All Colombians over the age of 18—with the exception of active-duty military and police as well as those who are incarcerated—have the right to vote in all elections. Women only gained the right to vote in 1954.

POLITICAL PARTIES

Historically Colombia has had a two-party system: the Conservative Party and the Liberal Party. The Conservative Party has traditionally been aligned with the Catholic Church and has favored a more centralized government, and followed the ideas of Simón Bolívar. The Liberal Party favored a federal system of governing, has opposed church intervention in government affairs, and was aligned with the ideas of Gen. Francisco Paula Santander.

The hegemony of the two largest political parties came to a halt in the 2002 presidential election of rightist candidate Álvaro Uribe, who registered his own independent movement and then established a new party called El Partido de la Unidad. Since then, traditional parties have lost some influence. A third party, the Polo Democrático, became a relatively strong force in the early 2000s, capturing the mayorship of Bogotá, but has since faded, leaving no clear representative of the left.

Political parties today have become personality-oriented, and many candidates have been known to shop around for a party—or create their own—rather than adhere to the traditional parties. In 2014, President Juan Manuel Santos won a second term representing the Partido de la Unidad (known as La U), defeating a candidate allied with the founder of La U, former president Álvaro Uribe.

ECONOMY

Colombia has a thriving market economy based primarily on oil, mining, agriculture, and manufacturing. The country's GDP in 2015 was US$274 billion and per capita GDP was US$5,800, placing it as a middle-income country. Growth over the past decade has been a robust 3.29 percent. Inflation has averaged 3.8 percent in the past five years and unemployment has hovered around 10 percent.

During the colonial period and up until the early 20th century, small-scale gold mining and subsistence agriculture were the mainstays of Colombia's economy. Starting in the 1920s, coffee production spread throughout the country and rapidly became Colombia's major export good. Coffee production is of the mild arabica variety and is produced at elevations of 1,000 to 1,900 meters (roughly 3,000-6,000 feet), mostly by small farmers. During most of the 20th century, Colombia emphasized increasing the volume of production, using the Café de Colombia name and mythical coffee farmer Juan Valdez and his donkey Paquita to brand it. A severe global slump in coffee prices during the past decade has led to a reassessment of this strategy and an increasing focus on specialty coffees. Today, coffee represents only 3 percent of all Colombian exports.

Colombia's wide range of climates, from hot on the coast to temperate in the mountains, means that the country produces a wide range of products. Until recently, sugarcane production, fresh flowers, and bananas were the only major export-driven agribusiness. However, improvements in security in recent years have resulted in a boom in large-scale agricultural projects in palm oil, rubber, and soy. Cattle ranching occupies an estimated 25 percent of the country's land. Commercial forestry is relatively underdeveloped, though there is considerable illegal logging, especially on the Pacific coast.

In recent decades, oil production and mining have become major economic activities. The main center of oil production is the Llanos, the eastern plains of Colombia, with oil pipelines extending from there over the Cordillera Oriental to Caribbean ports. Oil currently represents roughly half of all Colombian exports. There are also significant natural gas deposits, mostly dedicated to residential use. Large-scale mining has been focused on coal and nickel, with large deposits in the Caribbean coastal region. With the improvement of security conditions in the past decade, many international firms, such as Anglogold Ashanti, have requested concessions for large-scale gold mining, often with opposition from the community. Illegal gold mining, often conducted with large machinery, is a severe threat to fragile ecosystems, especially in the Pacific coast rainforest.

During the postwar period, Colombia pursued an import substitution policy, fostering the growth of domestic industries such as automobiles, appliances, and petrochemical goods. Since the early 1990s, the government has been gradually opening the economy to foreign competition and tearing down tariffs. In recent years, the country has signed free-trade agreements with the United States and the European Union. Today, the country has a fairly diversified industrial sector. The country is self-sufficient in energy, with hydropower supplying the bulk of electricity needs.

Until recently, tourism was minimal because of widespread insecurity and a negative image. Things started to change in the mid-2000s, and the annual number of international visitors has increased from 600,000 in 2000 to 2.3 million in 2015. While Bogotá and Cartagena still receive the bulk of visitors, almost the entire country has opened up for tourism, though there are still pockets of no-go zones. This boom in tourism has fostered a growth of community and ecotourism options, often with the support from government. The network of *posadas nativas* (guesthouses owned and operated by locals) is one initiative to foment tourism at the community level, particularly among Afro-Colombians. In recent years, Parques Nacionales has transferred local operation of ecotourism facilities in the parks to community-based associations.

People and Culture

DEMOGRAPHY

Colombia was estimated to have had a population of a little over 48.7 million in 2016 and has the third-highest population in Latin America, behind Brazil and Mexico and slightly higher than Argentina. Around four million Colombians live outside of Colombia, mostly in the United States, Venezuela, Spain, and Ecuador. The population growth rate has fallen significantly in the past two decades and was estimated at 1.01 percent in 2016. The population of the country is relatively young, with a median age of 29.3 years. Average life expectancy is 75.5 years.

Sixty percent of the Colombian population lives in the highland Andean interior of the country, where the largest metropolitan areas are located: Bogotá (9.8 million), Medellín (3.9 million), and Cali (2.6 million). On the Caribbean coast, Barranquilla is the largest metropolitan area (2 million), followed by Cartagena (1.1 million).

It is increasingly an urban country, with around 76 percent of the population living in urban areas. This trend began during La Violencia and accelerated in the 1970s and 1980s. At least 3.9 million persons have been internally displaced due to the armed conflict in Colombia, leaving their homes in rural areas and seeking safety and economic opportunity in large cities.

Most of the population (over 84 percent) is either mestizo (having both Amerindian and white ancestry) or white. People of African (10.4 percent) and indigenous or Amerindian (over 3.4 percent) origin make up the rest of the Colombian population. There is a tiny Romani or Roma population of well under 1 percent of the population, but nonetheless they are a protected group according to the constitution.

There are more than 80 indigenous groups, with some of the largest

Happy Monday!

Colombians enjoy a long list of holidays (over 20). With a few exceptions, such as the independence celebrations on July 20 and August 7, Christmas, and New Year's Day, holidays are celebrated on the following Monday, creating a *puente* (literally bridge, or three-day weekend).

During Semana Santa and between Christmas Day and New Year's, interior cities such as Bogotá and Medellín become ghost towns as locals head to the nearest beach or to the countryside. Conversely, beach resorts, natural reserves and parks, and pueblos fill up. Along with that, room rates and airfare can increase substantially.

The following is a list of Colombian holidays, but be sure to check a Colombian calendar for precise dates. Holidays marked with an asterisk are always celebrated on the Monday following the date of the holiday.

- Año Nuevo (New Year's Day): January 1
- Día de los Reyes Magos (Epiphany)*: January 6
- Día de San José (Saint Joseph's Day)*: March 19
- Jueves Santo (Maundy Thursday): Thursday before Easter Sunday
- Viernes Santo (Good Friday): Friday before Easter Sunday
- Día de Trabajo (International Workers' Day): May 1
- Ascensión (Ascension)*: Six weeks and one day after Easter Sunday
- Corpus Christi*: Nine weeks and one day after Easter Sunday
- Sagrado Corazón (Sacred Heart)*: Ten weeks and one day after Easter Sunday
- San Pedro y San Pablo (Saint Peter and Saint Paul)*: June 29
- Día de la Independencia (Independence Day): July 20
- Batalla de Boyacá (Battle of Boyacá): August 7
- La Asunción (Assumption of Mary)*: August 15
- Día de la Raza (equivalent of Columbus Day)*: October 12
- Todos Los Santos (All Saint's Day)*: November 1
- Día de la Independencia de Cartagena (Cartagena Independence Day)*: November 11
- La Inmaculada Concepción (Immaculate Conception): December 8
- Navidad (Christmas): December 25

being the Wayúu, who make up the majority in La Guajira department; the Nasa, from Cauca; the Emberá, who live in the isolated jungles of the Chocó department, and the Pastos, in Nariño. Departments in the Amazon region have the highest percentages of indigenous residents. In Vaupés, for example, 66 percent of the population is of indigenous background. Many indigenous people live on *resguardos*, areas that are collectively owned and administered by the communities.

Afro-Colombians, descendants of slaves who arrived primarily via Spanish slave trade centers in the Caribbean, mostly live along both Pacific and Caribbean coasts and in the San Andrés Archipelago. Chocó has the highest percentage of Afro-Colombians (83 percent), followed by San Andrés and Providencia (57 percent), Bolívar (28 percent), Valle del Cauca (22 percent), and Cauca (22 percent). Cali, Cartagena, and Buenaventura have particularly large Afro-Colombian populations. In the Americas, Colombia has the third-highest number of citizens of African origin, behind Brazil and the United States.

While Colombia has not attracted large numbers of immigrants, there have been periods in which the country opened its doors to newcomers. In the early 20th century, immigrants from the Middle East—specifically from Lebanon, Syria, and Palestine—arrived, settling mostly along the Caribbean coast, especially in the cities of Barranquilla, Santa Marta, Cartagena, and Maicao in La Guajira. From 1920 to 1950, a sizable number of Sephardic and Ashkenazi Jews immigrated. Colombia has not had a large immigration from Asia, although in the early 20th century there was a small immigration of Japanese to the Cali area.

RELIGION

Over 90 percent of Colombians identify as Roman Catholics, and it has been the dominant religion since the arrival of the Spaniards. The numbers of evangelical Christians, called simply *cristianos*, continue to grow, and there are other Christian congregations, including Mormons and Jehovah's Witnesses, but their numbers are small. In San Andrés and Providencia, the native Raizal population—of African descent—is mostly Baptist.

The Jewish community—estimated at around 5,000 families—is concentrated in the large cities, such as Bogotá, Medellín, Cali, and Barranquilla. There are significant Muslim communities, especially along the Caribbean coast, and there are mosques in Barranquilla, Santa Marta, Valledupar, Maicao (La Guajira), San Andrés, and Bogotá.

Semana Santa—Holy or Easter Week—is the most important religious festival in the country, and Catholics in every village, town, and city commemorate the week with a series of processions and masses. The colonial cities of Popayán, Mompox, Tunja, and Pamplona are known for their elaborate Semana Santa processions. Popayán and Mompox in particular attract pilgrims and tourists from Colombia and beyond. In cities such as Bogotá, Cali, and Cartagena, there are multitudinous processions to

Gay Rights in Colombia

In a country still struggling with armed conflict and basic human rights, it might come as a surprise that gay and lesbian rights have not been pushed aside. Colombia has some of the most progressive laws regarding the rights of LGBT people in the western hemisphere. Since 2007, same-sex partners have enjoyed full civil union rights with a wide range of benefits, such as immigration, inheritance, and social security rights.

However, when it comes to marriage, it's a little more complicated. In 2016, the top judicial body, the Colombian Constitutional Court, legalized marriage and adoption by same-sex couples. These rulings created a backlash with conservative politicians, who have vowed to hold a referendum to block the marriage and adoption rights.

---

mountaintop religious sites, such as Monserrate, the Cerro de la Cruz, and El Monasterio de la Popa, respectively.

LANGUAGE

Spanish is the official language in Colombia. In the San Andrés Archipelago, English is still spoken by native islanders who arrived from former English colonies after the abolition of slavery, but Spanish has gained prominence.

According to the Ministry of Culture, there are at least 68 native languages, which are spoken by around 850,000 people. These include 65 indigenous languages, two Afro-Colombian languages, and Romani, which is spoken by the small Roma population.

Three indigenous languages have over 50,000 speakers: Wayúu, primarily spoken in La Guajira; Páez, primarily spoken in Cauca; and Emberá, primarily spoken in Chocó.

Essentials

Getting There 148	Travel Tips 154
Getting Around............... 149	Health and Safety............. 156
Visas and Officialdom.......... 152	Information and Services 159
Accommodations and Food.... 153	

Getting There

AIR

Most visitors to Colombia arrive by air at the **Aeropuerto Internacional El Dorado** in Bogotá, with some carrying on from there to other destinations in the country. There are also nonstop international flights to the **Aeropuerto Internacional José María Córdova** in Medellín and to the airports in Cali, Cartagena, Barranquilla, and Armenia.

From North America

Avianca (www.avianca.com) has nonstop flights between Bogotá and Miami, Fort Lauderdale, Orlando, Washington, Los Angeles, and New York-JFK. From Miami there are also nonstops to Medellín, Cali, Barranquilla, and Cartagena.

American (www.american.com) flies between Miami and Dallas and Bogotá; Miami and Medellín; and Cali and Medellín. **Delta** (www.delta.com) flies from Atlanta and New York-JFK to Bogotá; they also fly between Atlanta and Cartagena. **United** (www.united.com) has flights from Newark and Houston to Bogotá.

JetBlue (www.jetblue.com) has nonstop service to Bogotá from Orlando and Fort Lauderdale; to Cartagena from New York and Fort Lauderdale; and to Medellín from Fort Lauderdale. **Spirit** (www.spirit.com) has flights from Fort Lauderdale to Bogotá, Medellín, Cartagena, and Armenia.

Air Canada (www.aircanada.com) operates nonstop flights from Toronto to Bogotá. **Air Transat** (www.airtransat.com) provides seasonal service to Cartagena and San Andrés from Montreal.

From Europe

Avianca (www.avianca.com) has service to Bogotá and Medellín from Madrid and Barcelona, and between Bogotá and London. **Air France** (www.airfrance.com) flies from Paris to Bogotá. **Iberia** (www.iberia.com) serves Bogotá from Madrid, as does **Air Europa** (www.aireuropa.com). **Lufthansa** (www.lufthansa.com) offers service between Bogotá and Frankfurt. **Turkish Airlines** (www.turkishairlines.com) flies between Bogotá and Istanbul. **KLM** (www.klm.com) serves Amsterdam from Bogotá with a stopover in Cali.

From Latin America

Avianca (www.avianca.com) flies to Bogotá from many capitals in Latin America, including Buenos Aires, São Paulo, Rio de Janeiro, Valencia, Caracas, Lima, Santiago, and La Paz in South America; Cancún, Guatemala

Previous: Medellín's efficient Metro; Jeep Willys at the ready in Salento.

City, Mexico City, San José, San Juan, San Salvador, and Panama City in Central America; and Havana, Santo Domingo, Punta Cana, Aruba, and Curaçao in the Caribbean. Aerolíneas Argentinas, AeroGal, Aeromexico, Air Insel, Conviasa, Copa, Cubana, LATAM, Gol, TACA, and Tiara Air Aruba also have connections to Colombia.

CAR OR MOTORCYCLE

A growing number of travelers drive into Colombia in their own car or with a rented vehicle. The most common point of entry is at the city of Ipiales on the Pan-American Highway, the site of the Rumichaca border crossing with Ecuador at Ipiales (Tulcán on the Ecuador side). This entry point is open 5am-10pm daily.

On the Venezuelan side, the border at Cúcuta and San Antonio del Táchira is open 24 hours a day. Although there are other border crossings with Venezuela, this is the recommended overland point of entry.

For those taking the Pan-American Highway southbound, note that you will run out of pavement in Panama. In the Darién Gap, the road is interrupted by the Darién mountain range. The road picks up again in the town of Turbo on the Golfo de Urabá. Many travelers ship their vehicle from Panama City to Cartagena, which is not difficult to arrange, and will set you back about $1,000 USD. It takes about 10 days to be able to retrieve your vehicle in Cartagena.

BUS

Frequent buses depart Quito bound for Cali (20 hours) or Bogotá (30 hours). You can also take a taxi from the town of Tulcán to the border at Ipiales and from there take an onward bus to Pasto, Popayán, Cali, or beyond. In Quito contact **Líneas de los Andes** (www.lineasdelosandes.com.co).

Getting Around

AIR

Air travel is an excellent, quick, and, thanks to discount airlines such as VivaColombia, economical way to travel within Colombia. Flying is the best option for those looking to avoid spending double-digit hours in a bus or for those with a short amount of time—and sometimes it's cheaper than taking a bus, as well. Airlines have excellent track records and maintain modern fleets.

Bogotá is the major hub in the country, with the majority of domestic **Avianca** (tel. 1/401-3434, www.avianca.com) flights departing from the Puente Aéreo terminal (not the main terminal of the adjacent international airport). Other domestic carriers **LATAM Airlines** (Colombian toll-free tel. 01/800-094-9490, www.latam.com), **VivaColombia** (tel. 1/489-7989, www.vivacolombia.co), **EasyFly** (tel. 1/414-8111, www.easyfly.com.co), **Satena**

(Colombian toll-free tel. 01/800-091-2034, www.satena.com), and **Copa** (Colombian toll-free tel. 01/800-011-0808, www.copaair.com) fly out of the new domestic wing of the international airport.

Medellín has two airports: **Aeropuerto Internacional José María Córdova** (in Rionegro) and **Aeropuerto Olaya Herrera.** All international flights and most large airplane flights depart from Rionegro, a town about an hour away from Medellín. The airport is simply referred to as "Rionegro." **Satena** (Colombian toll-free tel. 01/800-091-2034, www.satena.com) and **Aerolíneas de Antioquia-ADA** (Colombian toll-free tel. 01/800-051-4232, www.ada-aero.com) use the Olaya Herrera airport, which is conveniently located in town. This is a hub for flights to remote communities in the western and Pacific region, including Acandí and Capurganá near the Panamanian border.

For Leticia in the Amazon, the Pacific coast destinations of Bahía Solano and Nuquí, La Macarena (Caño Cristales) in Los Llanos, and San Andrés and Providencia in the Caribbean, the only viable way to get there is by air.

If you plan to fly to Caribbean destinations such as Cartagena, San Andrés, Providencia, and Santa Marta during high tourist season, be sure to purchase your ticket well in advance, as seats quickly sell out and prices go through the roof. If your destination is Cartagena or Santa Marta, be sure to check fares to Barranquilla. These may be less expensive, and that city is only about an hour away. Similarly, if you plan to go to the Carnaval de Barranquilla in February, check fares to both Cartagena and Santa Marta. If you are flying to the Coffee Region, inquire about flights to Pereira, Armenia, and Manizales, as the distances between these cities are short. The Manizales airport, however, is often closed due to inclement weather.

LONG-DISTANCE BUS

In order to thoroughly cover the country, you will have to hop on a bus at some point—just like the vast majority of Colombians. This is the money-saving choice and often the only option for getting to smaller communities. There are different types of buses, from large coaches for long-distance travel to *colectivos* for shorter distances. *Colectivos* (minivans) are often much quicker, although you won't have much legroom. There are also shared taxis that run between towns, a cramped but quick option. During major holidays, purchase bus tickets in advance if you can, as buses can quickly fill up.

When you arrive at a bus station with guidebook in hand and backpack on, you will be swarmed by touts barking out city names to you, desperately seeking your business on their bus. You can go with the flow and follow them, or, if you prefer a little more control and calm, you can instead walk past them to the ticket booths. Forge ahead and shake your head while saying *gracias*. You can try to negotiate better fares at the ticket booths, as there are often various options for traveling the same route. Find out what time the bus is leaving, if the vehicle is a big bus, a *buseta*, or minivan, and where your seat is located (try not to get stuck in the last row).

Be alert and aware of your surroundings and of your possessions when you arrive at bus stations, are waiting in the bus terminal, and are on board buses. Try to avoid flashing around expensive gadgets and cameras while on board. If you check luggage, request a receipt. During pit stops along the way, be sure to keep your valuables with you at all times.

During most bus rides of more than a few hours' length, you will be subjected to loud and/or violent films. Earplugs, eye masks, and even sleeping pills available at most pharmacies for those long journeys may come in handy, but make sure your possessions are well guarded. Expect the air-conditioning to be cranked to full blast, so have a layer or two at the ready. Pick up some provisions like apples or nuts before departing, because food options are generally unhealthy.

Bus drivers like to drive as fast as possible, and generally have few qualms about overtaking cars even on hairpin curves. Large buses tend to be safer than smaller ones, if only because they can't go as fast.

Buses may be stopped by police, and you may be required to show or temporarily hand over your passport (keep it handy). Sometimes passengers may be asked to disembark from the bus so that the police can search it for illegal drugs or other contraband. Young males may be given a pat-down. Even if it annoys you, it is always best to keep cool and remain courteous with police officers who are just doing their job.

CAR, MOTORCYCLE, OR BICYCLE

Although conditions are improving, driving in Colombia is generally a poor idea for international tourists. Roads are often in a poor state and are almost always just two lanes, speed limits and basic driving norms are not respected, driving through large towns and cities can be supremely stressful, signage is poor, sudden mudslides can close roads for hours on end during rainy seasons, and roads can be unsafe at night.

One exception is the Coffee Region, where the roads are excellent and often four lanes, distances are short, and traffic is manageable. If you are planning on spending some time visiting coffee farms and idyllic towns, this might be a good option.

There are car rental offices in all the major airports in the country. **Hertz** (tel. 1/756-0600, www.rentacarcolombia.co) and the national **Colombia Car Rental** (U.S. tel. 913/368-0091, www.colombiacarsrental.com) are two with various offices nationwide.

Touring Colombia on motorcycle is an increasingly popular option. One of the best motorcycle travel agencies in the country is **Motolombia** (tel. 2/665-9548, www.motolombia.com), based in Cali. A growing number of travelers are motoring the Pan-American Highway, shipping their bikes from Panama or the United States to Cartagena, or vice versa.

Every Sunday in cities across Colombia thousands of cyclists (joggers, skaters, and dog walkers, too) head to the city streets for some fresh air and exercise. This is the **Ciclovía,** an initiative that began in Bogotá in which city streets are closed to traffic. It may be difficult to find a bike rental place, but you can still head out for a jog.

Visas and Officialdom

PASSPORTS AND VISAS

U.S. and Canadian citizens do not need a visa for visits to Colombia of less than 90 days. You may be asked to show a return ticket.

There is an exit tax (Tasa Aeroportuaria Internacional) of around US$37 (COP$122,000). This is often automatically tacked onto your ticket price, but the airline agents will let you know upon check-in. If you are visiting for under 60 days, you are exempt. Prior to check-in, inquire with the airline if you qualify for an exemption. You may be directed to the Aeronáutica Civil booth across from the airline check-in counter, where you'll show your passport to get an exemption stamp.

To renew a tourist visa, you must go to an office of **Migración Colombia** (www.migracioncolombia.gov.co) to request an extension of another 90 days.

CUSTOMS

Upon arrival in Colombia, bags will be spot-checked by customs authorities. Duty-free items up to a value of US$1,500 can be brought in to Colombia. Firearms are not allowed into the country, and many animal and vegetable products are not allowed. If you are carrying over US$10,000 in cash you must declare it.

Departing Colombia, expect a pat-down by police (looking for illegal drugs?) at the airport. In addition, luggage may be screened for drugs, art, and exotic animals.

EMBASSIES AND CONSULATES

The **United States Embassy** (Cl. 24 Bis No. 48-50, tel. 1/275-2000, http://bogota.usembassy.gov) is in Bogotá, near the airport. In case of an emergency, during business hours contact the **U.S. Citizen Services Hotline** (business hours tel. 1/275-2000, after-hours and weekends tel. 1/275-4021). Non-emergency calls are answered at the American Citizen Services Section from Monday through Thursday 2pm-4pm. To be informed of security developments or emergencies during your visit, you can enroll in the Smart Traveler Enrollment Program (STEP) on the U.S. Embassy website. In Barranquilla, there is a **Consular Agency Office** (Cl. 77B No. 57-141, Suite 511, tel. 5/353-2001 or tel. 5/353-2182), but its hours and services are limited.

The **Canadian Embassy** (Cra. 7 No. 114-33, Piso 14, tel. 1/657-9800, www.canadainternational.gc.ca) is in Bogotá. There is a **Canadian Consular Office** (Bocagrande Edificio Centro Ejecutivo Oficina 1103, Cra. 3, No. 8-129, tel. 5/665-5838) in Cartagena. For emergencies, Canadian citizens can call the **emergency hotline** (Can. tel. 613/996-8885) in Canada collect.

Accommodations and Food

Most hotels include free wireless Internet and breakfast (although the food quality will vary). While all the fancy hotels and backpacker places have English-speaking staff—at least at the front desk—smaller hotels may not. Room rates usually depend on the number of occupants, not the size of the room. Except for some international chains and upper-end hotels, most hotels will not have heating or air-conditioning in their rooms.

Note that *moteles* are always, *residencias* are usually, and *hospedajes* are sometimes Colombian love hotels.

VALUE-ADDED TAX EXEMPTION

Non-Colombian visitors are exempt from IVA, a sales tax, which is around 16 percent. To qualify for the exemption, you must make your hotel reservation by email or phone from abroad, there must be at least two services included (such as the room fee and an included breakfast), and you must show proof of being in Colombia for less than six months.

HOTELS

Midrange hotels are often harder to find and their quality can be unpredictable. Beds can be uncomfortable, rooms may be small, views might be unappealing, and service hit-or-miss. Spanish is the most prevalent language spoken at these types of accommodations.

High-end hotels, including international brands, are in all large cities. In tourist centers such as Cartagena and Santa Marta, boutique hotels are good options for those seeking charm. Expect courteous service and comfort. The only place to expect international television channels and access for travelers with disabilities are at high-end international hotels.

HOSTELS

Hostels catering to backpackers are a relatively new phenomenon, and more are offering private rooms for those not interested in sharing a dorm room with strangers. Young people are drawn to hostels, but an increasing number of older travelers opt for hostels, as these, in addition to offering budget accommodations, are also the best places for information on activities. Most hostel staff speak English. **Hostel Trail** (www.hosteltrail.com) is a good resource for information on Colombian hostels. Hostels generally maintain updated information on their Facebook pages.

FOOD AND DRINK

In the major cities, a 10 percent tip is usually included in the price of a meal, but it is a requirement for the server to ask to include it. You can say no, but that would be considered harsh. If you are truly impressed with the service, you can always leave a little additional on the table.

In the Medellín area, the famed and hearty *bandeja paisa* is a dish made of red beans cooked with pork, white rice, ground meat, *chicharrón* (fried pork rinds), fried egg, plantains (*patacones*), chorizo, *hogao* sauce, *morcilla* (black pudding), avocado, and lemon. Eat what you can, but foreigners are forgiven if they can't finish a plate.

Vegetarians have decent options available to them, especially in tourist centers. A can of lentils can be a helpful travel companion in rural areas. In coastal areas it will be hard to avoid eating fish.

Be sure to try the many unusual fruits and juices in Colombia. Juice is either served in water or in milk, and sometimes has a lot of sugar. The same goes for freshly squeezed lemonade.

Breakfast almost universally consists of eggs, bread or arepas, juice, and coffee. Fresh fruit is not that common at breakfast. Arepas are important in Colombia: Every region has its own take on these starchy corn cakes. Arepas in Medellín are large, thin, and bland, while arepas in other parts of the country can be cheese-filled.

Travel Tips

ACCESS FOR TRAVELERS WITH DISABILITIES

Only international and some national hotel chains offer rooms (usually just one or two) that are wheelchair-accessible. Hostels and small hotels in secondary cities or towns will not. Airport and airline staff will usually bend over backwards to help those with disabilities, if you ask.

Getting around cities and towns is complicated, as good sidewalks and ramps are the exception, not the rule. Motorists may not stop—or even slow down—for pedestrians.

WOMEN TRAVELING ALONE

Women traveling alone should expect to be on the receiving end of flirting and various friendly offers by men and curiosity by everyone. Women should be extra cautious in taxis and buses. Always order taxis by phone and avoid taking them alone at night. Don't reveal personal information, where you are staying, or where you are going to inquisitive strangers.

GAY AND LESBIAN TRAVELERS

Colombia has some of the western hemisphere's most progressive laws regarding the rights of LGBT people. The Constitutional Court legalized same-sex marriage and adoption in 2016 after a torturous, decades-long struggle marked by court victories, legislative defeats, and much debate.

Colombia is a fairly tolerant country, especially in its large cities. Bogotá is one of the most gay-friendly cities on the continent, with a large gay nightlife scene and city-supported LGBT community centers. In many neighborhoods, passersby don't blink an eye when they see a gay couple holding hands on the sidewalk. The online guide **Guia GAY Colombia** (www.guiagaycolombia.com) has a listing of meeting places for LGBT people throughout the country.

Discrimination, especially against transgender people and even more so against trans sex workers, continues to be a problem in many cities and towns. The award-winning nonprofit group **Colombia Diversa** (www.colombiadiversa.org) is the main advocate for LGBT rights in the country.

Gay men in particular should be cautious using dating apps, keep an eye on drinks at nightclubs, and avoid cabs off the street when departing clubs.

Same-sex couples should not hesitate to insist on *matrimonial* (double) beds at hotels. Most hotels in cities and even in smaller towns and rural areas are becoming more clued in on this. At guesthouses, hostels, and at some midsized hotels, front desk staff may charge if you invite a guest to the room. At large international hotels and at apartments for rent, this is never the case.

CONDUCT AND CUSTOMS

Colombians are generally friendly to visitors and are often inquisitive about where you are from and how you like Colombia so far. This is most often the case in rural areas. Colombians are also quite proud of their country, after emerging from decades of armed conflict.

With acquaintances and strangers alike, it is customary to ask how someone is doing before moving on to other business. You're even expected to issue a blanket *buenos días* ("Good morning") in the elevator. When greeting an acquaintance, it's customary to shake hands (between men) or give an air kiss on the cheek (for women), although this is mostly the case in urban areas, especially with the upper crust.

Colombians are comfortable with noise—expect the TV to always be on and music blasting almost everywhere. Many Colombians you meet will ask about your family. Family ties are very important to Colombians. Sundays often mean lunch in the countryside with nuclear and extended family members.

While tourists get a pass on appearance, it's preferred that men avoid wearing shorts, especially at restaurants, except on the Caribbean coast. Dress up, like the locals do, when going out on the town.

Indigenous cultures are much more conservative, and women are expected to refrain from showing much skin.

Health and Safety

VACCINATIONS

There are no vaccination requirements for travel to Colombia. At present, proof of vaccination is no longer required in the national parks (namely Parque Nacional Natural Tayrona). However, having proof of vaccination may make life easier, especially if you plan on traveling onward to Brazil or other countries.

The Centers for Disease Control (CDC) recommends that travelers to Colombia get up-to-date on the following vaccines: measles-mumps-rubella (MMR), diphtheria-tetanus-pertussis, varicella (chicken pox), polio, and the yearly flu shot.

DISEASES AND ILLNESSES
Malaria, Zika, Chikungunya, and Dengue Fever

In low-lying tropical areas of Colombia, mosquito-borne illnesses such as malaria, dengue fever, chikungunya, and Zika are common. It is best to assume that there is a risk, albeit quite small, in all areas of the country.

Malaria is a concern in the entire Amazon region and in the lowland departments of Antioquia, Chocó, Córdoba, Nariño, and Bolívar. There is low to no malarial risk in Cartagena and in areas above 1,600 meters (5,000 feet). The Colombian Ministry of Health estimates that there are around 63,000 annual cases of malaria in the country, 20 of which result in death. Most at risk are children under the age of 15. Malaria symptoms include fever, headache, chills, vomiting, fatigue, and difficulty breathing. Treatment involves the administration of various antimalarial drugs. If you plan on spending a lot of time outdoors in lowland tropical areas, consider taking an antimalarial chemoprophylaxis.

The number of cases of **dengue fever** in Colombia has grown from 5.2 cases per 100,000 residents in the 1990s to around 18.1 cases per 100,000 in the 2000s. It is another mosquito-borne illness. The most common symptoms of dengue fever are fever; headaches; muscle, bone, and joint pain; and pain behind the eyes. It is fatal in less than 1 percent of the cases. Treatment usually involves rest and hydration and the administration of pain relievers for headache and muscle pain. **Chikungunya virus** has similar symptoms to dengue, and an infection, involving painful aches, can last for several months. It is spread, like dengue, by the *Aedes aegypti* mosquito, often during daytime.

Zika virus is the latest scare to grip South America, and is a concern to pregnant women, as there is a link between the virus and birth defects. Pregnant women should avoid traveling to low-lying areas (under 2,000 meters/6,000 feet), where Zika is present. This includes much of Colombia. Symptoms include fever, rash, joint pains, and conjunctivitis.

The Centers for Disease Control (www.cdc.gov) remains the best resource on health concerns for worldwide travel.

PREVENTION

Use mosquito nets over beds when visiting tropical areas of Colombia. Examine them well before using, and if you notice large holes in the nets request replacements. Mosquitoes tend to be at their worst at dawn, dusk, and in the evenings. Wear lightweight, long-sleeved, and light-colored shirts, long pants, and socks, and keep some insect repellent handy.

DEET is considered effective in preventing mosquito bites, but there are other, less-toxic alternatives, most available from online retailers.

If you go to the Amazon region, especially during rainy seasons, take an antimalarial prophylaxis starting 15 days before arrival, and continuing 15 days after departing the region. According to the CDC, the recommended chemoprophylaxis for visitors to malarial regions of Colombia is atovaquone-proguanil, doxycycline, or mefloquine. These drugs are available at most pharmacies in Colombia with no prescription necessary.

Traveler's Diarrhea

Stomach flu or traveler's diarrhea is a common malady when traveling through Colombia. These are usually caused by food contamination resulting from the presence of *E. coli* bacteria. Street foods, including undercooked meat, raw vegetables, dairy products, and ice, are some of the main culprits. If you get a case of traveler's diarrhea, be sure to drink lots of clear liquids, avoid caffeine, and take an oral rehydration solution of salt, sugar, and water.

Tap Water

Tap water is fine to drink in Colombia's major cities, but you should drink bottled, purified, or boiled water in the Amazon, the Pacific coast, the Darién Gap, La Guajira, and San Andrés and Providencia. As an alternative to buying plastic bottles, look for *bolsitas* (bags) of water. They come in a variety of sizes and use less plastic.

MEDICAL SERVICES

Colombia has excellent hospitals in its major cities. Over 20 hospitals in Colombia have been listed in the *América Economía* magazine listing of the top 40 hospitals of Latin America. Four hospitals were in the top 10. For sexual and reproductive health issues, **Profamilia** (www.profamilia.org.co) has a large network of clinics that provide walk-in and low-cost services throughout the country.

Aerosanidad SAS (tel. 1/439-7080, 24-hour hotline tel. 1/266-2247 or tel. 1/439-7080, www.aerosanidadsas.com) provides transportation services for ill or injured persons in remote locations of Colombia to medical facilities in the large cities.

Travel insurance is a good idea to purchase before arriving in Colombia, especially if you plan on doing a lot of outdoor adventures. One recommended provider of travel insurance is **Assist Card** (www.assist-card.com).

Before taking a paragliding ride or white-water rafting trip inquire to see whether insurance is included in the price of the trip—it should be.

CRIME

Colombia is safe to visit, and the majority of visitors have a wonderful experience in the country. For international travelers, there is little to worry about when it comes to illegal armed groups today. The threat of kidnapping of civilians and visitors has been almost completely eliminated. For updated travel advisories, check the website of the **U.S. Embassy** (http://bogota.usembassy.gov/) in Bogotá. The embassy always errs on the side of caution.

Street Crime

Cell phone theft continues to plague much of the country. Keep wallets in front pockets, be aware of your surroundings, and keep shopping bags and backpacks near you at all times. Muggings in major cities are not unheard of, but are quite rare. Be alert to your surroundings late at night.

Always order cabs instead of hailing them off the street. Fortunately, taxi crimes have diminished greatly in recent years, in no small part due to the advent of apps like Uber and Easy Taxi.

Police

From just about anywhere in the country, the police can be reached by dialing 123 on any phone. Otherwise, many parks are home to neighborhood police stations, called CAI (Centros de Atención Inmediata). Authorities may not be able to do much about petty theft, however.

Recreational Drugs

In Colombia, the legal status of the use, transport, and possession of recreational drugs can be best described as murky. A 1994 high court decision legalized a "personal dose" of recreational drugs for adults. The sale of drugs is prohibited. An attempt by President Uribe to criminalize recreational drugs failed in 2005. In practice, police may harass those caught with drugs, in addition to confiscating drugs, and may solicit bribes.

Medical use of marijuana was legalized in 2015.

Information and Services

MONEY
Currency
Colombia's official currency is the peso, which is abbreviated as COP. Prices in Colombia are marked with a dollar sign, but remember that you're seeing the price in Colombian pesos. COP$1,000,000 isn't enough to buy a house in Colombia, but it will usually cover a few nights in a nice hotel!

Bills in Colombia are in denominations of $1,000, $2,000, $5,000, $10,000, $20,000, $50,000, and $100,000. Some of the bills got a makeover in 2016, so you may see two different versions of the same amount. Coins in Colombia are in denominations of $50, $100, $200, $500, and $1,000. The equivalent of cents is *centavos* in Colombian Spanish.

Due to dropping oil prices, the Colombian peso has devalued to record levels, making the country a bargain for international visitors. In 2016, one US dollar was the equivalent of COP$3,000.

Most banks in Colombia do not exchange money. For that, you'll have to go to an exchange bank, located in all major cities. There are money changers on the streets of Cartagena, but the street is not the best place for safe and honest transactions.

Travelers checks are not worth the hassle, as they are hard to cash. Dollars are sometimes accepted in Cartagena and other major tourist destinations. To have cash wired to you from abroad, look for a Western Union office. These are located only in major cities.

Counterfeit bills are a problem in Colombia, and unsuspecting international visitors are often the recipients. Bar staff, taxi drivers, and street vendors are the most common culprits. It's good to always have a stash of small bills to avoid getting large bills back as change. Tattered and torn bills will also be passed off to you, which could pose a problem. Try not to accept those.

Consignaciones
Consignaciones (bank transfers) are a common way to pay for hotel reservations (especially in areas such as Providencia and remote resorts), tour packages or guides, or entry to national parks. It's often a pain to make these deposits in person, as the world of banking can be confusing for non-Colombians. On the plus side, making a deposit directly into the hotel's bank account provides some peace of mind because it will diminish the need to carry large amounts of cash. To make a *consignación* you will need to know the recipient's bank account and whether that is a *corriente* (checking) or *ahorros* (savings) account, and you will need to show some identification and probably have to provide a fingerprint. Be sure to hold onto the receipt to notify the recipient of your deposit.

ATMs

The best way to get cash is to use your bank ATM card. These are almost universally accepted at *cajeros automáticos* (ATMs) in the country. *Cajeros* are almost everywhere except in the smallest of towns or in remote areas. Withdrawal fees are relatively expensive, although they vary. You can usually take out up to around COP$300,000-500,000 (the equivalent of around US$150-250) per transaction. Many banks place limits on how much one can withdraw in a day (COP$1,000,000).

Credit and Debit Cards

Credit and debit card use is becoming more prevalent in Colombia; however, online credit card transactions are still not so common except for the major airlines and some of the event ticket companies, such as www.tuboleta.com or www.colboletos.com. When you use your plastic, you will be asked if it's *credito* (credit) or *debito* (debit). If using a *tarjeta de credito* (credit card) in restaurants and stores, you will be asked something like, *"¿Cuantas cuotas?"* or *"¿Numero de cuotas?"* ("How many installments?"). Most visitors prefer one *cuota* (*"Una, por favor"*). But you can have even your dinner bill paid in up to 24 installments! If using a *tarjeta de debito*, you'll be asked if it is a *corriente* (checking) or *ahorros* (savings) account.

Tipping

In most sit-down restaurants in larger cities, a 10 percent service charge is automatically included in the bill. Waitstaff are required to ask you, *"¿Desea incluir el servicio?"* ("Would you like to include the service in the bill?"). Many times restaurant staff neglect to ask international tourists about the service inclusion. If you find the service to be exceptional, you can leave a little extra in cash. Although tipping is not expected in bars or cafés, tip jars are becoming more common. International visitors are often expected to tip more than Colombians. In small-town restaurants throughout the country, tipping is not the norm.

It is not customary to tip taxi drivers. But if you feel the driver was a good one who drove safely and was honest, or if he or she made an additional stop for you, waited for you, or was just pleasant, you can always round up the bill (instead of COP$6,200 give the driver COP$7,000 and say *"Quédese con las vueltas por favor"* ("Keep the change"). Note that sometimes a "tip" is already included in the fare for non-Colombian visitors!

In hotels, usually a tip of COP$5,000 will suffice for porters who help with luggage, unless you have lots of stuff. Tips are not expected, but are certainly welcome, for housekeeping staff.

Value-Added Tax

Non-Colombian visitors are entitled to a refund of value-added taxes for purchases on clothing, jewelry, and other items if their purchases total more than COP$300,000. Save all credit card receipts and fill out Form 1344 (available online at www.dian.gov.co). Submit this to the **DIAN office** (tel.

1/607-9999) at the airport before departure. You may have several hoops to go through to achieve success. Go to the DIAN office before checking your luggage, as you will have to present the items you purchased.

INTERNET AND TELEPHONES

Being connected makes travel throughout Colombia so much easier. Free Wi-Fi is available at most hotels, restaurants, and cafés in major cities. An important Spanish phrase to learn is "*Como es la contraseña para el wifi?*" ("What's the password for the Wi-Fi?")

Obtaining a SIM card for your cell phone will ensure connectivity in all but the most remote locations. Sometimes low-tech phones work better than smartphones in very rural or remote locations like Providencia. SIM cards (*datos de prepago*) are available at mobile-phone carriers in all major towns and cities. Three main cell phone companies are Claro, Movistar, and Tigo.

Facebook and Whatsapp are often the best bets for contacting hotels, restaurants, and shops.

The telephone country code for Colombia is 57. Cell phone numbers are 10 digits long, beginning with a 3. To call a Colombian cell phone from abroad, you must use the country code followed by that 10-digit number. Landline numbers in Colombia are seven digits long. An area code is necessary when calling from a different region. To call a landline from a cell phone, dial 03 + area code + 7-digit number. To reach a cell phone from a landline, dial 03 + 10-digit number.

Resources

Spanish Phrasebook

Knowing some Spanish is essential to visit Colombia, as relatively few people outside the major cities speak English. Colombian Spanish is said to be one of the clearest in Latin America. However, there are many regional differences.

Spanish commonly uses 30 letters—the familiar English 26, plus four straightforward additions: ch, ll, ñ, and rr, which are explained in "Consonants," below.

PRONUNCIATION

Once you learn them, Spanish pronunciation rules—in contrast to English—don't change. Spanish vowels generally sound softer than in English. (*Note:* The capitalized syllables below receive stronger accents.)

Vowels

- **a** like ah, as in "hah": *agua* AH-gooah (water), *pan* PAHN (bread), and *casa* CAH-sah (house)
- **e** like ay, as in "may:" *mesa* MAY-sah (table), *tela* TAY-lah (cloth), and *de* DAY (of, from)
- **i** like ee, as in "need": *diez* dee-AYZ (ten), *comida* ko-MEE-dah (meal), and *fin* FEEN (end)
- **o** like oh, as in "go": *peso* PAY-soh (weight), *ocho* OH-choh (eight), and *poco* POH-koh (a bit)
- **u** like oo, as in "cool": *uno* OO-noh (one), *cuarto* KOOAHR-toh (room), and *usted* oos-TAYD (you); when it follows a "q" the **u** is silent; when it follows an "h" or has an umlaut, it's pronounced like "w"

Consonants

- **b, d, f, k, l, m, n, p, q, s, t, v, w, x, y, z, and ch** pronounced almost as in English; **h** occurs, but is silent—not pronounced at all
- **c** like k as in "keep": *cuarto* KOOAR-toh (room), *casa* KAH-sah (house); when it precedes "e" or "i," pronounce **c** like s, as in "sit": *cerveza* sayr-VAY-sah (beer), *encima* ayn-SEE-mah (atop)
- **g** like g as in "gift" when it precedes "a," "o," "u," or a consonant: *gato* GAH-toh (cat), *hago* AH-goh (I do, make); otherwise, pronounce **g** like h as in "hat": *giro* HEE-roh (money order), *gente* HAYN-tay (people)
- **j** like h, as in "has": *Jueves* HOOAY-vays (Thursday), *mejor* may-HOR (better)
- **ll** like y, as in "yes": *toalla* toh-AH-yah (towel), *ellos* AY-yohs (they, them)

- **ñ** like ny, as in "canyon": *año* AH-nyo (year), *señor* SAY-nyor (Mr., sir)
- **r** is lightly trilled, with tongue at the roof of your mouth like a very light English d, as in "ready": *pero* PAY-roh (but), *tres* TRAYS (three), *cuatro* KOOAH-troh (four)
- **rr** like a Spanish r, but with much more emphasis and trill. Let your tongue flap. Practice with *burro* (donkey), *carretera* (highway), and Carrillo (proper name), then really let go with *ferrocarril* (railroad)

Note: The single small but common exception to all of the above is the pronunciation of Spanish **y** when it's being used as the Spanish word for "and," as in "Ron y Kathy." In such case, pronounce it like the English ee, as in "keep": Ron "ee" Kathy (Ron and Kathy).

Accent

The rule for accents, the relative stress given to syllables within a given word, is straightforward. If a word ends in a vowel, an n, or an s, accent the next-to-last syllable; if not, accent the last syllable.

Pronounce *gracias* GRAH-seeahs (thank you), *orden* OHR-dayn (order), and *carretera* kah-ray-TAY-rah (highway) with stress on the next-to-last syllable.

Otherwise, accent the last syllable: *venir* vay-NEER (to come), *ferrocarril* fay-roh-cah-REEL (railroad), and *edad* ay-DAHD (age).

Exceptions to the accent rule are always marked with an accent sign: (á, é, í, ó, or ú), such as *teléfono* tay-LAY-foh-noh (telephone), *jabón* hah-BON (soap), and *rápido* RAH-pee-doh (rapid).

BASIC AND COURTEOUS EXPRESSIONS

Colombians use many courteous formalities. Whenever approaching anyone for information or some other reason, do not forget the appropriate salutation—good morning, good evening, etc. Standing alone, the greeting *hola* (hello) can sound brusque.

Hello. *Hola.*
Good morning. *Buenos días.*
Good afternoon. *Buenas tardes.*
Good evening. *Buenas noches.*
How are you? Colombians have many ways of saying this: *¿Cómo estás/ como está? ¿Qué hubo/Qu'hubo? ¿Cómo va/vas? ¿Que tal?*
Very well, thank you. *Muy bien, gracias.*
Okay; good. *Bien.*
Not okay; bad. *Mal.*
So-so. *Más o menos.*
And you? *¿Y Usted?*
Thank you. *Gracias.*
Thank you very much. *Muchas gracias.*
You're very kind. *Muy amable.*
You're welcome. *De nada.*
Goodbye. *Adiós.*
See you later. *Hasta luego. Chao.*

please *por favor;* (slang) *por fa*
yes *sí*
no *no*
I don't know. *No sé.*
Just a moment, please. *Un momento, por favor.*
Excuse me, please (when you're trying to get attention). *Disculpe.*
Excuse me (when you've made a mistake). *Perdón. Que pena.*
I'm sorry. *Lo siento.*
Pleased to meet you. *Mucho gusto.*
How do you say . . . in Spanish? *¿Cómo se dice . . . en español?*
What is your name? *¿Cómo se llama (Usted)? ¿Cómo te llamas?*
Do you speak English? *¿Habla (Usted) inglés? ¿Hablas inglés?*
Does anyone here speak English? *¿Hay alguien que hable inglés?*
I don't speak Spanish well. *No hablo bien el español.*
Please speak more slowly. *Por favor hable más despacio.*
I don't understand. *No entiendo.*
Please write it down. *Por favor escríbalo.*
My name is . . . *Me llamo . . . Mi nombre es . . .*
I would like . . . *Quisiera . . . Quiero . . .*
Let's go to . . . *Vamos a . . .*
That's fine. *Está bien.*
All right. *Listo.*
cool, awesome *chévere, rico, super*
Oh my god! *¡Dios mío!*
That's crazy! *¡Qué locura!*
You're crazy! *¡Estás loca/o!*

TERMS OF ADDRESS

When in doubt, use the formal *Usted* (you) as a form of address.

I *yo*
you (formal) *Usted*
you (familiar) *tú*
he/him *él*
she/her *ella*
we/us *nosotros*
you (plural) *Ustedes*
they/them *ellas* (all females); *ellos* (all males or mixed gender)
Mr., sir *señor*
Mrs., madam *señora*
miss, young lady *señorita*
wife *esposa*
husband *esposo*
friend *amigo/a*
girlfriend/boyfriend *novia* (female); *novio* (male)
partner *pareja*
daughter; son *hija; hijo*

brother; sister *hermano; hermana*
mother; father *madre; padre*
grandfather; grandmother *abuelo; abuela*

TRANSPORTATION
Where is . . . ? *¿Dónde está . . . ?*
How far is it to . . . ? *¿A cuánto queda . . . ?*
from . . . to . . . *de . . . a . . .*
How many blocks? *¿Cuántas cuadras?*
Where (Which) is the way to . . . ? *¿Cuál es el camino a . . . ? ¿Por dónde es . . . ?*
bus station *la terminal de buses/terminal de transporte*
bus stop *la parada*
Where is this bus going? *¿A dónde va este bús?*
boat *el barco, la lancha*
dock *el muelle*
airport *el aeropuerto*
I'd like a ticket to . . . *Quisiera un pasaje a . . .*
roundtrip *ida y vuelta*
reservation *reserva*
baggage *equipaje*
next flight *el próximo vuelo*
Stop here, please. *Pare aquí, por favor.*
the entrance *la entrada*
the exit *la salida*
(very) near; far *(muy) cerca; lejos*
to; toward *a*
by; through *por*
from *de*
right *la derecha*
left *la izquierda*
straight ahead *derecho*
in front *en frente*
beside *al lado*
behind *atrás*
corner *la esquina*
stoplight *la semáforo*
turn *una vuelta*
here *aquí*
somewhere around here *por aquí*
there *allí*
somewhere around there *por allá*
road *camino*
street *calle, carrera*
avenue *avenida*
block *la cuadra*

highway *carretera*
kilometer *kilómetro*
bridge; toll *puente; peaje*
address *dirección*
north; south *norte; sur*
east; west *oriente (este); occidente (oeste)*

ACCOMMODATIONS

hotel *hotel*
Is there a room available? *¿Hay un cuarto disponible?*
May I (may we) see it? *¿Puedo (podemos) verlo?*
How much is it? *¿Cuánto cuesta?*
Is there something cheaper? *¿Hay algo más económico?*
single room *un cuarto sencillo*
double room *un cuarto doble*
double bed *cama matrimonial*
single bed *cama sencilla*
with private bath *con baño propio*
television *televisor*
window *ventana*
view *vista*
hot water *agua caliente*
shower *ducha*
towels *toallas*
soap *jabón*
toilet paper *papel higiénico*
pillow *almohada*
blanket *cobija*
sheets *sábanas*
air-conditioned *aire acondicionado*
fan *ventilador*
swimming pool *piscina*
gym *gimnasio*
bike *bicicleta*
key *llave*
suitcase *maleta*
backpack *mochila*
lock *candado*
safe *caja de seguridad*
manager *gerente*
maid *empleada*
clean *limpio*
dirty *sucio*
broken *roto*
(not) included *(no) incluido*

FOOD

I'm hungry. *Tengo hambre.*
I'm thirsty. *Tengo sed.*
Table for two, please. *Una mesa para dos, por favor.*
menu *carta*
order *orden*
glass *vaso*
glass of water *vaso con agua*
fork *tenedor*
knife *cuchillo*
spoon *cuchara*
napkin *servilleta*
soft drink *gaseosa*
coffee *café, tinto*
tea *té*
drinking water *agua potable*
bottled carbonated water *agua con gas*
bottled uncarbonated water *agua sin gas*
beer *cerveza*
wine *vino*
glass of wine *copa de vino*
red wine *vino tinto*
white wine *vino blanco*
milk *leche*
juice *jugo*
cream *crema*
sugar *azúcar*
cheese *queso*
breakfast *desayuno*
lunch *almuerzo*
daily lunch special *menú del día*
dinner *comida*
the check *la cuenta*
eggs *huevos*
bread *pan*
salad *ensalada*
lettuce *lechuga*
tomato *tomate*
onion *cebolla*
garlic *ajo*
hot sauce *ají*
fruit *fruta*
mango *mango*
watermelon *patilla*
papaya *papaya*
banana *banano*

apple *manzana*
orange *naranja*
lime *limón*
passionfruit *maracuyá*
guava *guayaba*
grape *uva*
fish *pescado*
shellfish *mariscos*
shrimp *camarones*
(without) meat *(sin) carne*
chicken *pollo*
pork *cerdo*
beef *carne de res*
bacon; ham *tocino; jamón*
fried *frito*
roasted *asado*
Do you have vegetarian options? *¿Tienen opciones vegetarianas?*
I'm vegetarian. *Soy vegetarian(o).*
I don't eat . . . *No como . . .*
to share *para compartir*
Check, please. *La cuenta, por favor.*
Is the service included? *¿Está incluido el servicio?*
tip *propina*
large *grande*
small *pequeño*

SHOPPING

cash *efectivo*
money *dinero*
credit card *tarjeta de crédito*
debit card *tarjeta de débito*
money exchange office *casa de cambio*
What is the exchange rate? *¿Cuál es la tasa de cambio?*
How much is the commission? *¿Cuánto es la comisión?*
Do you accept credit cards? *¿Aceptan tarjetas de crédito?*
credit card installments *cuotas*
money order *giro*
How much does it cost? *¿Cuánto cuesta?*
expensive *caro*
cheap *barato; económico*
more *más*
less *menos*
a little *un poco*
too much *demasiado*
value added tax *IVA*
discount *descuento*

HEALTH

Help me please. *Ayúdeme por favor.*
I am ill. *Estoy enferma/o.*
Call a doctor. *Llame un doctor.*
Take me to . . . *Lléveme a . . .*
hospital *hospital, clínica*
drugstore *farmacia*
pain *dolor*
fever *fiebre*
headache *dolor de cabeza*
stomach ache *dolor de estómago*
burn *quemadura*
cramp *calambre*
nausea *náusea*
vomiting *vomitar*
medicine *medicina*
antibiotic *antibiótico*
pill *pastilla, pepa*
aspirin *aspirina*
ointment; cream *ungüento; crema*
bandage (big) *venda*
bandage (small) *cura*
cotton *algodón*
sanitary napkin *toalla sanitaria*
birth control pills *pastillas anticonceptivas*
condoms *condones*
toothbrush *cepillo de dientes*
dental floss *hilo dental*
toothpaste *crema dental*
dentist *dentista*
toothache *dolor de muelas*
vaccination *vacuna*

COMMUNICATIONS

Wi-fi *wifi*
cell phone *celular*
username *usuario*
password *contraseña*
laptop computer *portátil*
prepaid cellphone *celular prepago*
post office *4-72*
phone call *llamada*
letter *carta*
stamp *estampilla*
postcard *postal*
package; box *paquete; caja*

AT THE BORDER

border *frontera*
customs *aduana*
immigration *migración*
inspection *inspección*
ID card *cédula*
passport *pasaporte*
profession *profesión*
vacation *vacaciones*
I'm a tourist. *Soy turista.*
student *estudiante*
marital status *estado civil*
single *soltero*
married; divorced *casado; divorciado*
widowed *viudado*
insurance *seguro*
title *título*
driver's license *pase de conducir*

AT THE GAS STATION

gas station *estación de gasolina*
gasoline *gasolina*
full, please *lleno, por favor*
tire *llanta*
air *aire*
water *agua*
oil (change) *(cambio de) aceite*
My ... doesn't work. *Mi ... no funciona.*
battery *batería*
tow truck *grúa*
repair shop *taller*

VERBS

Verbs are the key to getting along in Spanish. They employ mostly predictable forms and come in three classes, which end in *ar, er,* and *ir,* respectively:

to buy *comprar*
I buy, you (he, she, it) buys *compro, compra*
we buy, you (they) buy *compramos, compran*

to eat *comer*
I eat, you (he, she, it) eats *como, come*
we eat, you (they) eat *comemos, comen*

to climb *subir*
I climb, you (he, she, it) climbs *subo, sube*
we climb, you (they) climb *subimos, suben*

Here are more (with irregularities indicated):

to do or make *hacer* (regular except for *hago,* I do or make)
to go *ir* (very irregular: *voy, va, vamos, van*)
to walk *caminar*
to wait *esperar*
to love *amar*
to work *trabajar*
to want *querer* (irregular: *quiero, quiere, queremos, quieren*)
to need *necesitar*
to read *leer*
to write *escribir*
to send *enviar*
to repair *reparar*
to wash *lavar*
to stop *parar*
to get off (the bus) *bajar*
to arrive *llegar*
to stay (remain) *quedar*
to stay (lodge) *hospedar*
to rent alquilar
to leave *salir* (regular except for *salgo,* I leave)
to look at *mirar*
to look for *buscar*
to give *dar* (regular except for *doy,* I give)
to give (as a present or to order something) *regalar*
to carry *llevar*
to have *tener* (irregular: *tengo, tiene, tenemos, tienen*)
to come *venir* (irregular: *vengo, viene, venimos, vienen*)

Spanish has two forms of "to be":

to be *estar* (regular except for *estoy,* I am)
to be *ser* (very irregular: *soy, es, somos, son*)

Use *estar* when speaking of location or a temporary state of being: "I am at home." *"Estoy en casa."* "I'm happy." *"Estoy contenta/o."* Use *ser* for a permanent state of being: "I am a lawyer." *"Soy abogada/o."*

NUMBERS

zero *cero*
one *uno*
two *dos*
three *tres*
four *cuatro*
five *cinco*
six *seis*
seven *siete*
eight *ocho*
nine *nueve*
10 *diez*
11 *once*
12 *doce*
13 *trece*
14 *catorce*
15 *quince*
16 *dieciseis*
17 *diecisiete*
18 *dieciocho*
19 *diecinueve*
20 *veinte*
21 *veinte y uno* or *veintiuno*
30 *treinta*
40 *cuarenta*
50 *cincuenta*
60 *sesenta*
70 *setenta*
80 *ochenta*
90 *noventa*
100 *cien*
101 *ciento y uno*
200 *doscientos*
500 *quinientos*
1,000 *mil*
10,000 *diez mil*
100,000 *cien mil*
1,000,000 *millón*
one half *medio*
one third *un tercio*
one fourth *un cuarto*

TIME

What time is it? ¿Qué hora es?
It's one o'clock. Es la una.
It's three in the afternoon. Son las tres de la tarde.
It's 4 a.m. Son las cuatro de la mañana.
six-thirty seis y media
quarter till eleven un cuarto para las once
quarter past five las cinco y cuarto
hour una hora
late tarde

DAYS AND MONTHS

Monday lunes
Tuesday martes
Wednesday miércoles
Thursday jueves
Friday viernes
Saturday sábado
Sunday domingo
today hoy
tomorrow mañana
yesterday ayer
day before yesterday antier
January enero
February febrero
March marzo
April abril
May mayo
June junio
July julio
August agosto
September septiembre
October octubre
November noviembre
December diciembre
week una semana
month un mes
after después
before antes
holiday festivo
long weekend puente

Suggested Reading

HISTORY

Bushnell, David. *The Making of Modern Colombia: A Nation in Spite of Itself.* Berkeley, CA: University of California Press, 1993. Mandatory reading for students of Colombian history. Bushnell, an American, is considered the "Father of the Colombianists".

Hemming, John. *The Search for El Dorado.* London: Joseph, 1978. Written by a former director of the Royal Geographical Society, this book explores the Spanish gold obsession in the New World. It's a great companion to any visit to the Gold Museum in Bogotá.

Lynch, John. *Simón Bolívar: A Life.* New Haven, CT: Yale University Press, 2007. This biography of the Liberator is considered one of the best ever written in English, and is the result of a lifetime of research by renowned English historian John Lynch.

Palacios, Marco. *Between Legitimacy and Violence: A History of Colombia, 1875-2002.* Durham, NC: Duke University Press Books, 2006. Written by a Bogotano academic who was a former head of the Universidad Nacional, this book covers Colombia's economic, political, cultural, and social history from the late 19th century to the complexities of the late 20th century, and drug-related violence.

THE DRUG WAR AND ARMED CONFLICTS

Bowden, Mark. *Killing Pablo: The Hunt for the World's Greatest Outlaw.* New York: Grove Press, 2001. This account of U.S. and Colombian efforts to halt drug trafficking and terrorism committed by drug lord Pablo Escobar was originally reported in a 31-part series in *The Philadelphia Inquirer.*

Dudley, Steven. *Walking Ghosts: Murder and Guerrilla Politics in Colombia.* New York: Routledge Press, 2004. Essential reading for anyone interested in understanding the modern Colombian conflict, this book is written by an expert on investigating organized crime in the Americas.

Gonsalves, Marc, Tom Howes, Keith Stansell, and Gary Brozek. *Out of Captivity: Surviving 1,967 Days in the Colombian Jungle.* New York: Harper Collins, 2009. Accounts of three American military contractors who were held, along with former presidential candidate Ingrid Betancourt, by FARC guerrillas for over five years in the Colombian jungle.

Leech, Garry. *Beyond Bogotá: Diary of a Drug War Journalist in Colombia.* Boston: Beacon Press, 2009. The basis for this book is the author's 11 hours spent as a hostage of the FARC.

Otis, John. *Law of the Jungle: The Hunt for Colombian Guerrillas, American Hostages, and Buried Treasure.* New York: Harper, 2010. This is a thrilling account of the operation to rescue Ingrid Betancourt and American government contractors held by the FARC. It's been called a flip-side to *Out of Captivity.*

NATURAL HISTORY

Hilty, Steven L., William L. Brown, and Guy Tudor. *A Guide to the Birds of Colombia.* Princeton, NJ: Princeton University Press, 1986. This massive 996-page field guide to bird-rich Colombia is a must for any serious bird-watcher.

McMullan, Miles, Thomas M. Donegan, and Alonso Quevedo. *Field Guide to the Birds of Colombia.* Bogotá: Fundación ProAves, 2010. This pocket-sized field guide published by ProAves, a respected bird conservation society, is a more manageable alternative to Hilty's guide.

ETHNOGRAPHY

Davis, Wade. *One River: Explorations and Discoveries in the Amazon Rain Forest.* New York: Simon & Schuster, 1997. From the author of *The Serpent and the Rainbow,* this is a rich description of the peoples of the Amazonian rain forest, and the result of Davis' time in the country alongside famed explorer Richard Evan Schultes.

Reichel-Dolmatoff, Gerardo. *Colombia: Ancient Peoples & Places.* London: Thames and Hudson, 1965. A thorough anthropological investigation of the indigenous cultures across Colombia by an Austrian-born anthropologist who emigrated to Colombia during World War II.

——. *The Shaman and the Jaguar: A Study of Narcotic Drugs Among the Indians of Colombia.* Philadelphia: Temple University Press, 1975. An examination of shamanic drug culture in Colombia, particularly among indigenous tribes from the Amazon jungle region.

ARCHITECTURE

Escovar, Alberto, Diego Obregón, and Rodolfo Segovia. *Guías Elarqa de Arquitectura.* Bogotá: Ediciones Gamma, 2005. Useful guides for anyone wishing to learn more about the architecture of Bogotá, Cartagena, and Medellín.

TRAVEL

Lamus, María Cristina. *333 Sitios de Colombia Que Ver Antes de Morir*. Bogotá: Editorial Planeta Colombiana, 2010. Colombian version of *1,000 Places to See Before You Die* (only available in Spanish).

Mann, Mark. *The Gringo Trail*. West Sussex: Summersdale Publishers, 2010. A darkly comic tale of backpacking around South America.

Nicholl, Charles. *The Fruit Palace*. New York: St. Martin's Press, 1994. A wild romp that follows the seedy cocaine trail from Bogotá bars to Medillín to the Sierra Nevada and a fruit stand called the Fruit Palace during the wild 1980s. The English author was jailed in Colombia for drug smuggling as he conducted research for the book.

Internet and Digital Resources

ACCOMMODATIONS

Hostel Trail
www.hosteltrail.com
Run by a Scottish couple living in Popayán, this is an excellent resource on hostels throughout South America.

Posadas Turísticas de Colombia
www.posadasturisticasdecolombia.gov.co
Find information on interesting accommodations alternatives, like home stays.

BIRDING

ProAves
www.proaves.org
Excellent website for the largest birding organization in the country.

ECO-TOURISM

Parques Nacionales Naturales de Colombia
www.parquesnacionales.gov.co
Colombia's national parks website has information on all of the natural parks and protected areas in the country.

Aviatur Ecoturismo
www.aviaturecoturismo.com
Package tours of the Amazon, PNN Tayrona, PNN Isla Gorgona, and more are available from one of Colombia's most respected travel agencies.

Fundación Natura
www.natura.org.co

The Fundación Natura operates several interesting eco-tourism reserves in the country.

EMBASSIES AND VISAS

U.S. Embassy in Colombia
http://bogota.usembassy.gov

The Citizen Services page often has security information for visitors, and is where you can register your visit in case of an emergency.

Colombian Ministry of Foreign Relations
www.cancilleria.gov.co

Offers information on visas and other travel information.

ENTERTAINMENT, CULTURE, AND EVENTS

Plan B
www.planb.com.co

Updated information on restaurants, entertainment, and cultural events in Medellín, as well as Bogotá and Cali.

Tu Boleta
www.tuboleta.com

The top event ticket distributor in the country, Tu Boleta is a good way to learn about concerts, theater, parties, and sporting events throughout Colombia.

Banco de la República
www.banrepcultural.org

Information on upcoming cultural activities sponsored by the Banco de la República in 28 cities in the country.

HISTORY AND HUMAN RIGHTS ISSUES

CIA World Factbook Colombia
www.cia.gov

Background information on Colombia from those in the know.

Centro de Memoria Histórica
www.centrodememoriahistorica.gov.co

Excellent website on the human toll of the Colombian conflict.

International Crisis Group
www.crisisgroup.org

In-depth analysis of the human rights situation in Colombia.

Colombia Diversa
www.colombiadiversa.org
Covers LGBT rights in Colombia.

LANGUAGE COURSES

Spanish in Colombia
www.spanishincolombia.gov.co
Official government website on places to study Spanish in Colombia.

MEDELLÍN

Medellín Living
www.medellinliving.com
This website run by expats is an excellent purveyor of insider information on the City of Eternal Spring.

NEWS AND MEDIA

El Tiempo
www.eltiempo.com
El Tiempo is the country's leading newspaper.

El Espectador
www.elespectador.com.co
This is Colombia's second national newspaper.

Revista Semana
www.semana.com
Semana is the top news magazine in Colombia.

La Silla Vacia
www.sillavacia.com
Political insiders dish about current events.

Colombia Reports
http://colombiareports.co
Colombian news in English.

The City Paper Bogotá
www.thecitypaperbogota.com
Website of the capital city's English-language monthly.

Colombia Calling
www.richardmccoll.com/colombia-calling
Weekly online radio program on all things Colombia from an expat perspective.

TRANSPORTATION
Moovit
This app will help you figure out public transportation in Bogotá.

Tappsi
To order a safe taxi in Colombia's large cities, first upload this excellent app.

TRAVEL INFORMATION
Colombia Travel
www.colombia.travel
This is the official travel information website of Proexport, Colombia's tourism and investment promotion agency.

Pueblos Patrimoniales
www.pueblospatrimoniodecolombia.travel
Find a pueblo that suits your needs at this informative website.

VOLUNTEERING
Conexión Colombia
www.conexioncolombia.com
This website is one-stop shopping for the nonprofit sector in Colombia.

Index

A
accommodations: 153
air travel: 148-150
Alborada: 29
Aldea Artesano: 87
Alto de la Cruz Mirador: 87
Alto de Ventanas: 54
Alumbrado Navideño: 29
animals: 118-122
Antigua Estación del Tren: 97
aquarium: 21
Armenia: 80-84; map 81
Ateneo: 28
Atlético Nacional: 30
ATMs: 160
auto travel: 149, 151

B
Banco de la República (Ibagué): 109
Banco de la República (Pereira): 97
bank transfers: 159
Basílica Menor de la Inmaculada Concepción (Jardín): 53
Basílica Menor La Inmaculada Concepción (Salamina): 72
beer/breweries: 25
Belalcázar: 106
Biblioteca EPM: 11
Biblioteca España: 8, 23
bicycling: 29-30, 31, 32, 45, 50, 67, 89, 98, 103, 151
birds/bird-watching: 54-55, 65, 77, 84, 95, 102, 107, 108
botanical gardens/arboretums: 21, 84-85, 97
bus travel: 149, 150-151

C
Cable Aéreo: 54
Café Jesús Martín: 9, 90
Calarcá: 86
Calle del Empedrado: 95
Calle del Recuerdos: 49
Calle del Tiempo Detenido: 95
Calle Peatonal: 109
Calle Real (Salento): 9, 87
Calle Real (Santuario): 106
Camino Herrera: 53
Camino La Salada: 53
Carabobo Norte: 20-22
Carmen: 8, 32
Carnaval de Riosucio: 53
car travel: 149, 151
Casa de la Cultura (Salamina): 72
Casa Museo Pedro Nel Gómez: 23
Casa Rodrigo Jiménez Mejía: 72
Casa Selva y Café: 9, 56
Cascada Santa Rita: 89
Catedral Basílica de Manizales: 62
Catedral de la Inmaculada Concepción (Armenia): 80
Catedral de Nuestra Señora de las Mercedes: 57
Catedral Inmaculada Concepción (Ibagué): 109
Caverna de los Guácharos: 47-48
caves/caverns: 47-48, 55
Cementerio San Esteban: 72
Centro Administrativo La Alpujarra: 11
Centro Cultural Lucy Tejeda: 98
Centro Historia de Jericó: 58
Centro Medellín: 20; map 21
Cerro Nutibara: 22
Cerro Tatamá: 107
Charlee Lifestyle Hotel: 8, 39
churches/temples: 44, 53, 57, 62-63, 72, 80, 95, 97, 104, 109
Ciclovía (Manizales): 67
Ciclovía (Medellín): 29
Ciclovía (Pereira): 98
Ciclovía Nocturna (Manizales): 67
Ciclovía Nocturna (Medellín): 30
climate: 116-118
climbing: 24, 79
Coffee Region: 60-110
coffee tours: 70-71, 88-89
Colombiamoda: 29
Conservatorio del Tolima: 109
consignaciones (bank transfers): 159
consulates: 152
credit cards: 160
crime: 158
Cueva El Esplendor: 55
currency: 159
customs regulations: 152

D
debit cards: 160
demographics: 143, 145
Deportivo Independiente Medellín: 31
Desfile de Yipao: 86

Día del Arbol Nacional: 93
Día Internacional de la Pereza: 29
disabilities, travelers with: 154
diseases: 156-157
Donde Ramón: 10
Droguería: 95
drugs, recreational: 158

E
economy: 142-143
Eco Parque La Estampilla: 106
Ecoparque Los Yarumos: 65-66
Edificio Carré: 11
Edificio Inteligente: 12
Edificio Vásquez: 11
El Cable: 9, 64-65
El Cedral: 103
El Poblado: 18-19, 32-34, 38-40; map 33
embassies: 152
Envigado FC: 31
Esquina de las Mujeres: 22
Estación Ferrocarril: 11
Estadio Atanasio Girardot: 31
Estadio Palogrande: 67
Estrella de Agua: 94
etiquette: 155
Exposición de Ganado Normando: 73

F
fauna: 118-122
Feria de las Flores: 29
Feria de Manizales: 66
Fernando Botero sculptures: 8, 20
Festival de Cine de Antioquia: 45
Festival Internacional de Poesía de Medellín: 28
Festival Internacional de Tango: 28
Festival Internacional de Teatro de Manizales: 67
Festival Nacional de la Música Colombiana: 109
Fiesta Nacional del Café: 86
Fiestas Cuyabras: 81
Filandia: 95-96
Finca Argentina: 95
Finca La Primavera: 94
Finca Las Nieves: 79
flora: 118-122
food/restaurants: 153-154

GH
gay and lesbian travelers: 146, 154-155
geography: 112-116
government: 140-141
gratuities: 160
Guatapé: 49-52
Hacienda Guayabal: 9, 71
Hacienda La Esperanza: 9, 54
Hacienda Napoles: 48-49
Hacienda Venecia: 9, 70-71
health: 156-158
Helipuerto route: 79
hiking: 23-24, 30, 76, 77-80, 89, 94-95, 103, 107-108
history: 123-140
Homenaje a la Raza: 11
horseback riding: 24, 45, 67, 88-89
hot springs: 66, 104-105

IJ
Ibagué: 109-110
Iglesia de la Vera Cruz: 10
illnesses: 156-157
Ingeominas weather station: 79
Inmaculada Concepción (Manizales): 63
Internet access: 161
Itagüi: 29
itineraries: 8-12
Jardín: 8, 52-57
Jardín Botánico de la Universidad Tecnológica de Pereira: 97
Jardín Botánico del Quindío: 84-85
Jardín Botánico de Medellín: 21
Jericó: 57-60
Jesús Dulce Mío-Mi Pueblo: 27
Juntas: 79

KL
kayaking/canoeing: 49
La Cuadra: 97
La Eliana: 9, 89
La Garrucha: 54
Laguna del Otún: 74, 77-78
Laguna Encantada: 108
La Montaña: 94
language: 146
La Piedra Peñol: 49-50
Las Brisas: 76
La Torre al Cielo: 64
lesbian and gay travelers: 146, 154-155
Lluvia de Semillas: 107

M
Magdalena Medio: 46-49
Manizales: 9, 62-69; map 63

Medellín: 18-43
Medellín and the Coffee Region, map of: 18
medical services: 157-158
Metrocable gondola: 8, 24, 26
Monasterio Santa María de la Epifanía: 49
money: 159-161
Montenegro: 85
Monumento a Cristo Rey: 106
Monumento Al Esfuerzo: 80
Monumento al Machete: 104
Monumento a los Colonizadores: 64
motorcycle travel: 149, 151
Museo Casa de la Memoria: 8, 22
Museo Cementerio de San Pedro: 22
Museo Clara Rojas: 53
Museo de Antioquia: 8, 20
Museo de Arte del Tolima: 109
Museo de Arte de Pereira: 97
Museo de Arte Moderno de Medellín: 24
Museo de Arte Religioso (Jericó): 58
Museo de Arte Religioso (Santa Fe de Antioquia): 44
Museo de Jericó Antioquia: 58
Museo del Agua: 12
Museo del Oro Quimbaya: 80-81
Museo Juan del Corral: 44
MUUA: 20

NOP

national parks: general discussion 117; Los Nevados 74-80, 95; Santuario de Fauna y Flora Otún-Quimbaya 102-103; Tatamá 107, 108
Nevado del Ruiz: 74
Nevado del Tolima: 74, 79-80, 95
Nevado Santa Isabel: 74, 77
Noche de las Luces: 73
Nuestra Señora de la Pobreza Catedral: 97
Once Caldas: 67
Otraparte: 28
Pabellón de Madera: 65
Palacio de la Cultura Rafael Uribe Uribe: 10
Palacio Nacional: 10
PANACA: 86
paragliding: 30, 51, 100
Paramillo del Quindío: 79-80, 95
Páramo de Romerales: 94
parks and gardens: 23-24, 49, 52, 81-82, 97, 104, 109
Parque Arví: 8, 23-24

Parque Bolívar (Belalcázar): 106
Parque Bolívar (Salento): 87
Parque Centenario: 109
Parque Central (Filandia): 95
Parque de las Luces: 11
Parque de la Vida: 81
Parque El Bosque: 82
Parque El Lago: 97
Parque El Salado: 24-25
Parque Explora: 21
Parque Jardines Montesacro: 32
Parque las Araucarias: 104
Parque Municipal Natural Planes de San Rafael: 107-109
Parque Nacional del Café: 85
Parque Nacional Natural Los Nevados: 74-80, 95; map 75
Parque Nacional Natural Tatamá: 107, 108
Parque Olaya Herrera: 97
Parque Principal: 9, 52
Parque Recreativo COMFAMA Guatapé: 49
Parque Regional Natural Ucumarí: 103
Parque San Antonio: 25
Parque Sucre: 81
passports: 6, 152
Peatonal Carabobo: 10, 19
Pereira: 96-101; map 98
phones: 161
Planetario Medellín: 21
plane travel: 148-150
planning tips: 6-7
plants: 118-122
Plaza Botero: 10, 19, 31
Plaza Cisneros: 11
Plaza de Bolívar (Armenia): 80
Plaza de Bolívar (Ibagué): 109
Plaza de Bolívar (Manizales): 62
Plaza de Bolívar (Pereira): 97
Plaza de Bolívar (Salamina): 72
Plaza de Bolívar (Santuario): 106
Plaza de la Libertad (Medellín): 11
Plaza de los Pies Descalzos: 10, 12
Plaza Mayor: 11, 12
Plaza Principal: 87
police: 158
politics: 140-141
Pueblito Paisa: 22
Puente de Occidente: 44

QR

Quebrada Risaralda: 108
Quimbaya: 86
rafting: 32, 45

Recinto del Pensamiento: 65
RECUCA: 85
religion: 145-146
rental cars: 151
Reserva Acaime: 9, 94
Reserva del Río Blanco: 65
Reserva Natural Río Claro: 46-48
resources: 162-179
Río Otún: 102-103

S
safety: 156-158
Salamina: 71-74
Salento: 9, 87-93
Salón Málaga: 8, 26
San Félix: 72
Santa Fe de Antioquia: 44-46
Santa Rosa de Cabal: 104-106
Santuario: 106-107
Santuario de Fauna y Flora Otún-
    Quimbaya: 102-103
Santuario La Milagrosa: 104
Semana Santa (Salamina): 72
Semana Santa (Santa Fe de Antioquia): 45
soccer: 30-31
spectator sports: 30-31, 67

T
Tarde de María La Parda: 73
taxes: 153, 160-161
Teatro Metropolitano: 12

Teatro Pablo Tobón: 28
telephones: 161
Templo de Santa Bárbara: 44
Templo María Inmaculada: 95
Temporada Internacional de Jazz: 67
Termales Balneario: 104
Termales de Cañón: 79
Termales del Ruiz: 66
Termales de Santa Rosa de Cabal: 104
Termales Otoño: 66
Termales San Vicente: 104
theme parks: 85-86
3 Cordilleras: 25
Tierra Viva: 66
tipping: 160
Tralala: 9, 90
transportation: 148-151

UVWXYZ
Universidad de Antioquia: 20
vaccinations: 6-7, 156
Valle de Cocora: 9, 93-95
Valle de las Tumbas: 76
Valle del Río Otún: 102-103
value-added tax: 153, 160-161
Vereda del Cocora: 79
visas: 6, 152
waterfalls: 51, 53, 89, 107
weather: 116-118
wildlife/wildlife-watching: 55, 102, 118-122
women travelers: 154
World Tango Championship: 28

List of Maps

Medellín and the Coffee Region: 16
Centro: 21
El Poblado: 33
Manizales: 63
Parque Nacional Natural Los Nevados: 75
Armenia: 81
Pereira: 98

Photo Credits

All photos © Andrew Dier except page 3 © Dubessonego | Dreamstime.com; page 4 (top) © Piccaya | Dreamstime.com, (bottom) © Toniflap | Dreamstime.com; page 5 © Diego Calderon-Franco; page 8 © Mardzpe | Dreamstime.com; page 11 © Pablo Hidalgo | Dreamstime.com; page 12 © Pablo Hidalgo | Dreamstime.com; page 13 © Jesse Kraft | Dreamstime.com; page 20 © Pablo Hidalgo | Dreamstime.com; page 37 © Rafael Bernal; page 104 © Jesse Kraft | Dreamstime.com

Also Available

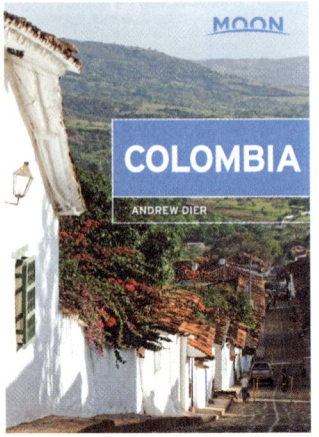
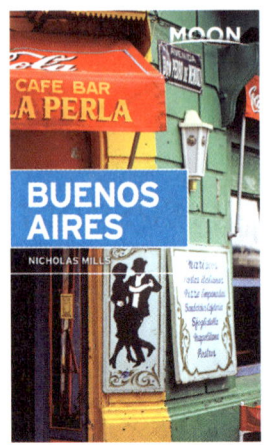

MAP SYMBOLS

≡≡≡	Expressway	★	Highlight	✈	Airfield	⛳	Golf Course
───	Primary Road	○	City/Town	✈	Airport	🅿	Parking Area
═══	Secondary Road	⊙	State Capital	▲	Mountain	⛰	Archaeological Site
·····	Unpaved Road	⊛	National Capital	+	Unique Natural Feature	⛪	Church
-----	Trail	★	Point of Interest			⛽	Gas Station
········	Ferry	•	Accommodation	🌊	Waterfall		Glacier
------	Railroad	▼	Restaurant/Bar	♣	Park		Mangrove
▬▬▬	Pedestrian Walkway	■	Other Location	🚩	Trailhead		Reef
⫶⫶⫶	Stairs	△	Campground	⛷	Skiing Area		Swamp

CONVERSION TABLES

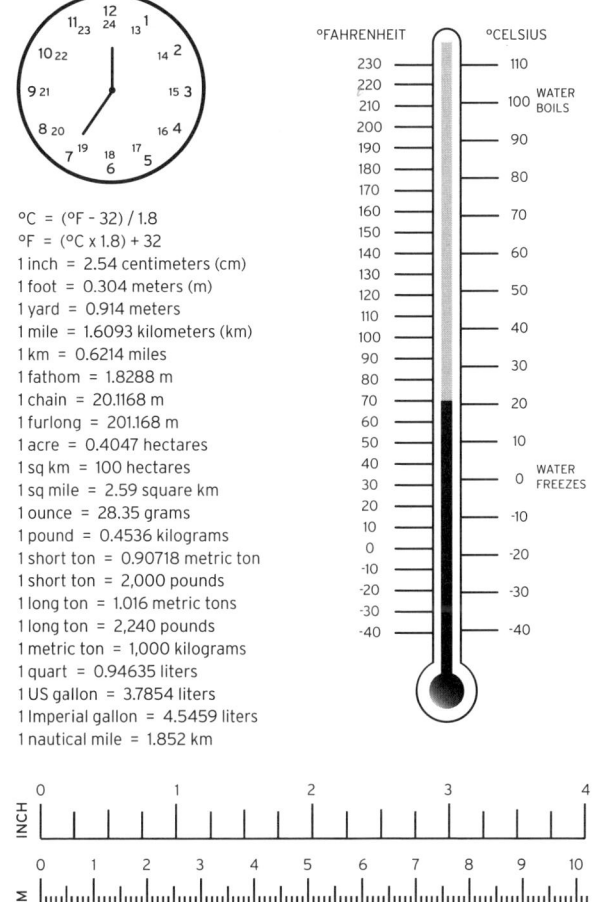

°C = (°F - 32) / 1.8
°F = (°C x 1.8) + 32
1 inch = 2.54 centimeters (cm)
1 foot = 0.304 meters (m)
1 yard = 0.914 meters
1 mile = 1.6093 kilometers (km)
1 km = 0.6214 miles
1 fathom = 1.8288 m
1 chain = 20.1168 m
1 furlong = 201.168 m
1 acre = 0.4047 hectares
1 sq km = 100 hectares
1 sq mile = 2.59 square km
1 ounce = 28.35 grams
1 pound = 0.4536 kilograms
1 short ton = 0.90718 metric ton
1 short ton = 2,000 pounds
1 long ton = 1.016 metric tons
1 long ton = 2,240 pounds
1 metric ton = 1,000 kilograms
1 quart = 0.94635 liters
1 US gallon = 3.7854 liters
1 Imperial gallon = 4.5459 liters
1 nautical mile = 1.852 km

MOON MEDELLÍN
Avalon Travel
a member of the Perseus Books Group
1700 Fourth Street
Berkeley, CA 94710, USA
www.moon.com

Editor: Leah Gordon
Series Manager: Kathryn Ettinger
Copy Editor: Brett Keener
Graphics Coordinator: Rue Flaherty
Production Coordinator: Rue Flaherty
Cover Design: Faceout Studios, Charles Brock
Moon Logo: Tim McGrath
Map Editor: Mike Morgenfeld
Cartographers: Brian Shotwell, Austin Ehrhardt
Proofreader: Deana Shields
Indexer: Greg Jewett

ISBN-13: 978-1-63121-590-2

Printing History
1st Edition — July 2017
5 4 3 2 1

Text © 2017 by Andrew Dier.
Maps © 2017 by Avalon Travel.
All rights reserved.

Some photos and illustrations are used by permission and are the property of the original copyright owners.

Front cover photo: cable car on metrocable extension, Medellín © Jane Sweeney/Getty Images.
Back cover photo: view from Rock of Guatape © Sevenkingdom | Dreamstime.com

Printed in Canada by Friesens

Moon Handbooks and the Moon logo are the property of Avalon Travel. All other marks and logos depicted are the property of the original owners. All rights reserved. No part of this book may be translated or reproduced in any form, except brief extracts by a reviewer for the purpose of a review, without written permission of the copyright owner.

All recommendations, including those for sights, activities, hotels, restaurants, and shops, are based on each author's individual judgment. We do not accept payment for inclusion in our travel guides, and our authors don't accept free goods or services in exchange for positive coverage.

Although every effort was made to ensure that the information was correct at the time of going to press, the author and publisher do not assume and hereby disclaim any liability to any party for any loss or damage caused by errors, omissions, or any potential travel disruption due to labor or financial difficulty, whether such errors or omissions result from negligence, accident, or any other cause.